Negative Sentences in the Languages of Europe

Empirical Approaches to Language Typology

16

Editors

Georg Bossong
Bernard Comrie

Mouton de Gruyter
Berlin · New York

Negative Sentences in the Languages of Europe

A Typological Approach

by
Giuliano Bernini
Paolo Ramat

Mouton de Gruyter
Berlin · New York 1996

Mouton de Gruyter (formerly Mouton, The Hague)
is a Division of Walter de Gruyter & Co., Berlin.

⊗ Printed on acid-free paper which falls within the guidelines of the
ANSI to ensure permanence and durability.

Library of Congress Cataloging-in-Publication-Data

Bernini, Giuliano.
    Negative sentences in the languages of Europe : a typological
approach / by Giuliano Bernini, Paolo Ramat.
      p.   cm. − (Empirical approaches to language typology ;
16) Includes bibliographical references (p.   ) and index.
    ISBN 3-11-014064-0
    1. Grammar, Comparative and general − Negatives.   2. Gram-
mar, Comparative and general − Sentences.   3. Grammar, Comparative and general − Quantifiers.   4. Typology (Linguistics)
5. Europe − Languages.   I. Ramat, Paolo.   II. Title.   III. Series.
P299.N4B47   1996
415−dc20
                              96-15690
                                  CIP

Die Deutsche Bibliothek − Cataloging-in-Publication-Data

Bernini, Giuliano:
Negative sentences in the languages of Europe : a typological ap-
proach / by Giuliano Bernini ; Paolo Ramat. − Berlin ; New York :
Mouton de Gruyter, 1996
   (Empirical approaches to language typology ; 16)
   ISBN 3-11-014064-0
NE: Ramat, Paolo:; GT

Typesetting and Printing: Arthur Collignon GmbH, Berlin.
Binding: Mikolai GmbH, Berlin.
Printed in Germany.

Contents

Abbreviations of grammatical terms

A	(negative) quantifier of the type *anybody*	INSTR	instrumental
		INT	interrogative
ABS	absolutive	LOC	locative
ACC	accusative	MASC	masculine
ADJ	adjective	N	negative quantifier of
ADESS	adessive		the type *nobody*
ADV	adverb	NEG	negative, negation
ALL	allative	'NEG$_{HOL}$'	holophrastic negation
ANIM	animate	'NEG$_{PRED}$'	sentence negation
ANT	anterior	NEUT	neuter
APFP	active perfect participle	NOM	nominative
		NP	noun phrase
APP	active past participle	NPI	negative polarity item
ART	article	OBJ	object
ASP	aspect	O$_D$	direct object
AUX	auxiliary	PART	partitive
COMM	comment	PARTC	participle
CONJ	conjunction	PASS	passive
DAT	dative	PERF	perfect
DECL	declarative	PFV	perfective
DEM	demonstrative	PL	plural
DET	determinative	PP	prepositional phrase
EMPH	emphatic	POSS	possessive
EQU	equative	PFP	perfect participle
ERG	ergative	PRED	predicate
FEM	feminine	PRES	present
FOC	focus	PRET	preterite
FUT	future	PROG	progressive
GEN	genitive	PRP	present participle
HAB	habitual	PTCL	particle
IMPER	imperative	REFL	reflexive
IMPF	imperfect	REL	relative
IMPFV	imperfective	S	existential quantifier of the type *somebody*
IND	indicative		
INDEF	indefinite	SG	singular
INESS	inessive	SJNT	subjunctive

SUBJ	subject	1,2,3	first, second, third
TOP	topic		person
UTR	'utrum'	*	indicates
Vb	verb		reconstructed form
Vf	verb in finite form	**	indicates
Vi	verb in infinitive form		ungrammatical form
VP	verb phrase		

Abbreviations of language names

a) Languages and dialects quoted in the text

Alb.	Albanian	Gév.	Gévaudanais
air	altirisch (Old Irish)	Goth.	Gothic
Arag.	Aragonese	Gr.	Greek
Arm.	Armenian	Hitt.	Hittite
Avest.	Avestan	Hung.	Hungarian
Bergam.	Bergamasque	Ice.	Icelandic
Bret.	Breton	IE	Indo-European
Bulg.	Bulgarian	It.	Italian
Bel.	Belorussian	Ir.	Irish
Cai.	Cairene dialect	Lat.	Latin
Cat.	Catalan	Latv.	Latvian
Corn.	Cornish	Lith.	Lithuanian
Dan.	Danish	Lom.	Lombard
Dolom.Lad.	Dolomitic Ladin	Mac.	Macedonian
Dut.	Dutch	Malt.	Maltese
Emil.	Emilian	MBret.	Middle Breton
Eng.	English	mcymr.	mittelcymrisch (Middle Welsh)
Est.	Estonian		
Finn.	Finnish	MDut.	Middle Dutch
Fr.	French	MEng.	Middle English
Fris.	Frisian	MHG	Middle High German
Frl.	Friulian	MWelsh	Middle Welsh
ScGael.	Scottish Gaelic	Milan.	Milanese
Gasc.	Gascon	Norw.	Norwegian
Georg.	Georgian	OBulg.	Old Bulgarian
Ger.	German	Occit.	Occitan

OE	Old English	Rum.	Rumanian
OFr.	Old French	Rus.	Russian
OHG	Old High German	Sansk.	Sanskrit
OIce.	Old Icelandic	Sard.	Sardinian
OIr.	Old Irish	Serbo-Cr.	Serbo-Croatian
ONor.	Old Norse	Slovk.	Slovak
OPers.	Old Persian	Sp.	Spanish
OPrus.	Old Prussian	Surs.	Sursilvan
OSax.	Old Saxon	Toch.	Tocharian
OSlav.	Old Slavonic	Ved.	Vedic (Sanskrit)
OSp.	Old Spanish	Wel.	Welsh
PIE	Proto-Indo-European		
Piedm.	Piedmontese	arch.	archaic
Pol.	Polish	class.	classical
Port.	Portuguese	coll.	colloquial
Prov.	Provençal	lit.	literary
(Rhaeto-)	(Rhaeto-)Romansh	mod.	modern
Rom.		w.	western

b) Symbols used in the charts

Afr	Afrikaans	Frl	Friulian
Alb	Albanian	(C) (L)Frs	(colloquial) (literary)
Arm	Armenian		Frisian
Bas	Basque	Gba	Gbaya
Bre	Breton	Ger	German
Bul	Bulgarian	Grg	Georgian
Bylr	Belorussian	Grk	Greek
Cat	Catalan	Hau	Hausa
Cz	Czech	Hun	Hungarian
Dan	Danish	Ice	Icelandic
Dcb	Dutch Creole of	Ir	Irish
	Berbice	It	Italian
Dut	Dutch	Lap	Lapp
Eng	English	Lith	Lithuanian
Est	Estonian	Ltv	Latvian
Ewe	Ewe	Mac	Macedonian
Fin	Finnish	Mlt	Maltese
Fr	French	Nor	Norwegian

Pan	Portuguese of Angola	ScGl	Scottish Gaelic
Pbr	Portuguese of Brasil	Scp	Spanish Creole
Pcp	Portuguese Creole of		Palenquero
	Príncipe	Scr	Serbo-Croatian
Pct	Portuguese Creole of	Sdr	Spanish of the
	São Tomé		Dominican Republic
Pol	Polish	Slk	Slovak
Por	Portuguese	Slv	Slovenian
Pro	Provençal	Spn	Spanish
Rmns	Rhaeto-Romansh	Srd	Sardininan
Rum	Rumanian	Swd	Swedish
Rus	Russian	Trk	Turkish
San	Sango	Ukr	Ukrainian
Sar	Sara	Wls	Welsh

Abbreviations of authors and texts

(Abbreviations of texts are given in italics)

Aesch.	Aeschylus	*KBo*	Keilschrifttexte aus
Bacch.	Bacchides		Boğazköy [Texts in
Cas.	Casina		cuneiform script from
Cat.	Orations against		Boğazköy]
	Catiline	*Lc.*	The Gospel according
Curc.	Curculio		to Luke
Cor.	Epistle to the	*L. L.*	De lingua latina [On
	Corinthians		the Latin language]
Cycl.	Cyclops	Lucr.	Lucretius
DB	Darius' Inscription at	Mart.	Martial
	Behistan	*Mc.*	The Gospel according
Gal.	Epistle to the		to Mark
	Galatians	*Mil.*	Miles gloriosus [The
Eurip.	Euripides		boastful soldier]
Hel.	Heliand	*Od.*	Odyssey
Hom.	Homer	Otfr.	Otfried
Il.	Iliad	*Nibel.*	Nibelungenlied
Joh.	The Gospel according	Plaut.	Plautus
	to John	*Prom.*	Prometheus vinctus

Pseud.	Pseudolus	*Tat.*	Tatian
RV	Hymns of the	*Tim.*	Epistle to Timothy
	RigVeda	*Truc.*	Truculentus
XII Tab.	Leges duodecim	Varr.	Varro
	tabularum [The laws	*Vid.*	Vidēvdād
	of the twelve tables]	*Y.*	Yašt
Tab.Ig.	Tabulae Iguvinae		
	[Tables from		
	Gubbio]		

0. Introduction

> Nā́ṣād āsīn, nó sád āsīt tadā́nīṃ
> 'There was not the non-existent nor the existent then'
> (RgVeda X, 129,1)

0.1. The rationale of the research

In recent years the trend in typological studies has been to examine specific phenomena in a more or less representative sample of languages in order to obtain a general overview: we have thus had monographs dealing with relative clauses (Chr. Lehmann 1985), comparative constructions (Stassen 1985), tense-aspect systems (Dahl 1985), etc.

The basic, intuitively highly plausible, assumption is that certain categories or structures, since they are reflexes of cognitive processes, are expressed in one way or another in every natural language. Every language, for example, will have one or more strategies for expressing comparison between comparable entities ('A is bigger/smaller than B') or for connecting a clause with a nominal head.

Negation (NEG) − and more specifically sentence negation − is one of these universals: every language will have one or more ways of negating the truth of an utterance: "It is not the case that P"; for example:

(1)   *The weather is not cold*
        ≅ [[it is not the case that] the weather is cold]

Every language will have some means of translating negative modality as it is expressed in another language (on NEG as modality see the following section). This assertion seems difficult to prove on the abstract theoretical level which encompasses definitional universals, 'conditio sine qua non' for the very existence of a possible human language (see Ramat 1987: 42). Yet it is a fact that there is no known language which does not have some means or another of expressing negation. What we are dealing with, then, is a 'pragmatic universal' which is related to the behavioural and cognitive functions encountered in every language (Ramat 1987: 48), and which is realized at the discourse level, as is the case with, e.g., interrogatives or imperatives.[1]

However, every language will, of course, have its own particular devices (phonological, morphological, syntactic, lexical, or a combination of devices at the various levels) for the linguistic realization of the operation 'negation'. This is further confirmed by the fact that the morphemes which express negation are not usually autonomous but are instead dependent upon other semantic units (sentences, phrases, lexemes) for their meaning (cf. Stickel 1975: 18).

This study is part of what may be called the 'onomasiological' perspective outlined above, the field of enquiry having been deliberately restricted to European languages for reasons that will become clear in due course: given the behavioural-cognitive universality of NEG we need to ask what strategies the various languages make use of to give it concrete realization. Since the investigation is restricted to the languages of Europe we do not in any way aim to draw conclusions of a general universalistic nature concerning the morphosyntactic properties of negative sentences from the sample under observation, as is, of course, the case with investigations whose scope is broader and which examine a sample representative of all the languages of the world.

0.2. On negation in general

Despite the non-universalistic nature of the research, it is nonetheless necessary to look in detail at certain general points already raised in the preceding section (see Ramat 1994).

It does not appear to be essential for our purposes to go into the discussion regarding the representation of NEG at the level of Logical Form (see Lyons 1977: 768–773, and also Bîtea 1984; Horn 1989, Moeschler 1992).

We shall shortly return to the status of Negation, and look into its general phenomenology. Here it will suffice to note that the strictly formal-logical view does not apply to language: "In logic, negation is a simpler matter than in the grammar of English (or of natural languages in general)", (Taglicht 1984: 105). It is not the case, for example, that two consecutive negations necessarily give an affirmative meaning in real languages ($:\neg\neg P = P$) as is the case in the Latin *non nullus* 'someone', *nullus non* 'each one' (: *Hac ratione potest nemo non esse disertus* (Mart., I, 27) 'in this way everyone may be eloquent'). Yet, at an informal, substandard level, Latin itself has many counter-examples: *iura te non nociturum esse homini … nemini* (Plaut., *Mil.* 1411), exactly like the Italian translation *giura che non farai male a nessuno* 'swear that you will (not) do harm to no-one' (see Molinelli 1988: 34–40; Orlandini 1991).

Consider also Givón's (1975: 75) persuasive arguments: *He ran as fast as he could* implies *He ran*; but *He didn't run as fast as he could* – with the modal adverb *as fast as* in the scope of NEG – does not imply *He didn't run*, but again *He ran*.

Likewise *Mark has not eaten much* − with the quantifier *much* in the scope of NEG − implies *Mark has eaten (something)*. (For the definition of 'scope' it will suffice to repeat what Koktová (1987: 176) writes from the Praguian viewpoint of the 'Functional Generative Description': "… 'scope' as standing for that part of the sentence […] which is directly semantically influenced by the scoping expressions, e.g. for what is negated (e.g. not)…").

Conversely, a sentence such as *They almost sold it, didn't they?* is understood as affirmative − as the 'tag question' in the negative shows − even though what is being stated implies the negative proposition 'They HAVEN'T sold it' (cf. Taglicht 1984: 108). The pragmatic presuppositions in the co-text and in the context of the communication seem to be what determine the functioning of negation (see Givón 1975: 62, 77ff; cf. also Krivonosov 1986; Contini-Morava 1989: 3ff). For example, it makes no sense to look for temporal reference in a non-event: *When did John arrive?*, but **/? *When did John not arrive?* (cf. again Givón 1975: 89). Furthermore − as we shall also see in relation to European languages − the temporal, aspectual and modal features of a negative sentence may be completely different to those of the corresponding affirmative sentence; there are languages, such as Somali or Swahili, which have different verbal paradigms for affirmatives and negatives (see (9) below and cf. Contini-Morava 1989: 11). Amharic has 2nd person singular jussive forms that are used only with NEG (cf. Palmer 1986: 113).

In the pragmatic dimension in which we have placed it, NEG is therefore a sentence operator, like interrogation or like the imperative (cf. Muller 1991: 17). From this viewpoint negation may well be considered in the same way as a particular kind of modality, concerning the sentence rather than the verb.

In fact, many of the linguistic modes of behaviour of NEG suggest a close interrelationship between negation and modality, like, for example, the use in the Romance languages of the subjunctive in a subordinate clause which is dependent on a negative main clause (even in cases where negation is expressed by a negative quantifier such as 'no-one') (cf. Palmer 1986: 218−221; on the concept of NEG as modality see Palmer 1986: 14−15):

(2)   French
        Guy   ne   croit   pas   que   Fifi   soit   bête
        Guy   NEG   thinks   NEG   that   Fifi   be:SJNT:PRES:3SG   stupid
        'Guy doesn't think that Fifi is stupid'

(3)   Italian
        Non   dubito   che   sia   (/*è)   Vivaldi
        NEG   doubt:1SG   that   be:SJNT:PRES:3SG   (/*INDIC)   Vivaldi
        'I don't doubt it's Vivaldi'

(4)   Spanish
            No   insisto   que   aprenda
            NEG insist:1SG that learn:SJNT:PRES:3SG
            'I don't insist on him learning'

(5)   *Nessuno che si*   possa   (/*può)   *dire*
            no-one that REFL can:SJNT:PRES:3SG (/*INDIC) say
            onesto   lo   farà
            honest   it   will.do
            'No-one who calls himself honest will do it'

(6)   *Ningún hombre que   se*   considere   (/*considera)
            no   man   that REFL think:SJNT:PRES:3SG (/*INDIC)
            honrado lo   haría
            honest   it   would.do
            'No man who considers himself honest would do it'

In (5) and (6) "the speaker does not commit himself to the existence of the men" (Rivero 1970: 646). The sentence is characterised by potential irreality, or at any rate, it is not strictly connected to the semantic feature [+realis] as is the prototypical declarative sentence in (1).

Although it does not reflect the vast complexity of the phenomenon negation, it will, nonetheless, suffice for our purposes to accept the metalinguistic definition of the negative sentence already given above: given a proposition P, the negative declarative sentence is that which denies the truth of P. "Negation is a distinct speech-act in language, that it is used largely to deny supposed beliefs of hearers in the context where the corresponding affirmative has been assumed" (Givón 1975: 102 – 103.; see also Forest's definition (1993: 2)).

In what follows we shall deal basically with the factive *not*, which is assigned the semantic feature [-irrealis], and which is found in the sentence *The weather is not cold*. The prohibitive sentence is different; as it contains a negative imperative or a device other than that which expresses reality, for example *Do not smoke*, which does not refer to a real state of affairs, but rather seeks to prevent the occurrence of a state of affairs (and is therefore characterised by the feature [+irrealis]; see briefly Chapter 1 and 5.6.). Note also that in *The weather is not cold* the presuppositions at discourse level ('pragmatic presuppositions') have an important role: this sentence usually has a meaningful discursive aim if whoever utters it has reason to believe that his interlocutor may think that the weather is cold (see in particular the Italian negative emphatic construction exemplified by *La giornata non è* mica *fredda* 'The weather is not at all cold' (cf. Cinque 1976).

Following Givón's (1975: 72) fitting example, when I say *My wife is not pregnant* I effect a felicitous linguistic act only if this sentence is the reply to a previous assertion that my wife is pregnant or if I have reason to believe that others may think my wife pregnant.

As the title suggests, this investigation will basically examine sentence negation — that is, cases where the sentential predication is within the scope of the operator NEG: [[It is not the case that]F]. However, apart from sentence negation in the strict sense of the term, we will also examine the way in which negative quantifiers function, since they have the same property of including the entire sentential predication in their scope: *No-one has injured me* means 'There does not exist an x such that x has injured me', or 'It is not the case that someone has injured me'.

Some languages, such as English and Italian, have a special construction for the so-called metalinguistic negation which is the "denial of the possibility of making an assertion about a particular propositional content", (Horn 1989: 371−445; Bernini 1992). It concerns utterences of the type *Non è che+S, It is not that+S:* in the sentence *It is not that this doesn't interest me: it shouldn't interest me* the effect of NEG is not to deny the truth of the dependent proposition (in reality the thing may well interest me) but to deny − controversially − the possibility of asserting such an interest. In this sense it may be considered a second level NEG. (Consider, on the other hand, the unambiguously negative sentence *This does not interest me* where the sequel *it shouldn't interest me* reinforces the first part on the deontic level.) NEG concerns the illocutionary aspect of the linguistic act itself (cf. Attal 1984, with examples of the type *Il ne me le dit plus: il ne cesse de me le répéter* 'He doesn't say that to me: he doesn't stop repeating it to me'; or *Elle n'est pas belle, elle est gracieuse* 'She isn't pretty, she is graceful', where NEG takes on a role of counter-argument at the pragmatic level.) Nølke (1992: 49) calls this type of negation 'négation polémique': *Paul n'est pas grand: il est immense* 'Paul isn't tall, he is huge'. The cases of metalinguistic negation cited by Payne (1992), such as *That's not a fistle, it's a thistle,* that is, the type "It is not A1 but A2", are more straightforward : their scope being not the truth value of the sentence and its presuppositions but simply the linguistic material which constitutes the sentence.

I'm not his daughter − he's my father (Payne 1992: 76) may also be considered an example of metalinguistic negation; uttered outside an appropriate context it is completely contradictory, yet makes sense if, for example, whoever utters it wishes to emphasize the simple physiological relationship while at the same time disputing any spiritual bond. In such cases it would perhaps be more appropriate to speak of the pragmatic strategies of NEG without overly stretching the concept of 'metalinguistic'.

So-called lexical negation (the type *continuous* > *discontinuous, proper* > *improper, trust* > *mistrust*) and phrase negation (the so-called constituent negation, or local negation) do not impinge on the positive/negative reading of the sentence (and for this reason they will not be dealt with in the following chapters). Consider *His achievements are (stable and) unstable* next to *His achievements are not (stable and) unstable*: the positive/negative value of the sentence is not influenced by the absence/presence of the negative adjective (see also Klima 1964). See also *Not all the arrows hit the target* and *Not all the arrows didn't hit the target* (where it is obvious that only the quantifier *all* is in the scope of the first NEG: 'some arrows did hit the target'); and *Gli uomini non onesti hanno sovente successo* (lit. 'Men not honest have often success') and *Gli uomini non onesti non hanno sovente successo* (lit. 'Men not honest not have often success'): the positive reading of the first examples and the negative reading of the second examples is not dependent upon the NP which is in the scope of the negative quantifier. For the same reasons, cases where NEG concerns a qualifying element (usually an adverb) will also be excluded from our investigation: in *Maria doesn't drive recklessly* (= 'with recklessness'), or *Maria doesn't drive like a formula-1 racer,* NEG obviously concerns the adverb or the modal adverbial ('like a formula-1 racer') and the sentence does not imply that Maria cannot drive, but in fact just the opposite (cf. the remarks above regarding *He didn't run as fast as he could*; see also Dik, Vester, Hengeveld, Vet (1990: 55ff)).

As far as phrase negation is concerned, the same sort of definition given above may also apply: given a phrase P, the corresponding negative phrase is that which denies the existence/truth condition of P or the possibility of asserting P (: *all the men* ∼ *not all the men, the men* ∼ *the non-men, incomparably (beautiful)* ∼ *not incomparably (beautiful), with gold* ∼ *not with gold*, etc.). However, further emphasising the difference between sentence negation and phrase negation is the fact that in the former case NEG does not apply only to either the predicator (usually a verb) or to its arguments (usually noun phrases) but rather to the predicative connection: *No-one flies / Everyone does not fly / Each does not fly* ≡ 'there does not exist an x such that x flies'. Regarding the various scopes of negation, cf. also the two Italian sentences *Puoi non dare l'esame oggi* and *Non puoi dare l'esame oggi* which correspond to the two readings of the English sentence *You may not take the exam today*: in the first case *non/not* belong to the subordinate clause (= 'You have the option of not taking the exam today'), but in the second case (with a pause after *not*, = 'You are not allowed to take the exam today') the modal verb as well is included in the scope of the negation: see Taglicht (1984: 131); which goes to show that NEG applies to the predicative connection.

0.3. The linguistic phenomenology of negation

The considerable variety of negative forms found in the world's languages can now be fully appreciated in the detailed descriptions of the negation systems of sixteen languages edited by Peter Kahrel and René van den Berg (1994). However the devices for expressing negation may essentially be reduced to four basic types (see Payne 1992: 75; Ramat 1994: 2770):

(a) a negative verb takes the entire positive clause as its complement. Note the way the Tongan (Austronesian family) negative verb *'ikai* functions:

(7)   Tongan (Payne 1985: 208)
  a. *Na'e   'alu 'a   Siale*
     PERF.ASP go   ABS Charlie
     'Charlie went'
  b. *Na'e   'ikai [F ke   'alu 'a   Siale]*
     PERF.ASP NEG   ASP go ABS Charlie
     'Charlie didn't go'
     (NB: *ke* is an aspectual marker found only in subordinate clauses)

(b) one or more negative markers have a position defined in relation to clause-level constituents, more specifically to the verbal predicate; cf., for example, Sinhalese (Indoeuropean, spoken in Śri Lanka), where NEG is prefixed to the verb form (and also to the nominal form):

(8)   Sinhalese (Matzel 1966: 123)
  Kuḍamassō viśvāsa no-kaḷa-ha
  fish   trust   NEG-did-they
  'The fish did not believe (i. e. what the stork said)'

  In Somali (Cushitic family), which has a special negative verbal conjugation, NEG instead invariably operates on the part of the sentence which constitutes the focus (which has its own grammatical marker) (examples from Antinucci 1981: 278 ff.):

(9)   *Axmed hadiyad* ma   keenin
        Axmed present NEG bring:NEG.PRET
        'Axmed did not bring a present'

(10)   a. *Axmed* ima   arkin
           Axmed me:NEG see:NEG.PRET
           'Axmed did not see me'

Compare the corresponding sentence with nominal focalization:

> b. *Axmed* baan   *i*   arkin
> Axmed NEG.FOC me see:NEG.PRET
> 'It is not Axmed who saw me'

The same is true for following languages:

(11)   Hausa (Kraft – Kirk-Greene 1973: 310)
        Yārinyà bà   *tà*   *tàfi gōnā* ba
        girl   NEG 3SG.FEM.PERF go farm NEG
        'The girl didn't go to the farm'

In Hausa (Nigeria) the particle *bà* (low tone, short vowel) must appear immediately before the pronoun used to indicate perfect aspect (: ** *tà bà*); *ba* (high tone, short vowel) in clause final position).

(12)   Afrikaans (den Besten 1986: 203)
        Hy het nie   *gesê, dat hy hierdie boek geskrywe het* nie
        he has NEG said that he this   book written has NEG
        'He has not said he wrote this book'

(13)   Afrikaans (Raidt 1983: 189)
        Ons beskuldig niemand *daarvan dat hy geld   gesteel het* nie
        we blame   no-one of.that that he money stolen has NEG
        'No-one blames us for him having stolen some money'

Note that the second *nie* after the subordinate clause also refers to the main clause (cf. 4.3.): its position at the very end of the sentence is fixed.

(14)   French
        Jean ne   *croit*   pas   *que Marie viendra*
        Jean NEG believes NEG that Marie will.come
        'Jean doesn't believe that Marie will come'

(15)   French
        Ça n'   *a*   ni   *queue* ni   *tête*
        That NEG has neither tail   nor head
        'That has neither head nor tail'
        (****Ça* n'a pas ni *queue* ni *tête*)

(c) a (quasi-)auxiliary negative verb is added to the predicate, and assumes, or may assume, all or some of the (morphological) properties characteristic of the main semantic verb in the corresponding positive sentence; as in Finnish (cf. 3.4.):

(16)   Finnish

    a. En   *juo*   *kahvia*
       NEG:1SG drink coffee:PART
       'I do not drink coffee'

    b. Emme   *voineet*   *odottae*
       NEG:1PL be.able:PL.PERF.PARTC wait
       'We couldn't wait'

(Note also the use of a special verb, distinct from the main semantic verb, in the English translation: see furthermore 0.3.1.). The difference between (a) where the entire positive sentence is the complement of the negative verb, and (c) with an AUX, may be represented as follows (from Payne 1985: 211, with reference to Tongan):

$$[_F \ Vb_{neg} \ [_F COMP \ Vb_{lexical} \ OBJ \ SUBJ]]$$
$$[_F \ [_{VG} \ Vb_{neg} \ COMP \ Vb_{lexical} \ OBJ \ SUBJ]]$$
(NB: VG = Verb Group)

In fact, in many languages (including, for example, the Uralic group) the negative construction shows that verbal categories are distributed between Vb_{neg} and $Vb_{lexical}$ according to hierarchical ordering (cf. Chapter 3, note 6).

(d) a bound morpheme occurs within the verbal inflection: cf. for example in Turkish

(17)   *gör*-mü-*yor-um*
       see-NEG-PRES-1SG
       'I don't see'

(18)   *gör-ül*-me-*yecek-ler*
       see-PASS-NEG-FUT-3PL
       'They will not be seen'
       (Wendt 1972 (1992): 71,171)

The NEG marker *-me-* (/*-ma-*, taking vowel harmony into account) is adjoined immediately after the verb root (or the expanded verb root).

In the light of types (a)-(d) we can see that the devices for expressing NEG are morphological, morphosyntactic, or lexical in nature (see Ramat 1994):
(i) a morphological device is the Turkish negation as exemplified in (17) and (18): a specific morpheme representing NEG is adjoined to the verbal morphology;
(ii) morphosyntactic is the type found in the Somali example of (10b): a special device for negatively marking the focus is adjoined to a specific negative conjugation;

(iii) a lexical device is the type found in German:

(19)   a. *Hans ist* nicht *fertig*
        Hans is   not   ready
        (= 'Hans has not finished')

as well as in English:

        b. Nobody *wounded me*

where the negativity of the sentence is assigned entirely to a particular lexeme (a negative quantifier). Existential negation ('there is not') may come under this heading in cases where it is expressed by a lexeme which differs from the existential affirmative ('here is') as happens in Turkish:

(20)   *Çay* var   *mi?*   Evet, var
        tea there.is INT Yes   there.is
        'Is there any tea? Yes, there is'

but:

(21)   *Çay var   mi?* Yok,   *çay* yok
        tea there.is INT There.isn't tea there.isn't

see also in Hungarian:

(22)   Van   *kenyér*
        There.is bread

but:

(23)   Nincs   *kenyér*
        There.isn't bread

    A mixed strategy is shown in Polish for negative statements:

(24)   a. *Jacek   jest w szkole*
        Jacek:NOM is   in school:LOC
        'Jacek is at school'

but

        b. *Jacka   nie   ma   w szkole*
        Jacek:GEN NEG has in school
        'Jacek is not at school'

the negative sentence has both a grammatical (Nominative > Genitive) and a lexical device (the verb is not *być* 'to be' but *mieć* 'to have' (see Kaczorowska 1994).

Purely syntactic strategies — like, for example, the special word order rules in Kwa (Niger-Congo family, see Dahl 1979: 82) — are altogether quite rare. The NEG marker may be accompanied by other different types of phenomena (secondary alterations due to negation), like the use of the subjunctive in dependent clauses seen in (2)-(6). In Igbo (Niger-Congo) the marker indicating incomplete aspect undergoes a tone change (*nà* > *ná*; see Payne 1985: 229). Alteration in the grammar is found in Russian: if the sentence is in the negative the object may appear in the genitive case:

(25)   a. *On čitaet* gazetu
           He reads newspaper:ACC
           'He reads the newspaper'

but:

        b. *On* ne   *čitaet* gazety
           he NEG reads newspaper:GEN
           'He doesn't read the newspaper'

In his vast study of the typology of sentence negation, which we will often refer to, Östen Dahl, examining a sample of approximately 240 languages representative of all the world's language families, adds these comments to the statistics that follow (see Dahl 1979): "NEG is most frequently expressed by either bound morphemes as part of the predicate (45%) or by separate particles (44.9%)". NEG auxiliaries make out only 16% of Dahl's sample, while the use of dummy auxiliaries as in English (see below) is quite rare.

The expression of NEG (according to Dahl 1979):	%
1. morphologically as part of the predicate	45.0
2. morphologically in an auxiliary verb	16.7
3. by a separate negative particle	
a. in pre-verbal position	12.5
b. in pre-auxiliary position	20.8
c. before verbal group	2.1
d. in post-verbal position	1.2
e. in post-auxiliary position	3.7
4. by a separate negative particle	
a. in sentence-initial position	0.4
b. in sentence-final position	4.2
3+4	*44.9*

(NB: The total runs above 100% because a number of languages have more than one type of NEG)

Negative imperatives, as already stated in 0.1., deserve a separate discussion; it is with this verbal category that negative auxiliaires most often occur – in other words it takes the highest position on the negativity hierarchy (see Comrie 1981a: 354).

Of the strategies set out above those that are especially attested in the languages of our corpus are (b) [negative markers in a fixed position]: cf. (14)-(15) for French, and (c) [(quasi-)auxiliary negative verbs], cf. (16) for Finnish with English translation. However, the Balto-Finnic languages generally tend to mark on the negative AUX only the present tense.

Of particular interest is Estonian, where the present tense of the negative verb is generalised in the form *ei* (3SG) – like the substandard English *don't* (*My Mama* don't *told me* in the song *That's all right mama*) – and is thus the forerunner of an invariable NEG marker, uniformly inflecting the Vb$_{lexical}$ (cf. 3.4., with reference also to spoken Finnish in a Massachussets settlement).

There is, then, development from a full Vb$_{neg}$ to an AUXneg to a fixed negative marker via numerous intermediate stages – as always happens in such cases – where it may be difficult to say whether the item in question already is or still is an AUX (which does not mean, of course, that every NEG marker derives from an AUX!).

On the subject of the phenomenology of NEG dealt with in this section, Welsh merits a particular mention for a phenomenon which is not amongst those already examined. In this language the pre-verbal NEG marker contrasts with a declarative marker (DECL) (and also with an interrogative marker: INT):

(26)   a. Nid   *yw John yn bwyta pysgod*
            NEG is John in eat   fish
            'John doesn't eat fish'
        b. Y   *mae John yn bwyta pysgod*
            DECL is   John   in eat   fish
            'John eats fish'

The Welsh negative declarative sentence is marked for modality in a way not dissimilar to the affirmative declarative sentence and to the interrogative, yet it is far more common for a negative sentence (in keeping with its cognitively more complex nature) to be morphologically more complex than the corresponding affirmative sentence;[2] cf.

(27)   a. *Mary loves John*

vs.

        b. *Mary* doesn't *love John*

and also

    c. Does *Mary love John?*

For further observations regarding the languages of Europe the reader is, of course, referred to subsequent chapters.

0.4. Organization of the work

In the first chapters of the book we present revised versions of earlier papers we wrote on negation.[3] After a short account of the current situation in the Romance languages with reference to so-called discontinuous negation (Chapter 1; cf. Molinelli – Bernini – Ramat 1987: 165 – 172), we shall concentrate on the diachronic approach which will lead to an attempt at reconstructing the syntactic pattern of the Indoeuropean negative sentence (Chapter 2; cf. Bernini 1987a). In fact, one of the reasons for restricting the research to the languages of Europe has been the very fact that as far as the large majority of them is concerned we are in the fortunate position of having at our disposal a vast documentation covering a span of many centuries. Due to its long tradition of contact between languages and cultures, which may be traced directly from original documents, Europe presents itself as a particularly favoured area of research, where it is possible to see developmental tendencies, including those of a typological nature, which are important not only for the light they shed on the classic problem of linguistic and cultural contact, with the associated phenomena of linguistic convergence and assimilation, but also for the more general speculations they give rise to concerning linguistic change and the role that typology plays in this.

    It would be highly inappropriate at this point to embark on a discussion of what Benjamin Lee Whorf called 'Standard Average European' (SAE: see Whorf (1956 >) 1978: 138), but there is no doubt that the family likeness that the main languages of Europe share, "the unanimity of major patterns", exists either because of a common Indoeuropean origin or because these languages "have long shared in building up a common culture; and because much of this culture, on the more intellectual side, is derived from the linguistic backgrounds of Latin and Greek" (Whorf (1956 >) 1978: 214). This is what comes out also from the large inquiry of the EUROTYP project of the European Science Foundation (both authors of this book have been involved in that inquiry whose results will be published in the very next times). It seems to us, then, that the reasons in favour of restricting the present research, in diachronic and 'eurocentric' terms,

particularly regarding languages with more extensive documentation, are justi-
fied: by no means we were led to this restriction by a 'nationalisme européen à
la mode', as a critic has strangely written in a review of a miscellaneous volume
containing also previous versions of two chapters of the present book (cf. *Bulletin de la Société Linguistique de Paris* 87/1992: 35).

In Chapter 2, taking as our starting point the situation as it has been reconstructed for Indoeuropean, we attempt to sketch out the course of development
of the types of negation not only in the Romance languages but also in the
Germanic, Celtic and Slavic languages.

In Chapter 3 we examine phenomena relating to the position of NEG in the
sentence: to do this it is necessary to overcome the limits of a purely syntactic
approach and instead deal with the strategies of focalization and topicalization
that speakers use during the communication from a pragmatic viewpoint (cf.
Ramat 1988b).

In Chapter 4 we come at last to the areal viewpoint and tackle a crucial
problem that arises in any work on diachronic typology: whether in the languages of Europe (and not only Europe) the various types of sentence negation
have developed independently or whether they have spread out from one or
more centres in different ways, at different times. In this framework, the genesis
of sentence final negation in Afrikaans, the offspring of Dutch in South Africa,
as a result of complex contact patterns will also be dealt with in some detail.

Following these chapters is the second part, strictly synchronic in approach,
which examines the responses to a Questionnaire developed with the aim of
capturing the way in which sentential NEG basically operates in the various
European languages (see the Foreword to Part two). First of all, the way in
which sentential negation and phrasal negation operate will be examined, then
the morphosyntactic behaviour of negative quantifier systems in the various
languages (for example, *nobody, nothing*). With this aim in mind we have tried to
set out a grid of the values of these same quantifiers in functional terms and to
project onto this grid the quantifier forms present in the individual languages
(for example, *nobody, anybody, somebody*). This, then, is a typically functional approach. From the, at times detailed, description of the individual facts we have
thus sought to bring to the typological level the underlying explanatory patterns.

In the conclusion we also consider a possible parametrization of typological
behaviour, which allows us, amongst other things, a more immediate representation in spatial terms of the phenomena examined, and as a result of this we are
able to deal with the problems discussed in Chapter 4, as well as in Chapters 6,
7 and 8, from a different point of view.

Part I

The diachronic and areal perspective

1. Types of negation in the Romance languages

It may be useful to start by examining the strategies of NEG which are found in the Romance languages. Piera Molinelli has sketched out the picture, with particular reference to the Italian situation, and given an indication of the socio-linguistic range (Molinelli−Bernini−Ramat 1987: 165−172; see also Molinelli 1984).

There are, essentially, three types of sentential NEG found in the Romance languages of Europe (see Donadze 1981: 298; Schwegler 1983; 1988):

> NEG1) : NEG + Vb
> NEG2) : NEG + Vb + NEG ('discontinuous NEG')
> NEG3) :   Vb + NEG

NEG1 is that which is found in Latin and prior to that in Indo-European (see 2.1.). It is normally found in Portuguese (Lusitanian: for Brazilian Portuguese the picture is somewhat different: see Schwegler (1991a) and 4.3. below.), Spanish, Italian, eastern Romansh and Rumanian.

(1)	a. Portuguese	*O João não come peixe*
	b. Spanish	*Juan no come el pescado*
	c. Italian	*Giovanni non mangia pesce*
	d. Rumanian	*Ion nu mănîncă peştele*
		(lit.: John not eat fish)
		'John doesn't eat fish'

NEG2 is found in French (:*Jean ne mange pas de poisson*) and in Catalan (:*Joan no menja pas peix*; see also with *cap* < Lat. *capu(t)* 'head': *No m'agrada cap, això* 'I don't like this at all', *No ho sé cap* 'I don't know (at all)': cf. Schwegler (1986: 290); for a more detailed description of the areal distribution of NEG2 see chapter 4). In Catalan postverbal *pas* is used to give the negative construction a particular adversative meaning on the pragmatic level; its use, comparable to that of *mica* in Italian, implies that the speaker presupposes that whatever he is denying is on the contrary considered true or understood as realizable by his interlocutor (Cinque 1976; Lepschy−Lepschy (1977 >) 1981: 116):

(2)	a. Catalan	A: *Li demanaré el libro.* − B: *No te'l deixarà pas.*
	b. Italian	A: *Gli chiederò il libro.* − B: *Non te lo darà mica.*
		'I'll ask him for the book. − He won't give it to you'

These are the only instances in the Romance languages where pragmatic pre-suppositions encroach upon the form of NEG, albeit in a not strictly grammaticalised way; as opposed to what is found, for example, in Classical Greek or Classical Armenian, respectively *mḗ* and *mi* (prohibitive) vs. *ouk* and *oč̣* (factive). Similarly, absent also from the Romance languages is the subtle distinction, characteristic of Latin, and having in this language a pragmatic (often rhetoric) purpose, between the various interrogatives in negative form; this may be schematized as follows: *ne* when a negative or a positive reply is expected, *an* when a positive reply is expected, *num* when an unequivocally negative reply is expected. Nor do we find the functional opposition between preverbal negative particles at the modal/aspectual level, typical, for example, of Classical Arabic (*lā, lam, mā*: see Bernini (1987b: 41−42)). All in all, with respect to the classical languages we have a simplification of the morphs available at the grammatical level, while on the other hand there is an increase in the pragmatically expressive forms, characteristic of NEG2.

NEG2 may be found not only in Catalan and French but also in the northern Italian dialects: those of Piedmont, Emilia Romagna, western Veneto as well as in central Romansh (see Molinelli 1988: 166−167; Donadze 1993):

(3)   a. Emilian (Atlante Italo-Svizzero, map 1678)
            sta   donna   ki   la   nem   pyaz̧   miga
            this woman here she NEG:me pleases NEG
            'I do not like this woman'
        b. western Lombard
            Kwela funna   li   no   me pyas   miga
            that woman there NEG me pleases NEG
            'I do not like that woman'
        c. Romansh
            Ke   co   nu   fatschi   britch
            that that NEG do:1SG NEG
            'that I don't do it at all'
            (emphatic; see Schwegler (1983: 309)).

Note also

(4)   Dolomitian Ladin
            ... ne   ste pa   a   davei   festidi   de nos
                NEG be NEG to give:you worries of us
            'Don't worry about us'
            (from a letter of an Italian World War I prisoner: Spitzer (1976: 28)).

NEG3 is the normal form of sentential negation in a continuous area stretching from Occitan to the Piedmontese, Lombard and western (and central) Romansh dialects:

(5)   a. Provençal
          Sabe   pas/ges
          know:1SG NEG
          'I don't know'

     b. Piedmontese (cf. (3 a,b)
          Sa   fumna   m   pyaz̧   nen
          this woman me pleases NEG

     c. western Romansh
          Kwela diuna   play   a   mi   buk
          that   woman pleases to me NEG
          'I don't like that woman'

     d. central Romansh
          Eu sai   beka
          I   know:1SG NEG
          'I don't know'

     e. eastern Lombard
          Sta fomna   la   m   pyaz̧   mia
          this woman she me pleases NEG
          'I don't like this woman'

     f. western Piedmontese
          Akella fremo   m   agrad   ren
          that   woman me pleases NEG
          'I don't like that woman'

     g. western Piedmontese
          Akella ffeme   me   pyay   pä
          that   woman me pleases NEG
          'I don't like that woman'

     h. Milanese
          Mi parli   no
          I   speak:2SG NEG
          'I don't speak'

(for postposed *no* cf. below 3.2.). The original negative morph (*non*) may also be
reinforced (in postverbal position however):

     i. Gévaudanais
          La Marjano manquet pas   non   res   de ço   que   l'   abiô
          la   Marjano forgot NEG NEG thing of that which him had
          dich
          told
          'Marie Jeanne didn't forget anything of what she told him'

(cf. Posner (1985: 174 ff.) for other data from Romance dialects).

The Romance and Germanic
negation words

◎ NEG₁ V NEG₂
○ V NEG₂
🌫 ne V kel; ni(d) V ddim
▒ NEG₂ = passu(m)
▓ NEG₂ = punctu(m)
    NEG₂ = micu(m)
▤ NEG₂ = ne ente(m)
▦ AUX not V
▨ T Vf (...) inte Vi
▥ nicht/kein
▦ ma-V-i
(...) discontinuous construc-
    tions which are possible
    in preverbal negation
    areas

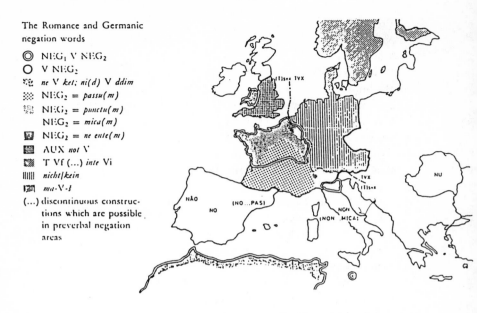

We draw attention here to the vast abundance of negative mophemes found
with NEG3, a point to which we will return in greater detail later on: *pas* and
pä < *passum* 'step', *ges* < *gentium* ('of the people'), *buk(a)* < *bucca* 'cheek, mouth',
beka < 'beak'?, *mia* < *mica* 'crumb', *ren* < *rem* 'thing' in addition to Piedm. *nein*
< *ne ente(m)* 'not (a) being', (cf. It. *niente* 'nothing'), Cat. *cap* < *capu(t)* 'head',
(formerly also Occ. *capdorn*, where *dorn* means 'fist': OFr. *do(u)r* < Wel. *dwrn*
'fist', as a unit of measure: see Schwegler (1986)), Arag. *brenca* < *branca* 'twig',
Gasc. *nada* , *(rem) nata(m)* 'born thing', Dolom.Lad. *nia* < *nullia* 'nothing'; cf.
Schwegler (1988).

As can clearly be seen from the map reproduced in this chapter, the three
types of negation in the Romance languages form three cohesive geographical
areas, and not a random pattern of distribution: NEG1 is distributed throughout
the southern Romance area (as well as Rumania); NEG2 is found in the central-
northern area; NEG3 doesn't belong to any standard Romance language, but is
distributed amongst the dialects of a vast area which overlaps with NEG2, with
which it is in competition (see Schwegler 1983; Molinelli – Bernini – Ramat 1987:
167; Molinelli 1988: 68). We will have to return later on to the inferences that
may be drawn from the geographical distribution of the various types of negation present in the Romance languages (see chapter 4), but note for the time
being that spoken French has a tendency to eliminate the first element of its
discontinous NEG (see Ashby 1981) – a construction in itself marked with
respect to a natural morphology (cf. 3.1.):

(6)   *C' est pas vrai, je viens pas,* etc.
        it is not true I come not
        'It isn't true, I'm not coming'

with a shift from NEG2 to NEG3.

As far as Italian is concerned, Piera Molinelli (1984; Molinelli—Bernini—Ramat 1987: 71) has clearly shown how this century has witnessed an increasing diffusion of NEG3 in some low varieties (so-called 'italiano popolare'). The reduction of NEG2 to NEG3 in sentences of the type exemplified in (7) is typical of substandard, colloquial and popular varieties (particularly in the north):

(7)   a. *Ma c'   era   niente   da fare* (instead of *Ma non c'era niente da fare*)
         but there was nothing to.do
         'But there was nothing we could do'
      b. *Seppi   nulla   fino a che   andai   a casa*
         knew:1SG nothing until to that went:1SG to home'
         'I hadn't known anything before I came home'
      c. *Politicamente erano   niente*
         politically   were:3PL nothing
         'As for politics, they weren't worth anything'
      d. *Davo   nemmeno un soldo   di valore   a quei   due*
         gave:1SG not.even a hap'orth of importance to those two
         'I considered those two worthless'

(political militants' texts from the Cremona area, published by D. Montaldi in 1971: see Molinelli (1984: 79)).

Even in Italian-speaking Switzerland a wealth of examples may be found (considerably more in the spoken than in the written language) such as:

(8)   a. *Abbiamo raggiunto niente*
         'We have achieved nothing'
      b. *Ci si   accorge   neanche   che è lunedi*
         one REFL realises not.even that is Monday
         'One doesn't even realise it's Monday'

(see Bianconi (1980), who also records the following interesting datum regarding speakers' self-evaluation: 48.1% of his Swiss interviewees consider *c'era nessuno* 'there was nobody' acceptable; 47.7%, that is, still a very high percentage, also accept *era mai stato in città* 'he had never been in town'; cf. Molinelli 1984: 83). In conclusion, it may be said that NEG3 is a construction consistently attested at a non-literary level, particularly in northern Italy (see Bernini 1992: 213).

Notice how postverbal NEG of the NEG3 type very often consists of negative quantifiers ('no-one', 'nothing') or negative adverbs ('not even', 'never'). We will return in the second part of the book to the behaviour of these forms; but this observation leads us to the diachronic examination of the Romance data.

2. The diachronic perspective

2.1. Towards a reconstruction of the negative sentence in Proto-Indo-European

Grammars of the old Indo-European languages, as indeed those of the original proto-language, deal extensively with NEG both at the phrasal and at the sentential level: a negative morpheme *nĕ̌, *mē̄ for sentence negation and a morpheme *n̥ for lexeme negation, may be reliably reconstructed as the *original* form (see Brugmann and Delbrück 1897, vol. IV: 519–540; Hirt 1937: 69–80).

On the other hand, amongst those concerned with the reconstruction of Proto-Indo-European within a typological framework in the Greenbergian (1966) tradition that studies the order of basic constituents, only W.P.Lehmann has examined the expression of NEG. According to Lehmann (1974: 153) sentential NEG in PIE was originally postverbal, in keeping with the basic OV (Object + Verb) order which required the sentential qualifier to be postposed to the verb. However, data from earlier attested languages do not seem to support this assumption (for a recent discussion of Lehmann's position see Dryer (1988: 106–109) where it is observed (p. 106) that "more OV languages place the negative before the verb than after it").

As far as sentential NEG morphemes are concerned the vast enquiry conducted by Östen Dahl (1979) (cf. also 0.2.) has shown that there is a strict correlation between the two main types of negative constructions (that is, syntactic constructions that make use of negative particles like *nĕ̌, *mē̄, on the one hand, and morphological constructions, such as the use of affixes or a negative auxiliary (AUX) in the Uralic languages, on the other hand) and the order of the basic elements (i. e. Greenberg's 'meaningful elements': Subject, Object, Verb). Morphologically based negative constructions usually follow the general rule which applies to the order of words and morphemes. Therefore suffixes are in strict correlation with orders which provide for the Vb in final position; and in the dominant VSO order an inflected AUX usually precedes the main verb, while in languages with a predominantly SOV order it follows the main verb (see Greenberg 1966, Universal 16); NEG particles in syntactic constructions instead show a clear TENDENCY to appear in PREVERBAL position (before the finite verb in compound forms), independently of whatever the predominant basic order may be (such preference for a NEG + Vb order is confirmed by Dryer's more recent survey on an even more extensive sample of languages: 345 (See Dryer 1988)).

In the vast majority of cases the old Indo-European languages follow this tendency:

(1)   Old Irish (Würzburger Glossen 8a4)
            ar-nach-n-aurchoissed
            that-NEG-him-would.detain:3SG
            'that he should not detain him'

where *nach* < **ne-kʷe* is the NEG form used before a personal clitic pronoun.

(2)   Gothic (Gal. 4,30)
            ni   nimiþ arbi   sunus þiujos
            NEG takes heredity son   slave:GEN
            'The slave's son does not inherit'

(3)   Lithuanian (Fraenkel 1950: 78)
            n-éra   kas   piauną· darą·
            not-there.is something to.harvest to.do
            'There is nothing to harvest, to do'

(4)   Old Bulgarian
            ašte ne   bi   otŭ   boga by-lŭ   sĭ,   ne
            if   NEG PTCL from God be-APFP such, NEG
            mog-lŭ   bi
            be.able-APFP PTCL
            'If he had not been thus by the will of God, he would not have been able (to do that)'

(5)   Albanian (Lambertz 1959: 83, where *nuk* < **ne-kʷod*)
            Skënder nuk   do   ta   turpëronte   Brahimin
            Skender NEG AUX him dishonour:IMPF:3SG Brahim:ACC
            'Skender would not dishonour him, Brahim'

(6)   Tocharian A
            ñātsey-ac   mā   kumnäṣ
            misery-in NEG reach
            'he will not fall into misery'

(7)   Old Persian (DB I 70−71)
            yaþā   Gaumāta hya maguš viþam tayām amāxam nayi
            so.that Gaumata the wizard house that of.us   NEG
            parābara
            destroyed
            'so that Gaumata the Wizard did not destroy our (royal) house'

(8)   Vedic (*RV* 3.59,2)
         ná   hanyate, ná jīyate   tuóto
         NEG is.killed not is.beaten helped.by.you
         'he was not killed, he was not beaten with your help'

(9)   Hittite (KBo 2 III 12−5)
         *karū   ERÍN-*MEŠ *Manda* (...)   *luzzi*   *natta   karp[ianzi]*
         before people-PL Manda:NOM service:ACC NEG lend:3PL
         sahhan   natta   īsser
         feudal:ACC   NEG   did:3PL
         'before, the people [of] Manda (...) did not lend their services (in
         the fields) nor did they do feudal labours' (where *natta* < **ne + id*?).

As can clearly be seen, attestations of NEG preposed to the Vb belong to
either VSO languages such as the Celtic ones, SVO languages such as Albanian
and the Baltic languages, SOV languages such as Persian and Hittite, as well as
Tocharian (SVO with SOV features).
   We may also add to these attestations those languages which do not retain
the IE **nĕ* but which nonetheless have NEG in preverbal position:

(10)   Armenian (*Lc.* 2,7)
         zi   oč   goyr noča teli   yijavanin
         since NEG was them place in.hostel.the
         'since there was no place for them in the hostel'

(11)   classical Greel (Aesch., *Prom.* 232)
         lógon   ouk éskhen   oudéna
         account not took:3SG any
         'he took no account (of it)'

   As far as Latin, Italic, Homeric Greek, Avestan and (Vedic) Sanskrit are concerned two NEG positions are possible: either sentence initial or in front of the
verb group:

(12)   Latin (*XII Tab.*, 5)
         si adgnatus   nec   escit, gentiles   familiam
         if close.relative neither exits distant.relatives family
         habento
         have:IMPER.FUT
         'if there is no close relative, those more distant shall have the family
         property'

(13)   Latin (Plaut., *Curc.* 713)
               non   ego   te   flocci   facio
               NEG   I   you   bean:GEN   do:1SG
               'You're not worth a bean'

and in particular with iterated NEG (in the type *nec...nec*) NEG is found in initial position (see also (22)):

(14)   a. Latin (*Annales* 186)
             nec   mi   aurum posco   nec   mi   pretium
             neither me:DAT gold   ask:1SG nor me:DAT price
             dederitis   nec...
             give:ANT.FUT:2PL   nor
             'neither do I ask for gold for me nor shall you pay me a price, nor...'
         b. Umbrian (*Tab. Ig.* VIa 6−7)
             erse   neip   mugatu   nep arsir
             then neither one.makes. a.noise nor with.dedications
             andersistu
             one.interrupts

as also in Homer:

(15)   *oúte ti mántis   eṑn   oút' oiōnôn   sápha   eidṓs*
             nor soothsayer being nor of.the.birds clearly knowing
             (Od. 1, 202)
             'being neither a soothsayer nor knowing the omens'

in Vedic (as sentence negation):

(16)   a. *ná   tắ   naṣanti; ná   dabhắti   táskaraḥ* (*R V* 6.28, 3)
             NEG they perish NEG damages thief
             'they will not perish nor will a thief harm them'

and also as phrase negation:

         b. *ná   tád   devó ná   mártyas tuturyād   yắni*
             nor that god nor mortal could.surpass the.things.that
             právṛddho vṛṣabháṣ chakắra (*RV* 8.96, 2)
             powerful bull   did
             'neither a god nor a man could surpass that which the powerful bull did'

and in Avestan:

(17)   a. *nōiṯ   ərəžəǰyōi*   *fraǰyāitiš   nōiṯ*
        NEG   for.he.who.lives.justly   destruction   NEG
        fšuyentē   *drəgvasū*   *pairī*   (*Y.* 29, 5)
        for.he.who.raises.cattle   in.the.friends.of.Drug   by
        '(let there be) no destruction by the friends of the Drug [Falsehood]
        for he who lives justly, nor for he who raises cattle'

also with repetition of NEG before Vb:

        b. *Nōiṯ   spō.bərətō*   *nōiṯ   maxši.bərətō*   *nasuš   narəm*
        NEG   dragged.by.dogs   NEG   dragged.by.flies   corpse   one
        nōiṯ   + āstārayeiti   (*Vid.* 5,3)
        NEG   makes.guilty
        'neither the corpse dragged by dogs, nor the corpse dragged by flies
        makes one guilty'

As can be seen from these examples, sentence NEG in initial position is
strongly emphatic (and sometimes its function almost overlaps with noun phrase
NEG, even though in Vedic *ná* may be used only with sentences containing a
finite verb (see Macdonell 1962: 235): cf. (15), (16ab) [and (17)?]). Concerning
Ved. *ná* Gonda (1951: 52) does observe that it is used in initial position with
the function of a strongly emphatic reaction to what was affirmed beforehand:
'it is not so that...'.

Again in initial position we find:

(18)   Homeric Greek (*Il.* 1, 24)
        All' ouk   Atreḯdēi   *Agamémnoni   hēndane   thumôi*
        but NEG   to.son.of.Atreus   Agamemnon   pleased   in.the.mind
        'but (that) did not please Agamemnon son of Atreus'

(19)   Avestan (*Y.* 51, 14)
        Nōiṯ   urvāpā   *dātōibyas-čā*   *karapanō*
        NEG   to.the.dispositions   to.the.laws.-and   the.karapans
        vāstrāṯ   *arəm*
        for.agriculture   obedient (are)
        'The karapans (false priests) will not obey the rules and laws of
        agriculture'

(20)   Vedic (*RV* 10.14, 2)
        na-íṣā́   gávyūtir   ápabhartavā   *u*
        NEG-it   pasture   is.to.be.taken.away   PTCL
        'this pasture is not to be taken away'

etc. etc.

The preverbal position is more or less obligatory with certain verbs such as 'to know, to want, to be able to'; cf. the Lat. forms *nescio* 'I don't know', *nolo* 'I don't want', *nequeo* 'I can't', and analogous formations in other languages (for example OE **nyllan, nellan* < *ne willan* 'not to want', OHG *nist* < *ne ist* 'not is', etc.).

In conclusion, therefore, it seems that sentential NEG was normally placed in front of the verb in PIE (we leave to those who maintain an original postverbal position the task of reconstructing the whys and wherefores of its supposed shift to preverbal position).[1]

From the typological point of view it will be observed furthermore that even a rigidly SOV modern IE language such as Hindi does not exhibit SOV+NEG but rather draws NEG into initial position in coordinate clauses; cf.

(21)   a. *na   mẽ bāzār   gayā,   na gha*
           NEG I   to.bazaar went:1SG   not to.house
           'I didn't go to the bazaar nor home' (Bhatia 1978: 25).

And yet NEG appears in preverbal position:

        b. *usne kām   nāhĩ̀   kiyā*
           he   work NEG   did
           'he didn't work' (Bhatia 1978: 23)

2.2. Diachronic developments

It will have already been noted in the examples recorded above that there is a tendency for the particle *ne to reinforce itself by uniting – especially in negative coordinates of the type 'neither...nor' – with some other morpheme, as in the case of OIr. *nach*, Goth. *nih*, and Umbrian *ne(i)p* < *ne-kʷe 'and not' (like Gr. *oú-te!*), OPrus. *neggi* 'neither', arch.Lat. *nec* < *ne-gi* (?) with the IE particle **-ghe/gho* that is found in OSlav. *ni-že* 'ne-que, and not', Lith. *ne-gì*, *ne-gù* 'no' (cf. the reinforcing Sansk. particle *gha, ha* after *ná*, Gr. *ou-khí*), Alb. *nuk* < *ne-kʷod, Hitt. *natta*, Ved. *ned*, OPers. *nayi* and Avest. *nōiṭ* < *ne-id 'not-that' then simply 'no'; the same is true for Lat. *non* < *ne-oinom (?) 'not-one' (neuter singular, like *nuk, ned, nayi, nōiṭ* just mentioned; cf. the analogous Gr. *oud-én* > Mod.Gr. *dén* 'not'). The formation of *nōn* is exactly comparable to that of *nūllum* < *ne oinolom 'not one (diminutive)', or of *nihil* < *ne hīlum 'not a thread' (see Ernout–Meillet 1951: 788).

The case of *non* broaches the subject of negative quantifiers and the new negative particles which arise out of the fusion of the negative morpheme (*nĕ, *mē) with other words, usually without negative meaning, like, for example, Eng. *none* < 'not one', or Ger. *nicht* 'not' < *ni eo wiht* 'not ever thing'.

As can be seen from Ved. *nákim, nákis* (also *mākim*), Avest. *naēčīm, naēčiš* 'no' (emphatic), reinforcement of NEG with a pronominal base is a very old process. It is immediately apparent that next to *nákim, nákis* with the meaning 'no' there is *nákis* 'no-one' (Avest. *naēkay-*).

The only negative quantifier that may be reconstructed for PIE is indeed *ne(i)-kʷos*, with the indefinite/interrogative pronoun *kʷo-/kʷi-* (see in fact Sanskr. *nákis*, Avest. *naēkay-*, OSl. *nikŭto* and Lith. *nĩekas*, Latv. *nekas*; also Hitt. UL *kuis* (with the ideogramme UL for 'not') (OIr. *nech* 'someone'?; see Sornicola (1988: 144)). The process is, however, repeated independently in the various IE linguistic traditions: see Gr. *oud-eís, oú-tis* 'not-one > no-one', like Goth. *ni ains-hun* (with the clitic *-hun* < IE *kʷu-ne*, again from the indefinite/interrogative stem *kʷo-* : cf. W.P. Lehmann (1986: 194)), ONor. *nein* < *ne-einn*, OE *nān* (OSax. *nēn*) < *ne ān*, OHG *neo-man, nio-man* 'no-man > no-one'; Lat. *nēmo* < *nē hemō*, Eng. *no-body*. Note that in all these cases NEG is represented (except, of course, in Greek) by IE *nĕ-*, sentential negation, not by *n̥*, word negation (as in *n̥-gnō-tos* > Gr. *ágnōtos*, Sansk. *ájñātā*, Lat. *ignōtus*, Goth. *unkunþs*, Arm. *ancanawt'* 'unknown'): this being an important indication of the fact that the expressions for 'no-one' were created inside the syntax of the sentence (originally perhaps with the indefinite pronoun in clitic form, in 'Wackernagel position', that is, in second place in the sentence: *né-kʷos* like *né-kʷe* (see note 1) with the well-known enclitic particle *kʷe*, which shares in all probability the same root as *kʷos*).

An element with an autonomous meaning affixed to the sentence NEG and this was then crystallised in a new morphological form − that, in fact, of the negative quantifier: see, for example, in OSax. *Ne mag that getellean man*, literally: 'not may that tell man' > 'no-one may tell that' which then became the new form of the 'negative pronoun' *nioman*, already cited (see Ramat 1988a: 137).

Note the position of the subject *man* after the non-finite verb, while *nioman* almost always appears preverbally if it is the subject (cf. 8.3. for this in more detail). Like *ne...man* the corresponding neutral 'nothing' may also appear divided: *ni...wiht* 'not...thing' (> *ni(c)ht* 'nothing'): Goth. *ni bigitiþ waiht* (Joh. 14, 30) 'he will not find anything' (liter. 'not he will find thing'); also with the reverse order *waiht...ni*: *jah sai andaugiba rodeiþ jah waiht du imma ni qiþand* (Joh. 7, 26) 'and lo, with candour he speaks and they don't say anything to him' (in Greek *kaì oudèn autôi légousin*), OHG *ni was wiht gitanes* (*Tat*.1, 2) 'factum est nihil' (liter. 'not (there) was thing of done'). We shall return in 7.6. to the different treatments of the negative indefinite subject or object; here it will suffice to show how there is a multiplicity of (new) formations (continually renewing themselves) to express these pronouns.

2.3. Reinforcement of NEG:
the creation of new negative morphemes

The phonetic autonomy of the negative particle *nĕ* was precarious however, as can be seen from the examples cited in note 1, and there was a danger of it becoming unrecognisable, particularly in specific circumstances, like, for example, before a nasal in a cluster such as OE *menn ne cunnon* [mɛn:ə kun:ō] 'the men didn't know'. This led to the creation, in very ancient times, of reinforced NEG forms such as Avest. *nōiṯ*, OPers. *naiy*, Lat. *nōn*, already seen in the previous section.

On the other hand, on the pragmatic − discourse − level, the tendency to express emphasis by reiterating the expression of the same concept (such as, for example, in Fr. *ce-lui-ci* 'this one', composed of three deictic elements) is well known.

In the case of sentential NEG originally 'full' words, those, that is, having an autonomous meaning of their own, undergo a development where they take on negative values, entirely analogous to the development that led to the formation of negative quantifiers of the type Lat. *nemo*, Eng. *nobody* (cf. above): see, for example, the already cited Ger. *nicht* 'not' < *ni eo wiht* liter. 'not ever thing', Eng. *not* < MEng. *nat, not* < *nought* < OE *nāwiht, nōwiht*, liter. 'not thing'; Lat. *nihil* (< *ne hīlum* 'not (a) thread' > 'nothing').

Note that in the same way that we have Goth. *ni...waiht* (for example, *ni rodida waiht* in Joh. 18,20 as translation of *elálēsa oudén* 'he said nothing' (cf. also the examples at the end of the preceding section)), so also we find in Latin *nec/ neque...hilum*: *nec defit ponderis hilum* (Lucr. 3.220) 'none of the load is missing', *neque dispendi facit hilum* (Ennius, apud Varr., *L.L.*V, 111, Chapter XXII) 'and of loss not a whit does she suffer' in other words 'she loses nothing':[2] in the example from Ennius it can be clearly seen how the element subsequently incorporated into the NEG appears originally autonomously, for example as DO (direct object) of the Vb, in postverbal position (:SVO). As for German, Otfried frequently uses *wiht* as the first or second element of a double-constituent NEG:

(22)   a. *Nist wiht suntar werde* (I, 5, 63)
              'there is not but there will be'
          b. *thie líut es wiht ni duáltun* (I, 1, 58)
              'these people did not hesitate'
          c. *wiht ni fórahtet ir iu* (III, 8, 29)
              'do not be afraid'

(note in (22b) and (22c) the position of *wiht* 'thing', before *ni*, as in the previous Gothic example (Joh. 7, 26): a literal translation of the two examples would be:

'these people of that (a) thing not hesitated' > 'these people not even a bit didn't hesitate' > 'these people didn't hesitate (at all)'; and '(a) thing not fear you ever' > 'do not fear not even a thing' > 'do not be (at all) afraid'.

This is the situation that we find in the French discontinuous NEG *ne...pas*, introduced in chapter 1, in which – as opposed to German – fusion of the two parts of NEG to form a new morpheme does not occur. The object (direct and 'of measure') of the verb falls, along with the same verb, within the scope of the preverbal NEG (the type *non vado passum* 'I do not go a step', *non bibo guttam* 'I do not drink a drop': recall the abundance of elements with negative value in postverbal position, already observed in chapter 1); it then acquires an intrinsically negative value, becomes a verbal modality qualifier and finally renders the negative adverb that precedes the Vb superfluous: *je ne vais* > *je ne vais pas* > *je vais pas* 'I do not go'. The same occurs in German and Dutch: *ih en sprehhe nicht* > *ich spreche nicht* 'I don't speak', where *en* represents the old preverbal NEG; not to mention in English: *he ne may nat wel deme* (Chaucer) > 'he may not well deem'.[3] Note that *pas, nicht* may in their turn be reinforced becoming *pas rien* (in the substandard *c'est pas rien*[4]), *pas du tout* and *nichts* (in Berthold *nihtsnit*, dial. *nichtst* < *nichtzit* < *nichtesnicht*, liter. 'nothing of nothing'). Even *du tout* itself acquires negative value and replaces *pas*:

(23)   *Croyez-vous que je blâme? Du tout.*
         (Balzac, *Le père Goriot*, éd. folio Gallimard, p. 151)
         'Do you think that I disapprove? Not at all'

This is the so-called 'negative polarization' of items which, like *pas, mica, goutte, wiht, trophen* etc., did not originally have negative value: appearing habitually, however, in (emphatic) negative contexts together with the Vb, in the same scope of the negation, they take on this value and become, in fact, Negative Polarity Items (NPI).

The process may repeat itself indefinitely, as can be seen from the expressions in spoken (and often vulgar) Italian *Non ci vedo un tubo/un accidente* 'I can't see a damn/bloody (thing)' and the like. There is a well-known joke about an American colonel posted to the NATO base in Verona who, having picked up Italian from the locals rather than having learnt it from books, thought that NEG in Italian was *un cazzo* , lit. 'a prick' (see the numerous idioms of the the sort *non ci vedo un c.* 'I can't see a fuck(ing thing)', *non ci capisco un c.* 'I don't understand a fuck(ing thing)' etc.). Note the obligatory presence of the article in these expressions (***non ci vedo tubo/accidente*) which shows clearly the original Object function of these NPIs, in the scope of NEG (see von Bremen 1986: 261). In Old French we still find

(24)   a. *N'   irai*   un pas *avant*
         NEG will.go:1SG a   step forward
         (St. Thomas Becket's Life, v. 5480)
         'I will not go forward a step'

where the negative emphasizer *un pas* is syntactically still an NP with its article and semantically retains its full-fledged value. In the corresponding Mod.French sentence

         b. *Je n'irai* pas *avant*

the NPI is totally "déréférentialisé, du fait de l' "article-zéro" qu'il faut postuler devant cet ancien nom" [dereferentialised, for the "zero article" which is to be assumed in front of this old name] (Forest 1993: 136).

The continually self-renewing expressivity explains the many NPIs found in the Romance languages and dialects as postverbal NEG (NEG2 and NEG3: cf. chapter 1). Otto Jespersen in his excellent essay on negation in English and other languages (1917: 32) cites the case of Eng. *devil* "(also without the article)…frequently used as an indirect negative"; for example *I am going back − The devil you are* (Trollope); *My parents are al dead, and the diuel a peny they have left me, but a bare pention* (Marlowe; see Jespersen (1917: 32)): see also the use of *fanden* 'devil' in Danish: *Jeg vil bevise af den sunde logica, at I er tyr − I skal bevise fanden* 'I will show you with sane logic that you are a beast − The devil you will!' (Jespersen 1917: 34). As for German, we may recall the case of *Tropfen* 'drop', frequently used by Otfried as the second element of NEG2 (around twenty examples):

(25)   *joh ír ouh wiht thes ni áhtot, ouh dróf es ni bidráhtot*
         'and you do not consider that at all nor do you think it worth a drop'
         (Otfr. III 25, 24)

Drof must have been available as a formative for the neutral negative pronoun in colloquial varieties of Old High German (cf. in the *Pariser Gespräche* [Conversations in Paris], a sort of handbook for the rapid learning of German from the 10th century:

(26)   *Semergot elfe ne haben ne trophen* (*si me deus adiuuet, non habeo nihil*)
         (1.48; in 1.74 the same *formula* is glossed as *non abeo quid*)).
         'God help me: I have nothing'

The Romance equivalent is found in Lombard *negót* (< *ne gutta(m)*).[5]

As for Middle Dutch we can draw an example from Karel ende Elegast (v. 440):

(27)   *In* [= *ik en*] *prise mijn lijf niet twee peren*
           'My life is not worth two pears'[6]

En is often found reinforced by *meer, bore* 'much', *oit* 'always', *twint* 'blink'. From the 17th century onwards we find *niet een myt* 'not a spit' (with indefinite article!), and in modern Dutch we have the type *ik geloof geen bliksem van* 'I don't believe it a bolt' (Weijnen 1971: 137, no. 1).

The same type of discontinuous NEG is also found in the Celtic languages:

(28)   Welsh
           Nid   wyf i ddim yn hoffi   coffi
           NEG am I NEG in to.like coffee
           'I don't like coffee'

(29)   Breton
           Ne   lavaro   ket   kement-se
           NEG say:FUT:3SG NEG all-that
           'He will not say it'

where *ddim, ket* are NPIs that originally had no intrinsic negative value at all (*dim* 'thing', *ket* 'indeed' (?)). Even *takenn* 'drop' (cf. *goutte, trophen* !), *tamm* 'penny, coin' (cf. *non quiero far en el monesterio un dinero de daño, Cid* 252!), *barr* 'gem', not to mention *poent, pas* of obvious French origin, could serve as the second element of NEG2 in Middle Breton. Note, furthermore, that in Breton the second element may also be *ebed* 'at all', like the Fr. *du tout* (cf. Ramat–Bernini 1990: 33) and 7.3.4., note 28).

(30)   *N'   em-eus   amezeg ebet   er gêr-mañ*
        NEG have:1SG friends at.all in city-this
        'I don't have any friends at all in this city'

In conclusion, the development of an emphatic sentence NEG displays the so-called 'NEG cycle' (see Schwegler (1988); cf. also Vennemann (1989) and of course Jespersen (1917; 1924: chapter XXIII)):

French   *ne* + Vb > *ne* + Vb + *pas* > Vb + *pas* (> *pas du tout* > *du tout*);
English   *ne* + Vb > *ne* + Vb + *not* > Vb + *not*;
German   *ni/en/ne* + Vb > *ni/en/ne* + Vb + *niht* > Vb + *nicht*.

What occurs in the numerous Romance dialects with NEG3 of the type *buc, mia, pas* etc. already mentioned may be interpreted in the same way:

(31)   Bergamasque
           Se nò la   sömériza la tàca   mía
           If no the seed   it takes.root NEG
           'Otherwise the seed will not take root'

(32)   Sursilvan
        Questa schlateina ven   buc   ad ir giù
        This   surname comes NEG to go down
        'This surname will not disappear'

(33)   Provençal
        Jan   manjo pas   de peissoun
        John eats   NEG of fish
        'John doesn't eat fish'

etc. alongside examples of NEG2 such as:

(34)   Sursilvan
        Ke   co   nu   fatschi   britch
        that that NEG do:1SG NEG
        'that I don't do it at all' (cf. chapter 1, example (3c))

(35)   Aragonese
        No   la tastaràs   brenca ista coca
        NEG it will.taste:2SG NEG this sweet
        'You will not taste this sweet at all'

(36)   Pyrenean Catalan
        No   se   cap
        NEG know:1SG NEG
        'I don't know'

(see Ramat–Bernini (1990: 29) with references to the preceding bibliography;
cf. also Zanuttini (1987: 167) for a brief presentation of analogous occurrences
in Piedmontese: *n(e)* + Vb > *ne* + Vb + *nent* > Vb + *nent/nein*; for some
criticisms of Zanuttini's approach see Berruto (1990, notes 24 and 26), who,
after having observed that Piedmontese represents a "textbook example of the
so-called 'Jespersen's cycle'", also records the possibility of typologically very
interesting sentences such as *a j-è pa ñün* 'there's no one at all', as a reinforced
form of *a j-è ñün*). Other languages, such as Breton, have stopped at the second
stage of the cycle, without arriving at NEG3: Bret. *ne* + Vb > *ne* + Vb (+
ket/takenn/tamm...) > *ne* + Vb + *ket*.

3. Word order and negation

3.1. Preverbal negation

From the syntactic point of view the complete NEG cycle occurs, however, in some creoles. In French-based creoles NEG [pa] (< *pas*) appears before the Vb, like the tense-aspect markers:

(1) a. Mauritius

   mo môte pa pe   travaj
   ma montre pas PROG travaill-
   my watch NEG PROG work
   'My watch doesn't work'

  b. *nu pa ti   pu rãtre*
   nous pas PRET FUT rentr-
   we NEG PRET FUT come.back
   'We would not have come back'

(2)   Seychelles

   person pa pu pik u
   personne pas FUT piqu- vous
   no-one NEG FUT sting you:PL
   'No-one will sting you'

(3)   Guyana

   mo pa ka dromi
   moi pas FUT dorm-
   I NEG FUT sleep
   'I won't sleep'

while in Louisiana creole postverbal NEG may still be found:

(4)   *mo kup pa* and *mo pa kup*
   moi coup- pas moi pas coup-
   I cut NEG I NEG cut
   'I do not cut';

see also

(5)   Guadeloupe

   Sa vo pa la pẽn and *Sa pa vo la pẽn*
   ça vaut pas la peine ça pas vaut la peine
   this be.worth NEG the pain this NEG be.worth the pain
   'It's not worth it'

(Green 1988: 450; Posner 1985: 180–181). The repositioning of NEG is in all likelihood connected to the general tendency for having NEG in preverbal position. Brugnatelli (1987: 59) notes that in the Maghreb Arabic dialects as well there is a tendency these days to reduce the discontinuous negation (NEG2) to a preverbal NEG (NEG1), either with the simple loss of the second element, or with the emergence of new negations. Such a tendency may be vouched for on the basis of a variety of data and has a psycholinguistic explanation. Both considerations merit some attention.

The various positions of NEG in the sentence make clear what is in each case its scope ('portée'), that is, which element is negated in each case. The following Swedish example is taken from Christina Heldner (1981: 15) (analogous German examples with *nur* are found in Koktová (1987: 180), taken from Jacobs (1983); see also 'cleft sentences' of the type *It wasn't JOHN who called me yesterday* vs. *It wasn't ME that John called yesterday* vs. again *It wasn't YESTERDAY that John called me*: cf. also Taglicht (1984: 103)):

(6)   a. *Kalle gav*   inte *Lisa en smörgas   med   korv*
           K.   gave not L.   a   sandwich with salami
           'Kalle *didn't* give Lisa a salami sandwich'
        b. *Kalle gav   L.* inte *en smörgas   med   korv,   utan ett kex*
           K.   gave L. not a   sandwich with salami but   a   biscuit
        c. *Kalle gav   L. en smörgas*   inte *med   korv,   utan med   ost*
           K.   gave L. a   sandwich not with salami, but with cheese
        d. Inte *Kalle utan Pelle gav   L. en smörgas   med   korv*
           not K.   but P.   gave L. a   sandwich with salami

The same happens in Italian, German (see Koktová 1987), French, English, Russian, Danish etc. The differences are due to different presuppositions: whoever utters (6b) intends to affirm that Lisa has in fact received a biscuit and not a sandwich (as he thinks his interlocutor believes); whoever utters (6c) intends to deny that the sandwich received by Lisa was with salami (as his interlocutor believes); whoever utters (6d) takes for granted that Lisa has received a salami sandwich but denies that it was Kalle who gave it to her (as he thinks his interlocutor believes). (6a) is in fact the simple negative predication, without any particular presuppositions (with postverbal NEG in Swedish).

Circumstantial adverbial phrases, where present, may reduce the scope of NEG:

(7)   a. *John didn't kick the ball that time*

and

        b. *John didn't kick the ball with enough force*

both presuppose that John hit the ball (but not on that particular occasion in question / but not with sufficient force): see Givón (1984: 329) (on the other hand, the same Givón (1975: 62−63) rightly recalls "the more marked presuppositional status of negatives" compared to the corresponding affirmative sentences).[1]

In the absence of such adverbials, that is, when NEG co-occurs with no more than the elements S, O and V only, its scope tends to coincide with the entire Verb Phrase (=VO/OV):

(8)   *Non* sv[*vado passum*]
           'I don't go (for) a step'

More generally, it may be said that there is a clear tendency to consider NEG as a Vb (or VP) operator, even in cases where NEG, as Horn (1978) puts it, is 'semantically sentential', since the Vb, being the PRED, is the central point of the sentence. Note in this context also the difference in standard Italian between

(9)   a. *È venuto* [SUBJ]*nessuno?*
              is come   no-one
              'Did anyone come?'

and

           b. **È venuto nessuno*
              'Came no-one';

between the indirect interrogative

(10)   a. *Si   domandava se sarebbe   venuto nessuno*
              REFL wondered if would.be come no-one
              'She wondered if anyone would come'

and

           b. ***Sapeva che sarebbe venuto nessuno*
              'She knew that would come no-one'

between

(11)   a. *Hai   sentito* [OD]*nessuno?*
              have:2SG heard   no-one
              'Did you hear anyone?'

and

           b. ***Hai sentito nessuno*
              'You have heard no-one'

The grammaticality of (9a), (10a) and (11a) — with *nessuno* postposed to, and no other NEG morph preceding, the Vb — is due to the fact that they are not declarative negative sentences, like (9b), (10b) and (11b), but rather interrogatives: the Vb falls within the scope not of NEG but of the interrogation. On the other hand the (b) examples are well-formed only if the negative quantifier is placed before the Vb, which will then fall within its scope (*nessuno è venuto*; *sapeva che nessuno sarebbe venuto*: see below, 7.6.).

Data from second language (L2) acquisition and from pidgins and creoles also confirm this tendency to place NEG in preverbal position, which is typical of what it may be appropriate at this point to consider a 'natural' syntax in the sense that Dressler, Mayerthaler, Wurzel etc. (1987) use the term (for pidgins and creoles cf. examples (1) — (5) above). The bibliography regarding L2 acquisition is enormous and it is not possible to give an exhaustive critical appraisal of it here (cf. Klein (1986); McLaughlin (1987); Schumann and Stauble (1983), who, significantly, deal with L2, pidgins and creoles together; see also Dal Negro (1994) on the interlanguage varieties of learners of German).

As far as the acquisition of negation in particular is concerned, sentences such as the following, produced by native Spanish speakers, are worth noting:

(12)   a. *Carolina no go to play*
        b. *I no can see*   (Klein 1986: 97)
        c. *This no is chicken* (Zobl 1980: 471)

which correspond exactly to those of speakers of the English based Guyana creole, produced in low varieties of the decreolization process ('basilang'):

(13)   a. *Hu na kyan afood it*
           'Those who cannot afford it'
        b. *Yu na taak tu di man neks de?*
           'Didn't you talk to the man next day?'
           (cf. Schumann and Stauble 1983: 262 f.).

Note the positioning of a NEG marker before the Vb in (12)−(13b). If mother tongue interference may be called upon to account for the Spanish speakers, this is certainly not the case for Norwegian or Japanese speakers whose languages have Vb + NEG, but who nonetheless in the initial stages of acquisition produce English sentences such as:

(14)   *I no like English. I no want many children.*

Sentences with a postposed NEG, where traces of L1 interference may be perceived, such as:

(15)   *He finds machinery no. Sells no.*

represent only 4% of the total (see Schumann and Stauble 1983: 273). The same goes for adult Turkish speakers (also an SOV language) learning German (a language with postverbal NEG!):

(16)   a. *Ich nich* [sic] *lesen*
           'I not read'
        b. *Vielleicht* [SUBJ]*andere türke nicht helfen*
           'Perhaps other Turk not help'
        c. *ich nicht blübe* (i. e. bleibe) *hier*
           'I not stay here'

(see Clahsen 1988: 22; Dal Negro 1994: 370). Meisel (1983: 130−131) reports data drawn from a longitudinal study of German and Swedish children (languages with Vb+NEG) from which the existence of a NEG+Vb phase emerges:

(17)   a. *Embla   inte   ha   täck-et*
           E.(name) NEG   have quilt-ART
           'Embla doesn't have the quilt'
        b. *Inte gatt   sönder*
           Not has.been broken
           'It has not been broken' (cf. also Clahsen (1988: 17)).

Leaving aside the general hypotheses concerning the difference between the mechanisms of L1 acquisition and those of L2 acquisition (see Clahsen 1988) it may therefore be concluded that 'natural syntax' calls for a negative element in preverbal position: the verb, being the predicate, the central pivot, of the sentence, does not come within the scope of NEG when the negativity applies to a specific part of the sentence (as in examples (6b)−(6d)) but rather when it applies to the entire sentence itself (:(6a)). The speaker and the hearer need a clear signal, before the central pivot, that the truth of the entire sentence is being denied (:'It is not the case that P'). This is also confirmed by the strategies , already alluded to, which children employ in learning their mother tongue: "In a variety of ways, children indicate in their restructuring of parental languages that the scope of negation should be the proposition, as indicated by the verb or the clause as a whole, rather than any particular nonverbal lexical item within the clause" (Slobin 1985: 222).

Note also, in this context, that in the initial stages of L2 acquisition NEG appears with great regularity before the main verb, more often than before the auxiliary, modal verb or copula[2] to the point of prompting Meisel (1983: 133) to formulate the strategy followed initially by learners as follows: "Place NEG immediately before the constituent to be negated" (which corresponds to what

has also been established from examples (6a) – (6d); cf. also Zobl (1980: 472):
"the type ANAPHORIC NEG + PREDICATE and NP + NEG + VP repre-
sent a presumably universal early stage in the acquisition of various language-
specific negation devices").

The rule which shifts the verb from final position in Basque when the sentence is negative may be defined in the same light:

(18)   *Etxe   bat dakusat*
          house a   see:1SG but
          'I see a house'

(19)   *Ez   dakusat etxe   bat*
          NEG see:1SG house a
          'I don't see a house'   (: Manandise 1987: 322).

3.2. Postverbal negation

If, however, the general tendency to place sentential NEG in preverbal position
is valid it is necessary to find an explanation for the postverbal NEG forms,
which do not seem to follow 'morphological naturalness'. A Vb + NEG order
is found not only in SOV languages but also in French (*je parle pas* 'I don't
speak'), in Italian dialects (Milan. *mi parli no* 'I don't speak'), in Brazilian Portuguese (*ele fala português não* 'he doesn't speak Portughese'): cf. Posner (1985); in
Middle English *I seye not,* in German *Ich sage nicht* 'I don't say', etc. Klima and
Bellugi (1966) also noted with regards to L1 acquisition of English – a language
with very complex negative morphology – that in the initial phases children
produce sentences such as:

(20)   *No wipe finger*

as well as

(21)   *Wear mitten no*

so that it seems as though Meisel's rule of strategic behaviour mentioned at the
end of the previous section should instead be reformulated: "Place the operator
of NEG either immediately before, or after the utterance to be negated". The
second possibility, as Eva Hajičová rightly observes in an interesting article
(1984: 101), occurs in the adult language only where the verb belongs to the
'topic' of the sentence.

This opens the way to a correct interpretation of postverbal negation, which is marked — as we have seen — from the point of view of a 'natural morphology'.

A negative sentence usually denies that which is affirmed (or else given as presupposed) in the corresponding affirmative sentence (cf. Introduction above): as Bergson says, an affirmative proposition represents an evaluation of a (noetic) object, a state of affairs; a negative proposition represents an evaluation of a proposition (see Molinelli—Bernini—Ramat (1987: 181); cf. Stickel (1975: 32)). "Negation is a distinct speech-act in language, that is used largely to deny supposed beliefs of hearers in the context where the corresponding affirmative has been assumed, rather than to impart new information in the context of the hearer's ignorance" (Givón 1975: 102—103). For this reason the situational presuppositions have a dominant role in negation (cf. again the Introduction).

NEG therefore belongs to the performative structure of a sentence, well before the grammatical structure (cf. Antinucci—Volterra 1975: 236; Bosque 1980: 12). It appears as a sentence operator/qualifier — as such it is linked to the central pivot of the sentence, the Vb (or the verb phrase): see Harris (1978: 23). Note that in Hungarian the negative sentence requires the preverbal particle to be shifted to postverbal position: *Péter felszáll* (unmarked) 'Peter goes upstairs' vs. *Péter száll fel* (marked) 'It's Peter who goes upstairs':

(22)   *Péter nem   száll   fel*
         P.   NEG   goes   upstairs
         'Peter doesn't go upstairs'

and not ***Péter nem felszáll* nor ** *Péter száll nem fel* (of the German type *P. steigt nicht auf*).

Being the focalised element NEG prevents the occurrence of another focalised element in preverbal position, which is characteristically what the Hungarian preverbal particle is.[3]

We may therefore consider a postposed negation as a sort of comment on the topic represented by the preceding (affirmative) part:

(23)   a. Milanese   TOP[Mi parli] COMM[no]   'I don't speak'
         b. Child English TOP[I sleep] COMM[no]

What turns out to be marked from a 'natural morphology' point of view may be an excellent functional strategy from a pragmatic, discourse, point of view. Postverbal NEG displays a tendency to emphasise the pragmatic organisation of the discourse rather than the syntactic, where the preverbal position is more 'natural'. Taking also into consideration the parallelism between the concepts of 'theme' and 'topic' on the one hand and 'rheme' and 'comment' on the other, the development into NEG morphemes of what were originally Objects (in SVO languages), which represent of course the 'rheme' with respect to the thematic part of the verb, may be included in this same perspective: *Non vado* [Rheme]*passum* 'I don't go a step', *Non bibo* [Rheme]*guttam* 'I don't drink a drop'. Thus, the dialectic interaction between the various dimensions of the phenomenon language, which has even recently quite rightly been considered as one of the main factors contributing to language change (see Vennemann 1989), reappears also under the phenomenology of NEG.

From the historical point of view it is, however, necessary to distinguish between the postposed NEG marker, as in (23a) and (23b), which is a continuation of the former Romance, Germanic and, in the final analysis, Indo-European negation, and the other NEG markers developed out of what were originally NPIs such as *pas, drof, nicht, not* (the latter with the incorporation of NEG). It has been seen that these NPIs arise in postverbal Object position (in a basically SVO order): obviously this does not apply to Milanese *no* or Portuguese *não* which were in themselves negative (sentential) adverbs.

In spoken Brazilian Portuguese three types of negative sentence exist today:

(24)   a. *Ele não fala português*
       b. *Ele não fala português não*
       c. *Ele fala português não*
          'He doesn't speak Portuguese'
          (cf. Schwegler 1991a)

NEG1, NEG2 and NEG3 are thus all present at the same time. They are found not only in declarative sentences but also in interrogatives and imperatives. Note however that the discontinuous construction (NEG2) is (24b) rather than:

       d. ***Ele não fala não português*

The second *não* is always found at the end of the sentence, except in the case of right dislocation of topicalised elements, as in

(25)   *Eu não   gosto muito não,   de peixe*
       I   NEG like   much NEG of fish
       'I don't like it much, fish'
       (see Schwegler 1991a)

NEG3 does not appear in subordinate clauses:

(26)   a. ***Eu imagino que você tem   dinheiro não*
          I   imagine that you have   money NEG
          'I think that you don't have any money'.

On the contrary we find

> b. *Eu imagino que você não ten dinheiro (não)*
> (see Schwegler 1991a)

Furthermore

(27)   *Eu não imagino que você tem dinheiro não*

does not mean **'I don't think that you don't have any money' but rather 'I don't think that you have any money ': the second *não* represents the second negative element of the main clause: *Eu não imagino [que você tem dinheiro] não* (Schwegler 1991a). It seems then that all the conditions are met to permit the conclusion that postverbal (or, more exactly, sentence final) *não*, though now grammaticalised in sentence final position, originally represented the 'comment' in the form of an 'afterthought' of the preceding negative sentence (see also 4.3.), its resumption in the form — indeed — of a comment, characteristic of the spoken language, in other words pertaining to the pragmatic dimension:

> resumptive negation […:] after a negative sentence has been completed, something is added in a negative form with the obvious result that the negative effect is heightened. […] In its pure form the suppplementary negative is added outside the frame of the first sentence, generally as an afterthought […] This is the case in a popular Swedish idiom, in which the sentence begins and ends with inte as in […] Wägner Northullsl.108 Inte märkte han mig inte ['He has not noticed me, no']. (Jespersen 1917: 72)

(notice that *inte* and not *naj* 'no' is used to reinforce NEG: this indicates that postposed *inte* is more rhematic than Italian *non*: **Egli non mi ha notato, non* 'He has not noticed me, no': cf. 5.2.); also in spoken French we may have:

(28)   *J'vais pas y aller, … moi, non*
          'I won't go there, I won't'

and in colloquial Spanish

(29)   *(Yo) no voy a ir allí, … no*
          'I won't go there, I won't'

etc. (Schwegler 1988: 39). Note also the following example taken from the French-based creole of the Mascarene Islands:

(30)   *Li   pas   connai (,)   non*
          He NEG knows   no
          'He doesn't know, no'
          (:Faine (1939: 106), cited as example (96) by Schwegler (1991b)).

It could be said that *pas* has become here the normal NEG marker, in preverbal position (cf. examples (1) – (3)) and that *non* is used to emphasise NEG, almost setting off a new cycle. The linguistic type represented by (24c) is the result of a normal process of grammaticalisation of a construction originally marked on the pragmatic level, for which the histories of various languages provide so many examples (cf. 2.3.).[4] At this stage Brazilian Portuguese has the potential to start a new NEG cycle, bringing *não* into the preverbal, morphologically unmarked, position as is in fact happening in the Scandavian languages.[5]

That which links NEG3 NPI and 'afterthoughts' (the types Vb+*pas* and Vb+*não* (#)) is thus the original emphatic function on the pragmatic level.

3.3. Discontinuous negation

Finally, regarding NEG2, that is, discontinuous NEG (the type *ne* ... *pas*), as already mentioned it is, like all discontinuous constructions, a strongly marked construction in terms of 'natural morphology'. Dan Slobin (1971) includes among the universals potentially relative to the ontogenesis of grammar the principle which tends to avoid interruption of linguistic units and, in the wake of Grégoire's studies on language acquisition (1937), quotes in fact French *pas*, the first form that French-speaking children use for NEG, as an example of elimination of discontinuous morphemes. According to Hagège's (1982: 86) statistical projections only 17% of the world's languages have discontinuous NEG (and generally these are SVO languages, like French). Comparing, therefore, the three types of possible syntactic order (NEG1, NEG2, NEG3: cf. 1.) it may be concluded that NEG1 turns out to be the most 'natural' syntactic construction due to reasons of a psycholinguistic nature.

3.4. The negative verb

Worthy of a separate discussion is the occurrence of an inflected negative verb, typical of Finnish: *e-n, e-t, e-i, e-mme, e-tte, e-ivät*,

(31)   *(hän) ei   lue;   emme   lue*
          (he) NEG:3SG read NEG:1PL read
          '(He) doesn't read'   'We don't read'

The verb expressing the lexical concept remains unchanged, while the negative form is inflected (in the present tense!): somewhat like the English translation. Consequently, in Finnish and in these particular English cases NEG turns out to be the 'head' ('operand', 'determinee') with the lexical verb being its specification ('operator', 'determiner'), if we accept the categorial grammar principle according to which the head of a phrase is that element which belongs to the same category as the entire phrase (see Vennemann 1989: 26). The relationship between Vb and NEG is therefore inverted with respect to the more diffused European type represented by Italian, German, French, etc.[6] In these latter languages NEG is expressed by an invariable element which is syntactically linked to that part of the sentence (usually the verbal predicate) which will come within its scope: Italian *Giovanni* [*non* [*mangia pesce*]] 'John doesn't eat fish', Polish *Jan* [*nie* [*je ryb*]], Basque *Jon*-ERG*ek* [NEG*ez*[AUX*du arrain*-PART*ik jaten*]], Welsh [*Ni* [*fwyty*] *Siôn* [*bysgod*]]; cf. also Georgian *Zoni* [NEG*ar* [VB*čams* OBJ*t'evzs*]]. Finnish, as well as Estonian and Lapp, makes use of a morphological expedient consisting of a phrase with the lexical verb (cf. Clahsen (1988: 6) and also Moreno Cabrera (1987: 81)). Lyle Campbell (1980) has shown that in the Finnish spoken in Fitchburg (Massachusetts) there is however a tendency to generalise the use of *ei* for all the negative forms of the verbs, substituting it, that is, for *en*, *et*, *eivät* etc. Even in Estonian *ei* is generalised in the present tense; and consequently the negative form of the verb has no inflection for person. This brings to mind the general use of *ain't* in Black English for *have*, *has*, *am* and *are* + *not*,[7] not to mention the use of *don't* as the only form of verbal NEG in the speech of adults learning English in a natural (as opposed to an educational) environment:

(32)   *He don't like it.*
        I don't saw him.

where "the sound cluster is perceived as another negation particle, a variant of *no*" (Klein 1986: 97). In these cases it seems as though an invariable NEG morph is reestablished, the very type of syntactic NEG found in Italian, French, German etc.

A final step towards morphological NEG is on the other hand found when NEG is expressed by a bound morpheme, as in Japanese, Swahili or in Turkish, a language which only marginally comes within our geographical perspective:

(33)   *bugün çok   çalış-ma-dı-m*
        today much work-NEG-PRET-1SG
        'Today I haven't worked much' (Clahsen 1988: 6).

The construction with an invariable NEG particle is, in conclusion, by far the most diffused amongst the world's languages: from this point of view the

European languages of IE lineage, with their clear tendency to adopt a single
NEG morph (cf. 2.1.), do not represent anything at all 'exotic'. Although the
term does apply to the English/Finnish type with negative AUX, known also
in other languages such as Telugu (: *le* 'cannot, be unable' (Zwicky—Pullum
1983: 510)).

4. The areal perspective

4.1. Geographical distribution

We have seen (cfr. 3.3.) that discontinuous NEG (the type *ne...pas*) turns out to be a strongly marked construction from a natural morphology point of view. Therefore, the distribution of this phenomenon amongst the languages of Europe turns out to be highly interesting. Dahl's sample (1979) clearly shows that NEG2 is concentrated among the Celtic, Romance and Germanic languages, with a very few sporadic cases here and there (: Pocomchi and Quiché among the Penutian languages, Kachin (Sino-Tibetan), Guaraní (Tupí-Guaraní)). It is found, furthermore, in Hausa (Afro-Asiatic), Gbeya, Mande (Niger-Congo) as well as in Amharic, Oromo (or Galla), Berber, Maltese, Modern Arabic: see, for example:

(1)   Algerian Berber
      Ud-ssarad.nt-ša   *ḍḍuft*
      NEG-they.wash:INDEF-NEG wool
      'They don't wash wool.'

(2)   Maltese
      Ġanni ma   jiekol-x   ħut
      G.   NEG eats-NEG fish
      'G. doesn't eat fish'

(3)   Cairene Arabic
      Ma-katab-ū-š
      NEG-write:PFV-3PL-NEG
      'They didn't write'

where *-š* derives from *šaʔ(an)* (indefinite accusative) 'thing' — on exactly the same lines as *rien* and *wiht* producing *nicht*! A discontinuous construction with a post-verbal morph is found in northern Berber: *(w)ur/(w)ul*+Vb+*k(é)ra* (once again with the meaning of 'thing'), also in a form with a palatal spirant *-š(a/i)* (*k*> *š*): cf. Brugnatelli (1987). In some of these languages NEG3 is also found alongside NEG2 — for example in Gbeya (as in other Niger-Congo languages such as Jukun, Senari, Sango); cf. Molinelli — Bernini — Ramat (1987: 177).

In this vast area, which extends from the Middle East to Egypt (spreading as far as Ethiopia) and to the whole north African coast as far as the Gulf of

Guinea, the dominant linguistic type is SVO (except for Galla, Mande and Am-haric — though in the latter SOV has recently replaced an older VSO). In Arabic, furthermore, SVO is the outcome of the older VSO order of Classical Arabic.

Returning to the area of Europe which mainly concerns us, we see that NEG2 and NEG3 are not found in the Baltic, Slavonic, Finno-Ugric and Balkan lan-guages. The whole of eastern Europe then constitutes an area which contrasts with western and Mediterranean Europe. As we shall see in the second part of this book, the eastern area is characterised by the obligatory presence of a negative morph in pre-verbal position, even when other words with a negative meaning are present (: Russian *nikto ne govorit* 'no-one speaks' vs. It. *nessuno (**non) parla*).

With regards to the areal perspective under discussion the Celtic languages are revealing: Irish and Scottish Gaelic (VSO type) have only NEG1:

(4)   Irish
        Ní   itheann Seán   iasc
        NEG eats   John fish
        'John doesn't eat fish'

(5)   Scottish Gaelic
        cha   robh   mi anns an   taigh
        NEG was:3SG I   in   the house
        'I wasn't in the house'

Welsh and Breton — that is to say the Celtic languages which come into closest contact with the NEG3 type (i. e. English, once NEG2 however!) and, respectively, NEG2 (i. e. French) — have instead only NEG2: cf. examples (28, 29) at the end of 2.3., to which may be added as being of particular interest to the problem of interlinguistic contact the following Breton example:

(6)   *evid nompaz dispign a dammig arhant*
        'pour ne pas dépenser son peu d'argent'
        'so as not to spend his little money'
        (see Trepos (1994: 253); cf. Ramat−Bernini (1990: 33):

the French origin of *nompas* (< *non pas*) is obvious.

Even the Romance area is divided: NEG2 and NEG3 are found only in French and adjoining (Gallo-)Romance dialects while it is unknown in Spanish, (Lusitanian) Portuguese, standard Italian and Rumanian (see Donadze 1993). Italian and Catalan, peripheral areas with respect to the Gallo-Romance lan-guages as a whole and languages in the main with NEG1, allow constructions with NEG2 with an emphatic meaning (adversative: cf. chapter 1) that fit well into the 'NEG cycle' described above:

(7)   Italian
         Non fa mica freddo qui
         'It's not at all cold here'

(8)   Catalan
         Joan no menja pas peix
         'John doesn't eat fish'

NEG3 is the normal form in German (both High and Low), Dutch, Frisian, Yiddish, and the Scandinavian languages, the end — as we have seen above — of the 'NEG cycle', that is, after having passed through a phase of discontinuous negation. The Scandinavian languages show a certain tendency to restore NEG1, the 'more natural' type: see chapter 3, note 5. Cf. Swedish subordinate clauses:

(9)   *det   var   synd att   han inte   kunde komma*
         that was pity that he   not could come
         'It was a pity that he couldn't come'

Modern English has developed a particular negative construction using an auxiliary verb followed by *n(o)t*, essentially a type of NEG3: *I do not believe it. I can't believe it. I wouldn't believe it. ...*

In the Middle East, Syrian, Iraqi and Saudi Arabian Arabic as well as Hebrew differ from Palestinian and Lebanese in having only preverbal NEG (Hebr. *lo*).

4.2. Areal typology

If we consider that:

(a) discontinuous negation is relatively rare and then highly marked as far as psycholinguistic strategies are concerned;
(b) the origin of NEG2 is the result of having followed significantly similar processes (if not, in some cases then directly corresponding) in the area in question;
(c) its areal distribution cuts across genetically related languages;
the conclusion, with all due caution, seems to point to the existence of a Celtic-Germanic-Romance isogloss with a partial extension towards other Romance, Celtic and even Arab areas (particularly western Arabic, of the North African

Coast: and from here also towards the Niger-Congo family and the rest of Afro-Asiatic).

Acknowledging the existence of a Gallo-Romance epicentre for NEG2 (and successive developments towards NEG3) does not, however, mean supposing a process of simple diffusion according to the 'wave theory' model. There are also significant chronological discordances in the attestation of NEG2 in the various areas: in the 12th century Icelandic seems to have reached NEG3, while in western Germanic NEG2 was still the norm. In the same period NEG2 had only just made its appearance in French; on the other hand Occitan had reached NEG3 by the 17th century when French had obligatory NEG2. The chronological 'décalage' may be inferred from table (10) (see Ramat−Bernini 1990: 32).

(10)

Century	N.Germanic	W.Germanic	Occitan	French	Breton
12th	Vb+NEG	NEG+Vb+NEG	NEG+Vb(+NEG)	NEG+Vb(+NEG)	NEG+Vb
17th	Vb+NEG	Vb+NEG	(NEG+)Vb+NEG	NEG+Vb+NEG	NEG+Vb(+NEG)
20th	Vb+NEG/NEG+Vb	Vb+NEG	Vb+NEG	(NEG+)Vb+NEG	NEG+Vb+NEG

Furthermore, in the majority of cases, what we are dealing with is obviously not diffusion of lexical material spreading out from a centre (the case of Bret. *nompas, poent, pas* is something of an exception).[1] We have seen that the NPIs that may give rise to NEG2 (> NEG3) are very disparate, they are not limited to meaning 'negligeable quantity' like 'crumb' or 'drop' and may be (re)constructed at any time in their expressivity.

They should therefore not be thought of so much as direct filiation but rather as the DIFFUSION OF A STRUCTURAL MODEL, rendered possible mainly by typological correspondances between languages not genetically related (unless in their distant common Indo-European origin − excluding, of course, Arabic). In fact, both the Romance and the Germanic languages have undergone the typological change SOV → SVO, that is to say from a type with the order Determiner + Determinee (or Operator + Operand) to one with the reverse order in which NEG, being a verbal Operator, should follow the Vb: the Milan. type *mi parli no*, lit. 'I speak no', is more coherent with the Romance order [Det.ee]*la casa* [Det.er]*bianca* 'The white house', [Det.ee]*il libro* [Det.er]*di Luigi* 'Luigi's book' etc. than is the Standard Italian *io non parlo*, lit. 'I not speak'. The development of postverbal NEG − which, let it not be forgotten, arises very often from an Object (direct or indirect 'of measure') in postverbal position: *non video guttam* : *je vois goutte*, lit. 'I (not) see drop' − may be facilitated by the principle of typological coherence, in both the Romance and the Germanic languages. Let it not be forgotten that the many expressions of emphatic reinforcement of NEG by means of a postverbal object complement in the oldest phases are progressively eliminated in favour of a single one (except, of course, for the possibility of forming ever new negative expressions, which may assign emphatic prominence to the negation): when *pas* ousts *goutte, point, mie* (a brief but clear summary of the philological data in Price (1986)), when in Middle High German *niawiht* (Ger. *nicht*) ousts *trophen* what is happening is grammaticalisation of a NEG morph whose origin is to be found in the pragmatic dimension, in the expressive discourse, with its focalisation strategies.

The Celtic languages, which have the order VSO, originally display NEG1 (cf. examples (4) and (5)). But the schema (NEG+)Vb+SUBJ+NEG (that is, NEG2 and NEG3) is developed here too: cf. Welsh:

(11)   *Nid   yw 'r   bachgen ddim   yn hoffi   coffi*
         NEG is the boy   NEG in to.like coffee
         'The boy doesn't like coffee' (Payne 1985: 224)

and with the elimination of the first negative element, in spoken Welsh:

(12)   *Eistaddais i ddim   yn y   gadair*
         sat   I NEG   in the chair
         'I didn't sit on the chair' (Payne 1985: 225)

(Not forgetting the etymology of *dim*: 'thing'!)

The same goes for the different varieties of Arabic, today SVO, from the older VSO order (like Celtic − and thus with O always after V).

This series of observations seems to lead to the plausible conclusion that it is internal factors (structural-typological) competing with external factors (inter-linguistic contacts) that is the cause of the diffusion of NEG3 and notably of NEG2, a construction strongly marked from the point of view of a 'natural morphology', so that the languages of Europe − at least those of central-western Europe − are from this point of view somewhat 'exotic': "the effects of drift can conspire with those of language contact", Bechert (1990: 139); Dahl (1990). See also in this regard the conclusions drawn by Vennemann (1989), who nonetheless seems in favour of the prevalence of internal factors.

4.3. Sentence final negation in Afrikaans and its Portuguese basis

4.3.1. Introduction

In the frame of the area typology perspective dealt with in the previous section we approach now a case study regarding the genesis of sentence final negation in

Afrikaans, a language which is relevant for the typology of European languages, although itself not spoken in Europe, having arisen as a result of the colonial rule of the Dutch in South Africa. The historical reconstruction argued for in this section links the development of Afrikaans negation to the pragmatically marked structures discussed at length in 3.2., which resort to the non-natural postverbal position of negative particles. This case study is also interesting because it illustrates well the kind of problems linguists are faced with when studying both areal and historical aspects of typologically relevant features.

Afrikaans arouses the curiosity of researchers because of many features of its grammatical and lexical organisation, which derive from its origins as a contact language of the Cape of Good Hope. From the second half of the seventeenth century onwards, Afrikaans developed out of the interaction between on the one hand the Dutch dialect of the seamen and employees of the Dutch East India Company, which had established an office at the Cape in 1652, and on the other hand the more or less rudimentary ways in which Dutch was learnt by the indigenous Khoekhoen, slaves deported from various parts of Africa and Asia, and/or the pidgin(/ised) varieties of it they used, as well as Europeans of various languages, who together outnumbered the immigrants from the Netherlands.

The influence of Dutch, however, while not great has always been constant (Holm 1989: 343), and Afrikaans shares with it, for example, the syntax of having the conjugated verb in second position in main clauses and in final position in subordinate clauses.[2] Negation in Afrikaans reflects well the ambivalent position of continuity and radical innovation with respect to Dutch. In fact, Afrikaans and Dutch share the same negative morphemes and their positioning rules, but they differ in that Afrikaans expresses negation a second time, redundantly, at the end of the sentence by means of the same morpheme used as standard negation, *nie* (< Dut. *niet*), as the following pair of examples show.[3]

(13)   a. Afrikaans[4]
        Jan   het   nie   geëet   nie
        John   have   NEG   eaten   NEG
        b. Dutch
        Jan   heeft   niet   gegeten
        John   has   NEG   eaten
        'John hasn't eaten'

The origin of this construction has been variously attributed to three main causes: derivation from Dutch dialects, interference from Khoisan languages; the influence of creolised varieties of Portuguese.[5]

Some time ago direct derivation of Afrikaans negation from forms of negation in Dutch dialects was reconsidered by Raidt (1983: 189–190), whose
studies form part of the tradition which seeks to explain the development of
Afrikaans on the basis of processes of linguistic change in the Dutch brought
to the Cape.[6] In fact, negative constructions similar to those in Afrikaans have
been described for Aarschot Brabantine by Pauwels (1958).[7] Its potential influence on Afrikaans, however, is rejected out of hand by Valkhoff (1966: 15–16)
with demographic and sociolinguistic arguments relating to the presence of
groups of speakers of these dialects at the Cape and their predominance during
the years when Afrikaans was being formed, while den Besten (1986: 203–210)
shows the lack of foundation in this position with a precise comparison of the
structures in question within the framework of a formal grammar model.

The second hypothesis on the origin of negation in Afrikaans, which traces
it back to phenomena of interference on the part of Khoisan languages, and in
particular Nama, goes back originally to Nienaber.[8] It has recently been developed with a wealth of argumentation along structural, sociolinguistic and historical lines by den Besten (1986) and is held by Holm (1989: 346) to be the most
probable explanation. According to this hypothesis, sentence final negation in
Afrikaans probably originated in the Dutch based pidgin of the indigenous
South Africans, called *Hottentots-Hollands* (cf. den Besten, 1986: 193, 212–218),
showing SOV constituent order, not normal for this type of simplified language,
which developed from the first contacts between Khoekhoen and Europeans at
the Cape. The indigenous people would have relexified the sentence final negative morphemes of their first language by using *nie(t)*, which would then have
been reanalysed as a scope marker, in that the main negation was already expressed within the sentence *Klammer* (den Besten 1986: 221).[9]

According to den Besten (1986: 198–199), the Cape Khoekhoen probably
had a prominent role as linguistic mediators for the slaves deported there as
well as for the Khoekhoen of the region to the east of the Cape and would
therefore probably have contributed to establishing the basis for the processes
of convergence with the more or less simplified varieties of Dutch spoken by
the whites. The new construction with sentence final NEG, therefore, would
have probably become, in Afrikaans, "a psychological, rhythmic and melodious
boon" (Nienaber 1955: 43, cited in Valkhoff 1966: 17).

Finally, the third of the hypotheses listed above, which traces sentence final
negation back to the influence of Portuguese creole, was elaborated by Valkhoff
(1966: 13–17), who developed ideas originally put forward by Hesseling at the
end of the last century.[10] Valkhoff (1966: 33, 146–191) highlights the role of
linguistic mediation played by the slaves of African and Asiatic origin who arrived at the Cape from 1685 onwards and the importance of Portuguese, both

'standard' and creole, in colonial trading during the sixteenth and seventeenth centuries.

This third hypothesis has not, however, received much support because most of the slaves deported to the Cape between 1677 and the mid eighteenth century came from India, Ceylon and Indonesia (but also from Madagascar and Mozambique) and the varieties of Portuguese creole attested for Asia do not possess this type of negation.[11] A second reason detracting from Valkhoff's hypothesis consists in the fact that the rare attestations of Portuguese creole found in the South African archives have only preverbal negation (den Besten (1986: 211).[12]

Outside of the realms of the study of Afrikaans, recourse to Portuguese creole varieties to explain Afrikaans negation is found in a few works by Schwegler (1991a, 1991b, 1992) on negation in Brazilian Portuguese, Palenquero (a Spanish-based creole of Colombia: see below) and varieties of Caribbean Spanish.

Despite the abundance of references, this third hypothesis on the origin of the unusual negation in Afrikaans still has aspects worth looking into because they have generally been overlooked. They concern in particular reconstruction of the origin and diffusion of such a construction in the source language, that is, Portuguese, or rather its colonial varieties, as well as reconstruction of the contexts that may have served as the means by which the construction in question penetrated Cape Dutch from Portuguese. Furthermore, the sociolinguistic conditions which allowed or favoured this influence must be identified.

These three questions will be examined more closely later on in this section, following a description of the negative structures of Afrikaans with the aim of defining its typological position (4.3.2.). In order to uphold the plausibility of the Portuguese origin of Afrikaans negation, recourse will be made to areal considerations relative to the two Atlantic coasts, where similar constructions are attested in different varieties of 'colonial' Portuguese and Caribbean Spanish, and in addition Schwegler's data (1991a, 1991b, 1992) (4.3.3.) will be discussed.

The Portuguese origin will then be reconstructed on the strength of structural considerations relating to the form and position of the morphemes concerned in Afrikaans and in Brazilian Portuguese. The origin of this structure may be traced back to the type of interaction that very probably characterised the contacts between the Portuguese and the slaves in the fifteenth century, from which the creolised varieties of Portuguese of the Atlantic Ocean and the Indian Ocean are derived (see 4.3.4.).

Although we aim at demonstrating the plausibility of a Portuguese base for Afrikaans negation, it must be borne in mind that the complex conditions of multilingualism in South Africa from the seventeenth century onwards do not allow the evolution from Dutch to Afrikaans to be explained in holistic terms. It is more likely to result from a combination of several factors, as many researchers have already highlighted, including den Besten (1986: 191) and, before him, Valkhoff, who concludes as follows his comments on the origin of Afrikaans negation, reconciling the three different positions set out above (1966: 17):

> So, both the creolized Dutch of the African slaves, who most likely knew a double negation in their own lingua franca, and that of the Hottentots, may have popularized a construction which sporadically occurred in the Netherlands

4.3.2. Typological profile of negation in Afrikaans

The typological profile of Afrikaans negation presented in this section is based on Burgers' (1971) grammar and also on data gathered by means of an 'intermediate' version of our questionnaire containing just 35 out of 38 sentences of its final version. The English version of this questionnaire was translated by two linguists, native speakers of Afrikaans.[13]

4.3.2.1. Inventory of negative forms

As has already been observed in 4.3.1., to a large extent Afrikaans shares with Dutch its inventory of negative morphemes (adverbs, prosentences, conjunctions, pronouns, etc.) all of which may be traced back to the same origin in Middle Dutch, as the following schema illustrates:

(14)   Inventory of negative morphemes
   a. Afrikaans
      nie 'not'; *nee* 'no'; *nòg...nòg* 'neither...nor';
      geen 'no' (adjective), *niemand, geeneen* 'nobody', *niks* 'nothing', *nooit* 'never', *nêrens* 'nowhere';
      moenie 'IMPERATIVE: NEG'
   b. Dutch
      niet 'not'; *nee(n)* 'no'; *noch...noch* 'neither...nor'
      geen 'no (adjective)/nobody', *niemand* 'nobody', *niets* 'nothing', *nooit* 'never', *nergens* 'nowhere'

The differences found between corresponding lexemes of the two inventories are mainly of a phonetic nature (for example *nie* vs. *niet*, *nêrens* vs. *nergens*) and reflect the rules of phonetic development in Afrikaans. In the case of *niks* vs. *niets*, the first form is also found in colloquial Dutch. Afrikaans, in this case, has maintained only the less literary form of the pair once present in the period of transition from Middle Dutch to Modern Dutch (*GWN* 1984). Finally, for *nòg* vs. *noch* the difference lies entirely in the spelling, in that <g> in Afrikaans corresponds to [x] as does in Dutch.[14]

The only real discrepancies are constituted by two Afrikaans elements which have no counterpart in Dutch. The pronoun *geeneen* 'nobody' (Burgers 1971: 88), derived from *geen* + *een* 'one', is a formation consistent with the other elements of the paradigm of Afrikaans quantifiers (cf. for example *enigeen* 'whatever' vs. Dut. *ieder*, cf. Burgers 1971: 42). On the other hand, *moenie* as an imperative negative morpheme is an Afrikaans formation derived from the fusion of the modal verb *moet* 'you must' and the negation morpheme *nie* (Burgers 1971: 138) and could represent a calque of the negative imperative of Portuguese creole *na misti*, literally 'it is not necessary' (den Besten 1986: 222, see also note 12).

4.3.2.2. The syntax of negation

The area of sharpest divergence with respect to Dutch is found instead, as has already been seen in example (13), in the syntax of negation, whose main characteristic may be summarised in the formula: each sentence must close with the morpheme *nie* or, optionally, with another negative morpheme.

This general formula interacts in particular with the constituent order of Afrikaans, where, like Dutch, in main clauses the conjugated verb is in second position, and infinitives, participles and 'separable' particles are in clause final position, while in subordinate clauses the conjugated verb is in final position.[15]

Since in main clauses negation is placed after the conjugated verb, this interaction predicts that if *nie* is not found in final position, as in (15), it is 'copied' in final position, as in (13), seen above, and in (16).[16]

(15)   *Jan   praat   nie   en   beweeg nie*
        John speak NEG and move NEG
        [S V NEG] *en* [V NEG]
        'John doesn't speak and doesn't move'   [Q3][17]

(16)   *Jan   eet   nie   vis   nie*
        John eat NEG fish NEG
        [S V NEG O NEG]
        'John doesn't eat fish'   [Q5]

The type of negative sentence with 'double *nie*' exemplified in (16) is in fact the more widespread one, as it is found whenever the final position of the corresponding positive main clause is occupied by a periphrastic finite verbal form as in (17), by a so-called 'separable' particle as in (18), or by a complement (excluding a pronominal direct object) as in (19) or by an adverbial as in (20).

(17)   *Ek het   dit   nie   gesien nie*
        I   have this NEG   seen NEG
        'I did not see it' (Burgers 1971: 205)

(18)   *Hy stem nie   toe   nie*
        he Vb NEG PTCL NEG   (the verb is *toestem* 'to agree')
        'He does not agree' (Burgers 1971: 89)

(19)   *Ek hou   nie   van hom nie*
        I   consider NEG of him NEG
        'I do not like him' (Burgers 1971: 92)

(20)   *Hy praat   nie   dikwels nie*
        he speak NEG often   NEG
        'He doesn't speak often' (Burgers 1971: 89)

Example (19), together with example (16) contrasts with (21), which contains a pronominal direct object, while (20) contrasts with (22), where *dikwels* is not included in the scope of the negation. Sentences (21) and (22) contain a single final *nie*.

(21)   *Ek is siek maar dit   skeel   hom   nie*
        I   is ill   but   this matter him:OBJECT NEG
        'I am ill, but it makes no difference to him' (Burgers 1971: 92)

(22)   *Hy praat   dikwels nie*
        he speaks often   NEG
        'He often doesn't speak' (Burgers 1971: 89)

Furthermore, when the final position in subordinate positive clauses is occupied by one or more verb forms, final *nie* is found in the corresponding negative sentences, cf.

(23)   *Ek weet   dat sy   nie   sal   skryf nie*
        I   know that she NEG FUT write NEG
        'I know that she will not write' (Burgers 1971: 162)

Of course, in most cases, the conditions listed here accumulate, as the following example shows.

(24)   *Júlle   kan gaan [...] maar ek gaan nie   daar onder in die*
        you:PL may go   but I go   NEG there under in the
        donker gange   rond-kruip   nie
        dark   passages around-crawl NEG
        'You can go [...] but I'm not going to crawl around down there in the dark passages!'
        (Burgers 1971: 188)

Where a negative clause governs a positive completive clause, be it finite (cf. 25) or non-finite (cf. 26), the copy of *nie* is placed to the right of the subordinate clause and indicates its strict structural dependence on the negative matrix clause, cf.

(25)　*Jan   het   nie   gedink   [dat iets   met   hom*
　　　John   have   NEG   thought   that anything   with   him
　　　sou   *gebeur]   nie*
　　　CONDITIONAL   happen   NEG
　　　'John didn't think that anything would happen to him'　　　[Q25]

(26)　*Dit   is nie   vir jou nodig   [om   dit   te   doen]*
　　　that is NEG   for you necessary   PTCL that PTCL do
　　　nie
　　　NEG
　　　'It is not necessary for you to do it' (Burgers 1971: 143)

Constituent negation behaves in a similar way to what has so far been seen for sentence negation. The phrase under negation must have as its final element the morpheme *nie*, which is a copy of the same *nie* which introduces the negated phrase.

(27)　*Jan   en   Marie het   mekaar   nie   by die skool   nie,*
　　　John and Mary have   each.other NEG   at the school NEG
　　　maar by 'n partytjie ontmoet
　　　but   at a party   met
　　　'John and Mary met not at school, but at a party'　　　[Q7]

In example (27) the preposition phrase *by die skool* is negatively focalised and is in contrastive relationship with the prepositional phrase *by 'n partytjie* by means of the conjunction *maar*. Both the phrases in contrastive focus belong to the positive clause which ends with the past participle *ontmoet*. As can be clearly seen, negation is expressed on the first of the two phrases in contrastive focus with the 'double *nie*' structure (that is, *nie* PP *nie*) which has already been seen with sentence NEG.

In (28) there is a negated adverbial phrase in sentence initial position. Note that here the two negative morphemes surround the entire phrase, even though the negation actually relates only to one of its elements, namely *baie*. The example should in fact be read in the sense of 'days afterwards, but not many'.

(28)　*En nie   baie dae daarna nie   het   die jongste seun*
　　　and NEG many days after NEG have the youngst son
　　　alles bymekaargemaak en   weggereis na   'n ver   land
　　　all   gathered   and left   towards a distant land
　　　'and not many days afterwards, the youngst son took up everything and left for a distant land'

(*Afrikaanse Bybel*, from the "Parable of the prodigal son", verse 13, recorded in Valkhoff 1966: 265)

Remember that according to the general formula of Afrikaans negation, the sentence final morpheme *nie* interacts, not only with itself, but also with other negative morphemes of the inventory discussed in 4.3.2.1. In fact, the first negative morpheme of the sentence, as well as being the principal morpheme *nie*, may also be the negative imperative morpheme *moenie* or one of the indefinite pronouns or adverbs listed in (14a), or also a prosentence or a negative conjunction.

For example, in the case of a negative imperative, the sentence has *moenie* as its first negative element, followed by at least the base form of the main verb, and closes with the morpheme *nie*, as example (29) illustrates.

(29)   *Moenie   bog   praat   nie!*
        IMPERATIVE:NEG rubbish speak NEG
        'Don't talk rubbish!' (Burgers 1971: 229)

On the basis of their position in the sentence, the elements listed in (14a) may be divided into three groups:

(a) elements which are never found in sentence final position: *geen* 'no' (adjective), *moenie*, *nòg* ...*nòg* 'neither...nor';
(b) elements which may also be found in final position: *niemand, geeneen* 'nobody', *niks* 'nothing', *nooit* 'never', *nêrens* 'nowhere';
(c) elements which are always found in final position: *nee* 'no'.

As far as the elements in group (a) are concerned, *geen* and *moenie* always require the sentence final morpheme *nie*. For *moenie* see example (29), for *geen* see instead the following example:

(30)   *Daar is geen brood nie*
        there is no   bread NEG
        'There is no bread'   [Q31]

In the case of *nòg*...*nòg*, however, the grammars do not prescribe the use of sentence final *nie* (for example Burgers 1971: 89), although it does appear in some of the replies to our questionnaire, cf.

(31)   a. *Nòg   Jan,   nòg sy   maats   wou   vertrek*
           neither John nor his companions wanted leave
        b. *Nòg   Jan   nòg sy   vriende wou   weggaan nie*
           neither John nor his friends wanted go.away NEG
           'Neither John nor his companions wanted to leave'   [Q4]

(32)   a. *Ek weet dat Jan nòg praat nòg beweeg*
            I   know that John neither speak nor move
        b. *Jan praat nòg beweeg nie*
            John speak nor move NEG
            'John neither speaks nor moves'[18]   [Q3]

As far the elements in group (b) are concerned, if they are not found in sentence final position then final *nie* is obligatory. Otherwise the final *nie* is optional. Similarly, with the single element of group (c), that is, the prosentence *nee*, the addition of *nie* is not obligatory. Cf.:

(33)   a. *Daar is niemand hier nie*
            there is nobody here NEG
        b. *Hier 's niemand (nie)*
            here is nobody NEG
            'There's nobody here'   [Q29]

(34)   *Het jy   (vir) Jan gesien? - Nee (, nie)*
        have you:SG ACC John seen   no   NEG
        'Have you seen John? – No'   [Q1]

The rules which govern the behaviour of the elements in group (b) also apply in negative subordinate clauses, as the following example shows:

(35)   *Jan het gehoop dat niks   met hom sou*
        John have hoped that nothing with him CONDITIONAL
        gebeur nie
        happen NEG
        'John hoped that nothing would happen to him'   [Q23]

What has been put forward in this section concerning the syntax of Afrikaans negation may therefore be summarised by the following schemata, where *niks* stands for any of the negative elements listed in (14a) with the exception of *nie*, X for any number of non-negative elements, XP for any phrasal category, # for the boundary to the right of the sentence. According to usual practice, round brackets contain optional elements and braces alternating elements.

(36)   a. {nie, niks} X nie#   (cf. 13, 15−20, 23−26, 29, 30, 31b, 32b, 33a, 35)
        b. niks (nie)#   (cf. 33b, 34)
        c. nie#   (cf. 15, 21, 22)
        d. nòg...nòg X#   (cf. 31a, 32a)
        e. nie XP nie   (cf. 27, 28)

Before concluding this description of the syntax of Afrikaans negation, it must be remembered that according to the grammars main clauses containing complements and/or adverbials may take only final negation. This occurs in contexts in which "a short sentence bears an exceptional emphasis" (Burgers 1971: 89), like the following:

(37)   *Dit is nutteloos - die man verstáán   die werk eenvoudig nie!*
       that is useless   the man understand the work simply   NEG
       'It is useless − the man simply does not understand the work!'
       (Burgers 1971: 89)

These types of sentences, which come under section c of (36), are pragmatically marked and the interpretation of the single final *nie* which marks them would be worth a study in itself, based on data from spoken Afrikaans. Suffice it, for the purposes of the present work, to bear in mind that this possibility also exists; its importance in a comparative context will become clear in 4.3.3.3.[19]

4.3.2.3. Sentence final nie

Following the description of the main rules of the syntax of Afrikaans negation, it will be appropriate to devote some attention to the role of the sentence final morpheme *nie*, which, as can be seen in the resumptive schema in (36), is characteristic of the majority of Afrikaans negative sentences. There are three points to consider concerning final *nie*: its compatibility with other negative elements, restrictions on its occurrence and its role as a marker of the right-hand boundary of the negative sentence.

From what has been seen in 4.3.2.2., final *nie* may occur with any of the elements of the inventory of negative morphemes recorded in (13a) except for the coordinating conjunction *nòg...nòg*, although this is possible to a limited extent in some varieties, cf. examples (31) and (32). Furthermore, final *nie* is sufficient to indicate sentence negation in the pragmatically marked cases illustrated by (37).

The only strong restriction on final *nie* is constituted by contexts in which the last word of the negative sentence is already the same *nie*: the sequence **nie nie* at the end of a negative sentence is ungrammatical (cf. (15)). This has an important consequence in the case of complex sentences consisting of a main clause and a completive clause, both negative, closed by a single final *nie*, cf.

(38)   *Jan   het   nie   gedink   dat   niks   met   hulle*
       John have NEG thought that nothing with them
       sou   gebeur   nie
       CONDITIONAL happen   NEG
       'John didn't think that nothing would happen to them'   [Q24]

According to the rules examined in 4.3.2.2., every negative clause, whether main or subordinate, is closed with *nie*. In the case of a negative main clause governing a completive clause, *nie* is placed at the end of the completive. But the ungrammatical sequence of two *nie*s which it would give rise to, with the first *nie* pertaining to the completive and the second to the main clause (as in (39a, b)), is avoided by leaving only one *nie*, which refers to both the main and the completive clauses (as in (38) and (39c)).

(39)   a. [MAIN Jan het nie gedink [COMPL dat *niks* met hulle sou gebeur *nie* COMPL] nie MAIN]

        b. *Jan het nie gedink dat *niks* met hulle sou gebeur *nie* nie

        c. Jan het nie gedink dat *niks* met hulle sou gebeur *nie*

A weaker restriction on the occurrence of final *nie* is constituted by the presence of other negative elements in final position. In such cases, as already seen in 4.3.2.2., final *nie* is optional. Otherwise, *nie* may be adjoined to whatever lexical category appears at the end of the sentence. This entails that with *geen* 'no' in adjectival function there is always a final *nie*, because adjectival *geen* is always followed by at least a noun which occupies the last position in the phrase, (see again (30)).

Finally, in the case of constituent negation there are no restrictions on final *nie*, which, as often noted, accompanies a duplicate of itself and is adjoined to a non-negative lexical category, such as a noun (cf. (27)) or an adverb (cf. (28)).

A role of *nie* as a scope marker seems clearly to emerge from these observations (the definition is den Besten's, see above 4.3.3.1), a role which is emphasised by the restriction on the co-occurrence of **nie nie* and which may be weakened merely by the presence of another final negative element, that is, cases which could be defined, respectively, as entirely or partially redundant.

Its function as a scope marker is also triggered in the restricted cases of holophrastic replies which substitute for sentences of negative polarity (see example (34)), and elliptical replies consisting of negative quantifiers, as illustrated by example (40).

(40)   *Het   jy   enigiets   gesien? - Nee,   niks (nie)*
        have you:SG something seen   No nothing NEG
        'Have you seen anything? – No, nothing'   [Q12]

On the other hand, final *nie* also has the function of establishing the right-hand boundary of a sentence. Yet adverbial subordinate clauses in a negative sentence do not come within the scope of final *nie*, as the following concessive clause shows.

(41)   *Hy het   nie   kom   werk   nie,   alhoewel   hy   gesond   was*
        he   have   NEG   come   work   NEG   although   he   healthy   was
        'He did not come to work, although he was well' (Burgers 1971:
        159)

The position of final *nie* is particularly significant in the case of dislocated constituents, as it reflects the extent of their structural link with the sentence. In example (42) (for which cf. also (27)), the phrase *by 'n partytjie* is outside the negative clause, and is in fact also separated from it by the adversative conjunction *maar.*

(42)   *Jan   en   Marie het   nie   op   skool   ontmoet nie,   maar by*
        John   and   Mary have   NEG   on   school   met   NEG   but   at
        'n partytjie
        a   party
        'John and Mary didn't meet at school, but at a party'

Also in example (43) the 'heavy' constituent introduced by the preposition *vir* comes within the scope marker constituted by *nie,* , although placed to the right of the auxiliary *het*, which in subordinate clauses is usually in final position,

(43)   *en   dan   het   hy geweet   dat   hy* [...] *hom nie   losgeskud*
        and   then   have   he   known   that   he   him NEG   liberated
        het   vir   die herstel   van sy   energie   uit die   diepste   bronne
        have   for   the recovery   of   his   energy   of   the   deepest   sources
        in die natuur en   in sy   eie   gees   nie
        in   the   nature   and   in his   own   spirit   NEG
        'and then he knew that he [...] had not shaken himself free (lit. 'loose') for the recuperation of his energy from the deepest sources in nature and in his own spirit' (Burgers 1971: 194)

By way of conclusion to this section, Afrikaans negation may be defined in general terms within the framework of the typology drawn up in the work by Dahl (1979) often referred to in this volume. With respect to the morphology of sentence negation, Afrikaans conforms to the more general tendency, according to which affixes and particles are found in around 80% of cases. The 'particle' *nie* is in fact a free morpheme, though weak, given its tendency to become enclitic (see note 16). With respect to its syntax, however, Afrikaans goes against the distinct tendency in Dahl's sample to prepose the NEG particle to the conjugated verb regardless of constituent order. Regarding the first *nie* therefore, Afrikaans conforms to the postverbal type of negation found in Dutch and the other Germanic languages. Regarding the second, sentence final, *nie* Afrikaans appears instead to belong to a separate and rather unusual type of discontinuous negation, as will be seen in 4.3.3.

4.3.3. The Afrikaans type of negation in the areal perspective

The type of discontinuous negation found in Afrikaans, with the second negative element of the main clause positioned after a positive dependent clause is also found in other languages spoken on both sides of the Atlantic Ocean, and in particular varieties of Romance (Brazilian and African Portuguese, Caribbean Spanish), Romance based creoles (those of the islands of the Gulf of Guinea, based on Portuguese; Palenquero), some West African languages (for example Ewe). The Romance varieties and Palenquero have been studied 'in the field' by Armin Schwegler (1988, 1991a, 1991b, 1992), who was the first to draw up a description and interpretation of this type of negation in a diachronic and typological perspective and to whose work frequent reference will be made here.

The distribution of this type of negation is illustrated by the examples in 4.3.3.1., 4.3.3.2., 4.3.3.3., which reproduce, for the majority of the languages quoted, the 'diagnostic' example of a positive completive clause embedded in a negative main clause. Before examining these data, however, a few methodological remarks regarding the languages to be compared with Afrikaans are in order.

On the one hand, the Afrikaans type contrasts with the type of discontinuous negation in which two particles are placed on either side of the finite element of the verbal complex, as in the case of French *Jean n'a pas parlé* 'John has not spoken', discussed in 1. Leaving aside discontinuity, there are two features which differentiate this type from the one under discussion here: the syntactic position of the second particle which in French is linked to the verb and not to the sentence final position; the different etymological origin of *pas* and *nie*, since the former has been grammaticalised from expressions of minute quantity which originally had the function of negative polarity items in object position (cf. 2.3.). Bantu languages such as Yaunde (Boretzky 1983: 103) or Kikongo (Holm 1988: 174), often cited in the creole literature, which appear to have a construction with particles (or affixes) bound to the verb, do not therefore belong to this type.

On the other hand, the Afrikaans type of construction, especially with regards to the final particle, is considered distinct from the type of negation which has a sentence final morpheme, characteristic of many SOV languages according to Dahl's (1979) and Dryer's (1988) generalisations. The most important difference is obviously constituted by the fact that in this type of language the construction is not discontinuous.[20] Furthermore, the Afrikaans construction is not linked to

a constituent order with the verb at the end of the sentence, despite the plausibility of a basic OV order. In fact, as seen in 4.3.2.3., final *nie* in Afrikaans is
not sensitive to the lexical category to which it is adjoined. Finally, it may also
be observed that in SOV languages the subordinate clause normally precedes
the main clause and it is therefore not possible for a completive clause to be
followed by the main clause final negative particle as is the case in Afrikaans.
See example (44), taken from eastern Ijo (Kalabari variety), one of the African
languages excluded from the comparison.

(44)   [*iyeí á   tu̯bó̱-áā   é̱ré̱sí̱*]   *árị   ị   ḅala-áā*
          I   her child-NEG REASON she me care-NEG
          'It is because I am not her child that she doesn't care for me'
          (Kouwenberg 1992: 284)

The languages listed above and exemplified in the remainder of 4.3.3 are
SVO, not SOV languages showing discontinuous negative constructions which
have the second element in sentence final position, that is, with the schema S
NEG V O NEG, or, in the case of Afrikaans, X V NEG O NEG. This type
will henceforth be refered to with the description 'NEG…NEG#', where '#'
represents the sentence boundary.

The Afrikaans type of negation also contrasts with a third type of construction which is not discontinuous but which has a single sentence final negative
element and is found in SVO languages, although sporadically (cf. Dryer 1988:
104); we will label it as 'NEG#'. Unlike the two types already considered, i. e.
…NEG V NEG… and X V NEG, the position of the sentence final element,
which follows the object (and the completive clause), makes this third type
suitable for comparison with the Afrikaans NEG construction. Aside from the
structural aspect, comparison with this type is appropriate for the fact that in
some of the varieties under consideration it seems to have developed out of the
type 'NEG…NEG#' by elimination of the first element. See, below, Brazilian
Portuguese, Palenquero, Principense and, perhaps, the Afrikaans case exemplified in (37) as well.

4.3.3.1. *Romance varieties*

The 'NEG…NEG#' type of construction is found in Brazilian Portuguese,
already mentioned in 3.2. (cf. examples (24) − (27)) and may again be exemplified
in (45), taken from Schwegler (1991a: 199).

(45)   Brazilian Portuguese
          Ele não   sabe   que   o   pai   chegou   não
          he NEG knows that the father arrived NEG
          'He doesn't know that his father arrived'

Unlike Afrikaans, in Brazilian Portuguese this type competes on the one hand with the construction with only one negative preverbal element as in Lusitanian standard Portuguese, and on the other hand with a construction having a single final element, that is, 'NEG#', similar to that noted in Afrikaans (cf. example (37) in 4.3.2.2). As Schwegler's (1991a) detailed description reveals, the choice between alternative constructions, one with double *não* and one with a single final *não*, is governed mainly by pragmatic factors, such as the type of utterance or the function of more or less emphatic contradiction with respect to the context of the discourse (imperatives and replies favour the two contructions more than declaratives). This is illustrated by the following examples, taken from a well-known Brazilian author.[21]

(46)   "Quem vem lá?" – disse Ferreira. "É homem. *Não* é bicho *não*"
        'Who's coming? – said Ferreira. It's a man, it's not an animal'

(47)   Gabriela iria com ele [...] Ela fez que não com a cabeça [...] disse
        apenas: – Vou pro mato *não*, Clemente.
        'Gabriela would have gone with him [...] She shook her head [...]
        she only said: I'm not coming (*literally*: going) into the forest, Cle-
        mente'

The type 'NEG...NEG#' is also attested in Angolan Portuguese and on the island of São Tomé (see Schwegler 1992, example (32) and note 19). In these cases as well there is competition with the standard Lusitanian construction, but data regarding this are thin on the ground.[22]

Identification of the discontinuous negation under discussion here in Caribbean Spanish is a result of recent research in the field by Armin Schwegler (1992), who has described it for the Dominican Republic in particular. It is exemplified in (48).

(48)   Dominican Republic Spanish
        Yo no sé decirle por dónde queda San Marero no
        'I can't tell you where San Marero [street] is'
        (Schwegler 1992, his example (21))

In the work quoted here, Armin Schwegler describes the conditions governing alternation of this construction with the standard European construction, again linked to the pragmatic factors already illustrated for Portuguese. Our construction is attested in Cuba and the environs of Cartagena in Colombia, where, however, it is in decline or has disappeared in favour of the construction with a single preverbal *no*, and also, outside the Caribbean area but still in Colombia, on the Pacific coast (Tierras Bajas; cf. Schwegler 1992).

4.3.3.2. *Creoles*

Amongst the creoles mentioned above, Spanish-based Palenquero[23] seems to echo the situation in Portuguese and Spanish seen in 4.3.3.1. both from the functional point of view and from that of the expression. The type 'NEG...-NEG#' is realised by means of the same morpheme *nu* (cf. 49). Furthermore the type 'NEG#' is also found and expresses a strong contradiction with respect to the context of the discourse.

(49)   Palenquero
I nu   dudà   ke   bo   a-ten   plata   aí
I NEG doubt that you TENSE/ASPECT-have money there
banko nu
bank NEG
'I don't doubt that you have money in the bank'
(Schwegler 1991b: 191)

Apart from one case, the other creoles, instead, display a construction of the type 'NEG...NEG#' consisting of two different morphemes and, apparently, subject to no variation with other constructions. The relevant Portuguese-based creoles in this respect are those of the islands of the Gulf of Guinea, and in particular the islands of São Tomé (São-Tomese and Angolar[24]) and of Annobón (today Pagalu, part of Equatorial Guinea). Cf.

(50)   São-Tomese
bo   na   be   ũa bisu ku pasa fa   õte   taji?
2SG NEG see a bird that pass NEG yesterday afternoon
'You did not see a bird that passed yesterday afternoon?'
(Valkhoff 1966: 109)

(51)   Angolar
kolómbá na   tá   methé pa nɔ tá ʒuntu
whites NEG TENSE/ASPECT want for us be together
nɛ   wa
them NEG
'The whites didn't want us to live near them'
(Schwegler 1992, his example (46b))

(52)   Annobonese
m-ã   sebe   xa-ŋ   fe-f
1SG-NEG know what.thing do-NEG
'I do not know what to do'
(Valkhoff 1966: 101)

In Príncipe Island creole, again Portuguese based and with close affinities with the other two, a construction with only sentence final negation has developed from 'NEG...NEG#', as example (53) shows.[25]

(53)   Principense
        kada-ni-ŋé (na) *sebe falá purtugezi*   fa
        each   NEG know speak Portuguese   NEG
        'Not everybody can speak Portuguese'
        (Valkhoff 1966: 101)

In these creoles the discontinuous construction involves a preverbal particle *na* (cf. (50), (51), (53)), which in Annobonese is reduced to *ã* and fused with the first person singular pronoun (cf. (52)), and the particle *fa* (or *wa*) in sentence final position. *Na* is linked to both Portuguese *não* and to its older fifteenth and sixteenth century form *nom* (Teyssier 1986: 597). *Fa* and *wa* are ascribed an African origin: these particles in fact echo the 'NEG...NEG#' or 'NEG#' constructions which are found in some of the West African languages (discussed below, in 4.3.3.3.), but their etymology is still obscure.[26]

While on the subject of creoles, a few words are in order concerning the Dutch-based creole of the county of Berbice in Guyana, recently (re)discovered but in the process of extinction.[27] In this creole, which has SVO word order, negation is expressed at the end of the sentence by the particle *kanε*, as illustrated in (54).

(54)   Dutch creole of Berbice
        o   habu bwa kanε
        3SG have leg NEG
        'It doesn't have legs'
        (Kouwenberg 1992: 282)

Unlike what has been said regarding the creoles of the Gulf of Guinea, the origin of this particle has been reconstructed with some certainty. It is made up of two elements. The first, *ka-*, is a continuation of the sentence final particle *-ka* which appears, with different phonetic forms, in varieties of eastern Ijo, the SOV language of the majority of the slaves deported to Guyana after the foundation of the colony by the Dutch in 1627, and which forms a large part of the Berbice creole lexicon.[28] The second element fused into the particle, that is, *-nε*, is instead a reflex of the Dutch *nee* 'no', which the colonials and/or the slave merchants probably used as a reinforcement of negation at the end of a negative sentence (cf. again 3.2. for a discussion of this feature in European languages). This point will be taken up again and examined in greater detail in 4.3.4.

4.3.3.3. Languages of Africa

As far as the languages of Africa are concerned, on the basis of available documentation, the construction of the type 'NEG…NEG#' is attested with certainty for Ewe, a language of the Kwa group, cf.

(55)   Ewe
        nye-mé-*lè,   háfi   wòvá   o*
        I-NEG-be then/when come:3SG NEG
        'I wasn't there, when he came'
        (Boretzky 1983: 102)[29]

Hausa, a language of the Chad group, has a 'NEG…NEG#' construction in so-called verbal sentences, except where they have continuous aspect or are in the subjunctive, in which case there is a single preverbal morpheme, *báa* and *kádà* respectively. The same applies in the case of existential sentences (with *bâa* or *báabù* 'there is not'); in equative sentences a discontinuous construction is used, but the two morphemes surround the predicative element and the second element is not in sentence final position (Newman 1987: 715, 721). The discontinuous construction has been already exemplified in the Introduction and reference should be made to example (11) reported there; (56) illustrates the construction found in equative sentences.

(56)   Hausa
        Shii báa   *sóojà*   bá   *nèe*
        he NEG soldier NEG EQUATIVE:M
        'He is not a soldier' (Newman 1987: 721, spelled as in the original)

In Africa there are then various SVO languages with sentence final but not discontinuous negation, that is, of type 'NEG#'. This type, as already stated, is not widely distributed (Dryer 1988: 104) and it is therefore significant that 10 out of the 13 cases included in Dryer's (1988: 123) sample are concentrated in central-western Africa.[30] The ten cases are two Afro-Asiatic languages of the Chad group (Margi, Tera), five Niger-Kordofanian languages (Duka, Gbaya Kara, Gbeya Bossangoa, Nzakara, Sango), three Nilo-Saharan languages (Kresh, Sara-Ngambay, Shatt). All these languages are spoken in a vast area which includes southern Chad, northern Nigeria, the Central-African Republic and the bordering areas of Cameroon, Zaire and Sudan (cfr. Moseley–Asher 1994). Two examples will suffice to illustrate the NEG strategy used in these languages, one from Kresh and one from the variety of Sango used as lingua franca in the Central-African Republic, and which developed from the last decade of the last century onwards. We leave aside the nonetheless relevant question of whether this is to be considered a pidgin in the process of creolisation or the result of processes of koiné formation (cf. Holm 1989: 562–563).

(57)   Kresh
              Kôkó ãnjã mömö 'dĩ
              Koko he:go home NEG
              'Koko did not go home'
              (Brown 1994: 166)[31]

(58)   Sango
              lo bâ ε tongàna ʐo   āpὲ
              he sees us as   person NEG
              'He doesn't consider us people'
              (Diki-Kidiri 1977: 59)

4.3.3.4. Areal observations

Having reviewed the distribution of the type of negation via a sentence final particle (regardless of whether it occurs alone or is preceded by another negative morpheme) amongst languages of different genetic affiliation, we now turn to observations on its geographic distribution, represented in a very schematic may in (59).

(59)   Geographic distribution of negative constructions with a sentence
              final particle
              Afr: 'NEG…NEG#'
              Dcb: 'NEG#'
              Pbr: 'NEG…NEG#' & 'NEG#'
              *: both constructions compete with preverbal negations
              n.b.: for the language symbols see the list of abbreviations on p. x

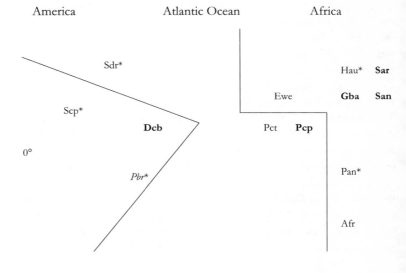

Negative constructions with a sentence final particle are concentrated on the two sides of the southern Atlantic. They do not, however, constitute a linguistic area in the strict sense of the term, which is characterised by the presence of the same features in geographically contiguous languages, as in the 'classic' case of the Balkan area (cf. Banfi 1985), nor do they represent areal *continua* of different types, as in the case of postverbal negation in Germanic, Romance and Celtic, as discussed in 4.2.

Nevertheless, the distribution schematised in (59) is interesting from an areal point of view, particularly in view of the fact that the languages included represent the unusual combination of SVO constituent order and negation expressed, redundantly or also exclusively, in sentence final position. They are in fact 'marked' both from the point of view of the more 'harmonious' combinations of constituent order and negative particles – already illustrated on the basis of Dahl's study (1979) – and also from the point of view of crosslinguistic distribution (cf. Croft 1990: 83). In both the continents, Africa and America, the territory surrounding that of the languages mapped in (59) is characterised by sentence final types of negation only where there is SOV order, as in the cases of Ijo (Nigeria), recorded above in 4.3.3.2., the Khoisan languages (cf. 4.3.1.), and also some of the Amazon languages such as Canela Krahô or Pirahã (Derbyshire – Pullum 1986).

Otherwise there are languages with SVO order and non sentence final negation, usually in preverbal position. In Africa this applies, amongst the Kwa languages, to Yoruba (which in this respect differs from Ewe discussed in 4.3.3.3.), and to the Bantu family in general, along the entire Atlantic coast of the Gulf of Guinea as far as Namibia. As for America, note instead the varieties of Spanish spoken in Colombia, Venezuela, Uruguay, and Argentina, and, amongst the original languages of the continent, Guaraní.

The type of negation discussed here is also exceptional with respect to creole languages as a whole, which are distributed along the Atlantic coasts of the two continents. In French-based creoles (all in America: Haiti, the Antilles, French Guyana) the postverbal particle *pas* of the lexifying language is used in preverbal position (cf. Haitian *Li* pa-*t-koné*, 'He didn't know'. literally 'He NEG-ANTE-RIOR-know', Holm 1988: 171; cf. also 3.1.). In English-based creoles in both America (creoles of the Atlantic coast of central America and of the West Indies, Jamaican, Guyanese, Sranan, Saramaccan, Ndjuka) and Africa (Krio and other varieties of western Africa) the preverbal negative particle reflects English *no* or *never* (cf. Sranan *ma Jezus* no *gi hem pasi vo dati*, 'But Jesus didn't let him do it', literally 'but Jesus NEG give him permission for that' (*Njoe Testament nanga dem Psalm*, Surinaams Bijbelsgenootschap, Paramaribo, 1980; Mark 5, 19).

Amongst the few Spanish-based creoles, on the American coast Papiamentu contrasts with Palenquero, with only preverbal negation (cf. *Ma Jesus* no *a permi-*

ti'é 'But Jesus didn't let him do it', literally 'but Jesus NEG ANTERIOR allow him', *E Testament Nobo di nos Señor y Salbador Jesu Christo*, Sociedad Biblica Neerlandesa, Amsterdam, 1952; St. Mark 5, 19). Amongst the Dutch-based creoles, still on the American coast, the so-called Negerhollands of the Virgin Islands in the Antilles, now extinct, contrasts with Berbice creole (and, of course, with Afrikaans) (cf. Negerhollands: *die* no *hab kaes* 'there is no cheese', literally 'there NEG exist cheese', Holm 1989: 328). Finally, contrasting with the Portuguese-based creoles of the Gulf of Guinea are, still on the African coast, the creoles of the island of Cape Verde and Guinea Bissau with preverbal *ka*, from Port. *nunca* 'never' (cf. Guinea Bissau *i ka bin inda*, 'He has not yet come', literally 'he NEG come yet', Teyssier 1986: 597).[32]

Outside the Atlantic region, the preverbal NEG is also characteristic of the Portuguese creoles of the Indian Ocean (cf. again Teyssier 1986) as well as creoles with other lexical bases: Indian Ocean French-based creoles, Spanish-based creoles of the Philipines and the numerous varieties of pidginised/creolised English of the Pacific (cf. for all of these the review in Holm 1989).[33]

Finally, we have also seen that in the colonial varieties of European languages, whether they belong to their diasystems (cf. Portuguese, Spanish) or not (cf. Afrikaans vs. Dutch), sentence final negation is an innovation.

Taking a more detailed look now at the languages in schema (59), and linking this to what has already been discussed in 4.3.3.1., 4.3.3.2., 4.3.3.3., the types of negation with a final element (that is, 'NEG...NEG#' and 'NEG#') seem to be more stable in Africa than in America. Here they compete with each other and with the preverbal type of negation, except in Berbice creole. However, it is clear that the alternation is found in particular in Romance varieties (Brazilian Portuguese, Dominican Republic Spanish and, in Africa, Angolan Portuguese, where the influence of the European standard is stronger) as well as in Palenquero; in Hausa (cf. 4.3.3.3.) the two constructions are in complementary distribution according to sentence type and are not subject to pragmatic factors.

The type 'NEG#' is well represented in Africa, while in America it is stable only in Berbice creole and is subject to the alternations mentioned above for the other (varieties of) languages. As for the African languages listed in 4.3.3.3. it is not possible to say anything concerning the origin of this type. Regarding Berbice creole, however, the hypothesis that a lexical and syntactic loan is responsible for the particular conditions determining the formation of this creole, discussed in 4.3.3.2., is convincing. In fact, as far as the other cases are concerned, 'NEG#' is the outcome of a development of type 'NEG...NEG#' with omission of the first negative element in certain conditions of emphasis (see 4.3.3.2.). Note that, on the one hand, this process is not entirely absent from Afrikaans, cf. example (37), while on the other hand it seems actually to be completed in Principense (cf. again 4.3.3.2.).

To sum up, the languages which share the discontinuous type 'NEG...-NEG#' may ultimately be divided into languages which use two distinct morphemes, all concentrated in Africa (Hausa, Ewe, São Tomese, Angolar, Annobonese) and those which use the same morpheme, found in both Africa (Afrikaans, Angolan Portuguese) and America (Dominican Republic Spanish, Palenquero, Brazilian Portuguese). As may be noted, only languages and language varieties of a European colonial stamp are included in this second group.

In the light of these observations, an attempt may be made to explain the origin of the Afrikaans negative construction in the context of European, and not only Dutch, colonial expansion on both Atlantic coasts. Colonisation, as is widely known, was started in the fifteenth century by the Portuguese, who opened the trade routes to India and the far East circumnavigating Africa (1488) and, in the following century, setting foot in Brazil (1532). In the seventeenth century the Dutch replaced the Portuguese along the African routes to the far East, where they imposed their colonial dominion (Batavia, Djakarta, 1610). The Cape colony, which as will be remembered was founded in 1652, served as an intermediate station along this very route to Asia.[34]

These brief observations on the historical foundation of the geographical distribution of the languages under discussion here with respect to their negative constructions, also contribute to the plausibility of the attempt to seek the foundations of Afrikaans in the phenomena of linguistic contact which characterised the history of the southern Atlantic in those centuries and which saw Portuguese in a dominant position as an 'international language' (Valkhoff 1975).

4.3.4. Diachronic hypotheses

The problem of the diachronic development of Afrikaans negation may now be tackled, and an attempt made to trace its origin in the varieties of colonial Portuguese of the sixteenth and seventeenth centuries. To this end we will first of all discuss the development of the type 'NEG...NEG#' in Portuguese and will then pass on to Afrikaans. In each of the two cases, the diachronic hypotheses will concern the structural level, the communicative context which may have favoured the rise and grammaticalisation of the 'NEG...NEG#' construction with identity of the negative morphemes involved, and finally the means by which the construction may have been diffused. We shall not discuss the same type of construction (with different negative morphemes) found in the creoles of the Gulf of Guinea, for which, as has been said, the influence of an African substratum has been invoked, and we shall touch only marginally on the type 'NEG...NEG#' in Caribbean Spanish, for which the reader is refered to Schwegler's already cited work (1992).

4.3.4.1. 'NEG...NEG#' in Portuguese

The discontinuous construction 'NEG...NEG#' found in varieties of colonial Portuguese has been explained as the result of a process whereby an original negative prosentence (as It. *no*) added to an already negative sentence for emphasis is reanalysed as a negative marker within the sentence, cf. in particular Schwegler (1991b: 208–109), but already Jespersen (1917: 72). This process is illustrated schematically in (60) and exemplified in (61) on the basis of example (45).

(60)   a. $_S$[...NEG V ...] $_S$[NO]
        b. $_S$[...NEG V ...(][)NO]
        c. $_S$[...NEG V ... NEG]

(61)   a. *Ele* não   sabe   que   o   pai   chegou.   Não!
           he NEG   knows   that   the   father   arrived   no
        b. *Ele* não   sabe   que   o   pai   chegou,   nao!
           he NEG   knows   that   the   father   arrived   no
        c. *Ele* não   sabe   que   o   pai   chegou   não
           he NEG   knows   that   the   father   arrived   NEG
           'He doesn't know that his father arrived'

As can be seen from (60), at the syntactic level the reanalysis involves weakening and elimination of the sentence boundary (cf. (60b) and (60c)), which is reflected on the prosodic level in the reduction of the intonational contours and, in particular, in the weakening of the original prosentence (*Não!*). In addition, on the lexical level there is recategorisation of the prosentence as a sentence negation marker (cf. *não* in (61c)).[35]

At its origin, this process is made possible by lexical identity of the sentence negation (NEG in the scheme (60)) and the negative prosentence (NO), which differ only in their prosodic features, the first being unstressed and the second, which on its own may assume the function of a sentence, being stressed. Identity of the two forms, apart from prosodic features, is a fait accompli in sixteenth century Portuguese, with the older unstressed sentence negation morpheme *nom* (originally pronounced [nũ]) assimilated to the phonetics of the prosentence *nam* (old spelling for *não*) as part of the wider process of adjustment of final *-ão, -an* and *-on*, both stressed and unstressed (cf. Teyssier 1980: 57–58).[36]

We can also imagine the communicative contexts which might have favoured the frequency of structures of the type exemplified in (60a) in the asymmetrical interactions between the Portuguese and their slaves, probably oriented towards warnings and prohibitions. The Portuguese probably exploited the same types of interaction in varieties of foreigner talk, where strategies of simplification (especially in morphology) and of clarification are adopted simultaneously (cf. Ferguson 1971). The addition of *não!* may have made a warning or a prohibition stronger (and clearer) to those with very little knowledge of Portuguese who, for their part, could interpret the prosentence as a sentence final negation marker.

This hypothetical pragmatic scenario is indirectly confirmed by the sentence final negative particle in Berbice creole, namely *kanɛ*, where *-nɛ* derived from Dutch *nee* 'no' (cf. Kouwenberg 1992: 285; cf. 4.3.3.2.). This element could well have originated in emphatic negative utterances such as the one reported in a modern Dutch version in (62), where, again, emphasis is obtained by means of an added negative prosentence in 'afterthought' (i. e. final) position.[37]

(62)   *het kan* niet   *waar zijn*(,) nee! (cf. (61b))
        it can NEG true be   no
        'It can't be true, no!'

The process whereby this element penetrated the creole may be reconstructed as follows:

(63)   a. (foreigner talk) Dutch.: s[...niet...] s[nee]
        b. Dutch pidgin: *s[...ka (][) ne]
        c. Berbice creole: s[...kanɛ]

Unfortunately, as far as Portuguese is concerned, solid documentary proof confirming the hypothesis advanced here is not available, and we have bare indications.

Valkhoff (1966: 13) takes the following example, uttered in 1627 by a black, from Silva Neto's introduction to Brazilian Portuguese, although in this case it is not possible to determine the category of the second *não* (prosentence or already NEG particle?).

(64)   Não   *retira*   não, *sipanta, sipanta!*
        NEG retreat NEG follow follow
        'Do not retreat, chase him, chase him!'

In the literary sources of the so-called 'reconnaissance language' discussed by Naro (1978) with the aim of showing that many features of Portuguese creole originate in the contact between Africans and Portuguese in Portugal, there is only one attestation of sentence final negation, but preceded by *nunca* 'never', which is the source of the negative particle of almost all the Portuguese-based creoles. Cf.

(65)   Nunca   *a mi cadella* nam
        never/NEG I   dog   no
        'I am not a dog' (Naro 1978: 330)[38]

Although unique, this example is important because it bears witness to the stage hypothesised in (60a). In fact, the written form *nam* enables us to interpret the final negation as a stressed, and therefore relatively independent, element.

Clements (1992) quite rightly points out that Naro's 'reconnaissance language' reflects nothing if not a form of foreigner-talk learnt and used by the first Africans brought to Portugal to be trained as interpreters. In his scant Portuguese foreigner-talk data no mention is made, however, of the possibility of having an emphatic negation at the end of the utterance.

On the other hand, it is surprising, although of course not conclusive, to find the negative reply in standard European Portuguese consisting of repetition of the verb of the question in negative form, to which is added the prosentence *não*. In Vázquez Cuesta – Mendes da Luz's grammar (1988: 546) this is the only structure given for a negative reply,[39] cf.

(66)   *Achou   a   corrida melhor do   que   a   do   ano*
        found:3SG the   race   better of:the that the of:the year
        passado? - Não achei,   não.
        passed   not found:1SG   no
        'Have you found the race better than last year's? *I haven't found, no*'
        [= No]

(67)   *Foste   lá? - Não fui,   não, minha senhora.*
        was:3SG there   not was:1SG   no   my   lady
        'Were you there? *I was not there, no,* madam' [= No,…]

Three constructions with double *não*, but, again, without the possibility of establishing with certainty the categorial nature of the second element, are attested in the last century by Schuchardt (1888: 252) for the contact varieties of Portuguese found in Angola and adjacent areas.[40] Again, they concern negative replies to questions, cf.

(68)   *Estás   doente? -* Nao *está* não
        are:2SG ill   NEG is   NEG/no
        'Are you ill? – No'

These last three types serve at least to show the plausibility of the diffusion of final *não* as a means of emphasis at least in the context of replies, where it is important to underline the potential negativity of the reply itself.

As far as the last of the questions relevant to the hypotheses on the origin of the discontinuous construction in Brazilian Portuguese is concerned, that is, identification of the ways in which it was diffused, attention has always been focused on the groups of west African slaves deported to America in the sixteenth and seventeenth centuries and on the hypothetical Afro-Portuguese pidgin (or semi-creole) spoken by them (cf. Schwegler 1992: 5 and the preceding literature cited there). In essence, this hypothesis relates the role the islands of the Gulf of Guinea played in the Portuguese dominated trade and deportation of slaves to the Americas, with the fact that in the creoles of the islands of São Tomé, Príncipe and Annobón themselves there are constructions with a sentence final negative element (cf. 4.3.3.2.). However the creoles of the three islands of the Gulf of Guinea constitute an exception with regards to other Portuguese creoles and to creoles (and pidgins) in general with different lexical bases, characterised by preverbal negation (cf. above in 4.3.3.4.).

The role that may have been played by the aforementioned varieties of contact Portuguese that developed along the Portuguese trade routes in Africa south of the Gulf of Guinea (see example (68)) should not be overlooked. They are probably more or less simplified varieties ("ein mehr oder weniger verdorbenes Portugiesisch" according to Schuchardt, 1888: 243), in use alongside real and proper Portuguese on the one hand and Bantu languages on the other in transactions between Africans and Europeans. These varieties, attested by Schuchardt (1888) for Africa, were diffused along all the routes held by the Portuguese and with the decline of their power were adopted by the Europeans, such as the Dutch, English and Danish, who replaced them (cf. Schuchardt, 1888: 244 for the use of Portuguese by the Danish on the Gold Coast in the second half of the seventeenth century).[41]

Passing now to Caribbean Spanish, we have to underline the perfect homology of form and function between Portuguese *não* and Spanish *no*, both of which serve as negation and prosentence: we can imagine that the 'NEG...NEG#' construction penetrated Spanish from varieties of contact Portuguese, with the groups of slaves deported to the Caribbean playing a possibly decisive mediation role.[42]

By bringing to the forefront the role played by varieties of contact Portuguese in the Atlantic a different light may be thrown on the Portuguese creoles of the Gulf of Guinea and Spanish-based Palenquero in Colombia. The islands of São Tomé, Príncipe and Annobón ('NEG...NEG#', but with different morphemes, the first of which is a reflex of *não* and not *nunca*) are in fact found on the fringes of the territory where the varieties of contact Portuguese mentioned above developed.[43] Furthermore, these islands had the ports where, especially in the second half of the sixteenth century, the African slaves were sorted out before being embarked for America (Holm 1989: 278). And this fact suggests a stronger Portuguese linguistic presence than in the situation typical of the plantations.

4.3.4.2. 'NEG...NEG#' in Afrikaans

Turning finally to the negative construction in Afrikaans, it must above all be noted that it has its origins in the transitional phase during which the discontinuous construction *en* V *niet* of Middle Dutch, attested in documents of the seventeenth century (see chapter 2, example (27) and cf. Raidt 1983: 189), develops into the modern postverbal construction, which must, however, have already been diffused in the spoken language. No traces of the discontinuous negation of Middle Dutch remain in Afrikaans.

As is evident from the discussion in 4.3.2., the 'NEG...NEG#' construction cannot be traced back to the processes of reanalysis described for Portuguese, as the result would have been a construction with two different morphemes, *nie* the first and *nee* the second, as exemplified in (69), which echoes example (62). Although under different conditions, this has happened in the Dutch-based Berbice creole.

(69)   a. Dutch
        Het kan niet   *waar zijn*(,) nee!
        it   can NEG true be   no
        'It can't be true, no!'
    b. Afrikaans
        *Dit kan nie   *waar wees* ne(e)
        it   can NEG true be   NEG
        'It can't be true'

On the other hand, the colonial Portuguese construction arisen from the reanalysis of the prosentence as exemplified in (61c) and the Afrikaans construction are homologous with respect to the type of morpheme used as well as the syntactic schema, apart from the position of the first element (*não* preverbally, *nie* after the conjugated verb in main clauses). The hypothesis that this homology is a result of the direct influence of the varieties of colonial Portuguese on Afrikaans is plausible. According to this hypothesis the Afrikaans construction would be a calque of the Portuguese construction. We illustrate this possibility by means of scheme (71), rephrasing in (70) with modern lexical items one of the first attestations of the construction in Brazilian Portuguese, as recorded above in (64).

(70)   Dut. *Wijk* niet   *terug*
            run   NEG back
        Afr. *Wyk* nie   *terug* nie[44]
            run   NEG back NEG

Port. Não *retira*   não
NEG retreat NEG
'Don't retreat/Don't run away!'

(71)

Dut		Wijk	niet	terug	Ø
Afr.		Wyk	nie	terug	nie
Port.	Não	retira			não

The calque consists in repeating the negative particle as the last word in the sentence, whilst the position of the first NEG particle in Afrikaans and Portuguese is different according to the syntactic rules of the two languages.

The calque hypothesis can also account for the restriction in the occurrence of two sentence final *nie*s: the process of repeating the negative particle at the end of the sentence is blocked by the fact that the NEG particle is already in sentence final position. See (72), constructed on one of the Portuguese examples recorded by Schuchardt (1888: 252) for the Angolan coast.[45]

(72)   Port. *Vaes   passear?* - Não *vae   não*
go:2SG walk   NEG go:3SG NEG
Afr. *Gaan jy   wandel?* - *Ek gaan* nie
go   you walk   I   go   NEG
'Are you going for a walk? — I'm not going'

The calque hypothesis implies that the construction was first established in sentences which did not contain negative indefinites, as in the hypothetical example (70); in fact it is only in this case that the conditions are found for the calque process, which essentially consists in doubling the negative particle, as (73) also shows.[46] Consequently we may suppose that the sentence final particle was extended by analogy to sentences with negative quantifiers only later.

(73)   Port.   Não *tem   pão*   não
NEG there.is bread   NEG
Afr.   *Daar is* geen *brood*   nie
there is no   bread   NEG
??

It must, however, be borne in mind that it is probable that co-occurrence of negative quantifiers and the particle *niet* was also available in the Dutch brought to the Cape, as is known from the history of Dutch and its modern dialects.[47] Even though it is not from native Dutch, an example of this is found in (74), which Raidt (1983: 189) considers the first attestation of our construction. The sentence is taken from the will of Kaspar Meister, a German from Osnabrück, written in 1716.

(74)   ..., *want   ik heb   geen vrinde   niet*
                 because I   have no   friends NEG
                 'Because I don't have any friends'

The example, as den Besten also argues (1986: 209), cannot be considered an instance of the 'NEG...NEG#' construction with certainty, but it is without doubt a case of double negation. On the basis of what has been put forward above, cases of this type, in which the particle *nie(t)* is found in sentence final position even though not duplicated, may have contributed to establishing the result of the calque as reconstructed above and to extending it to different types of negative sentences (those with negative quantifiers included).

From the historical and sociolinguistic point of view, the processes hypothesised here imply that at the Cape, at least in the seventeenth and eighteenth centuries, those crucial for the formation of Afrikaans, there was widespread, although imperfect, bilingualism in Dutch and Portuguese.

The point is dealt with in detail by Valkhoff (1966: 146–191) and (1972), who, unlike other authors, especially the South Africans, claims that there was already knowledge of Portuguese at the Cape in the seventeenth century.[48] Valkhoff goes back to direct evidence: for example, the travel chronicles of the Jesuit Guy Tachard for 1685 and of François Valentijn (1966: 162–169; 1972: 86–90, 95–96). He also records indirect evidence, such as, for example, the 1657 decree of commissioner Rijklof van Goens (cf. 1966: 163–164) urging Jan van Riebeeck, the founder of the colony at the Cape, not to use any other language but his mother tongue (that is, Dutch) with the slaves newly arrived from Guinea and Angola, thus setting a good example to the officials, who were presumably used to dealing with the slaves in some variety of Portuguese. In fact, widespread knowledge of Portuguese is inferred from the historical circumstances of Dutch colonisation which substituted Portuguese colonisation along the Asiatic routes which, circumnavigating Africa, had in the colony of the Cape an important intermediate supply station.

More important, however, is the question of the variety of Portuguese to which the documentation examined and discussed by Valkhoff refers. At several points he speaks of 'High Portuguese' and 'Low Portuguese', intending with the first expression the literary language, and with the second "a pidginized, creolized or simplified Portuguese" (Valkhoff 1972: 94), for which he also metaphorically uses the term *lingua franca*, (of course not referring to the lingua franca of the Mediterranean). Alongside the literary language, or rather the standard language, spoken in particular by the officials,[49] more or less simplified varieties of Portuguese must have been in use, including also the more properly creolized varieties, which, given the origin of the slaves deported to the Cape, were probably Asiatic and not African strains (cf. 4.3.1.).[50] However, the Asiatic strains must have had a less important role, since preverbal negation in them goes back to the Portuguese etymon *nunca*, which does not lend itself to the calque mechanism discussed above.

From a methodological, general perspective, the case study discussed here has shown how contact situations may cause the emergence and establishment of otherwise 'marked' constructions such as Afrikaans negation, thanks to the particular communicative conditions which the imperfect knowledge of a lingua franca or of foreign languages contribute in creating. This also shows up from the areal diffusion of constructions similar to the Afrikaans one in the Atlantic Ocean along the routes of Portuguese colonisation.

It is clear that historical and sociolinguistic remarks play an important role in the typological discussion when dealing with problems of language contact (see 4.3.1.). The 'NEG...NEG#' type in the southern Atlantic may have been active at various times and in various places, but proof of its having occurred may be shown only through reconstruction of the communicative conditions which may have favoured it and which may have operated over time and space.

Part II

The analysis of the Questionnaire

Foreword

The questionnaire, the type of inquiry

The wider field of research encompassed the preparation of a questionnaire in English and in Italian comprising 38 sentences, which potentially covered more or less the major types of negative sentence. This questionnaire was distributed amongst persons of a high level of education (to fellow linguists wherever possible) who were requested to translate the sentences in the more or less standard form of their respective languages. As often happens in such cases, as a consequence of the replies we were receiving, the questionnaire itself underwent modifications and additions during the course of the enquiry with the aim of rendering it more effective. In fact sentences containing an existential or locative negative construction (*There is no bread/There was no bread; John isn't there/John wasn't there; There's nothing here/There's nobody here*) were not examined: given the type of problems that they entail, including those of an extra-linguistic nature, they would require a special discussion.

Obviously such a procedure may raise more than one problem from a methodological point of view. Firstly, the replies were written rather than elicited during the course of a normal conversation. This entails a drastic reduction in scope to only the structural level, it not being possible to take into account potential conversational implicatures, excluded by definition from a written questionnaire.

Furthermore, the level of standardisation and of the linguistic variety chosen by the informant may depend upon his or her personal sensitivity and even cultural level. The diastratic range is missing from our replies; nor is there any diatopic dimension within a particular linguistic tradition: it is highly probable that, at least in some cases, the translation offered do not exhaust the possibilities which effectively exist among equivalent sentences within a given linguistic tradition, as each of us may be aware of with respect to our own mother tongues. It is, on the other hand, obvious that the sentences of the test have been formulated on the basis of a particular linguistic experience, specifically Italian, mother tongue of the two authors. For this reason it is possible that certain details may escape our questionnaire, as, for example, the contrast between factive NEG and prohibitive NEG (e.g. Greek *dén* vs. *mén*), which do not have distinct morphs in English or Italian, escaped the first version of it.

"If what we have said here is true, one may ask how anyone could be so stupid as to choose translations as a basis for an investigation of language use. The simple answer is that this is the only realistic method for large-scale data collection in typologically oriented linguistic research. We simply have to accept that it is unreliable and try to use the data with the necessary care", Dahl (1985: 50). We subscribe wholeheartedly to this position. In reality, in wide ranging enquiries, this is indeed the only procedure effectively possible: in a collection of spontaneously produced sentences it would never be possible to document the entire array of negative sentences brought together in this questionnaire. Furthermore, such a procedure allows for a real homogeneity, and therefore an immediate comparison of the data interlinguistically.

Nor should a fundamental fact be forgotten: the aim of the enquiry is of a typological nature. What is important, in this context, is that a certain type of sentence exists or not, whether it is possible or otherwise; not how widely it is used or how popular it is within a given linguistic community. For these reasons we have taken into account only those replies with which we have been supplied, ignoring possible variants not directly attested in them (except for checking, where it may have seemed necessary, the grammars of the various languages for the answers we got). Otherwise one runs the risk of making certain languages − those of which the authors have a greater knowledge − appear as having a wider range of possibilities than the others. This, too, is obviously but inevitably a limitation and a simplification of the linguistic reality.

Dealing with a relatively restricted area (Europe), the procedure has been aimed at completeness rather than sampling. Despite this, problems have arisen: should we consider, alongside Castillian, only Catalan or also Galician, Valencian and Asturian? If Sardinian and Ladin are included, what about Sicilian, Neapolitan and Ligurian? We have replied implicitly to these questions with an empirical decision dictated by practical reasons and which does not in the least enter into the much debated question of the relationship between language and dialect, which evidently goes beyond the problem in hand: we have simply taken into consideration those linguistic traditions which are widely agreed on as being autonomous 'languages', having their own particular physiognomy, and not 'dialects' of another linguistic tradition in some way superordinate to them. We have therefore not sought native speakers of Gascon or Neapolitan, even though they undoubtedly have − at least in the latter case − a celebrated linguistic and also literary tradition.

Regarding the geographical range, we chose to limit the enquiry by including only Georgian as representative of the Caucasian languages, only Turkish as representative of the Turkic languages, and excluded furthermore the non-Ugro-Finnic Uralic languages, even though all of these belong to Europe from a strictly geographical point of view. While not exluding the possibility of influences between these and the Slavic languages (in particular Russian, at least from the period following the Soviet revolution), they certainly do not fall within the cultural-historical panorama of the European languages, of which Russian is in

reality the extreme eastern boundary. Furthermore, as far as the European Cau-
casus area is concerned, for the Indo-European family, Armenian has been
briefly considered.

Even a perfunctory (but not overly arbitrary) decision such as that taken is
not without criticism: there remain borderline cases such as Maltese (included
in our corpus). Ineichen (1979: 104) observes: "Ob man (...) das Maltesische
als eine europäische Sprache betrachtet oder als Ableger des angrenzenden semi-
tischen Bereichs, ist nicht eine Frage des 'Europabegriffs', sondern der Linguistik". [Whether Maltese is considered a European language or an offshoot
of the neighbouring Semitic group is not a question pertaining the 'notion of
Europe', but a question pertaining linguistics]. There is here a curious overlapping of two criteria which should, instead, remain distinct: on the one hand the
geographical, and on the other hand the genealogical. The fact that Maltese
belongs to the Semitic group of languages is beyond question even if, hypotheti-
cally, it were to be spoken in Sicily or ... the Isle of Man. What is important
rather is the fact that Malta, given over to Christianity during the reign of
Frederik II, passed then to the Angevins and to the Aragonese, and from 1522
the seat of the famous order of knighthood, has a history inextricably linked to
that of Europe, with political, economic and cultural − and therefore also linguistic − contacts oriented more often towards Europe than towards the African shores; in this sense it may be considered a 'European language', even
though genetically Semitic. In any case we maintain that these are only marginal
examples which do not undermine the essential validity of the (historical and)
geographical criteria adopted.[1]

5. Sentence and phrase negation

5.1. The sentence Q1: negation in replies to 'yes/no' questions ['NO']

The first seven sentences in the questionnaire (along with sentence Q34) constitute a homogeneous block, while in the sentences from Q8 onwards other phenomena are examined.

(1)   = Q1 A. *Have you seen John?* –   B. *No* (,*I haven't*)
                 A. *Hai visto Giovanni?* –   B. *No*

Here we are dealing with the negative reply to so-called 'yes/no' questions ['NO', It. *NO*, Eng. *NO*], to which the term 'short answers' may also be applied: see Bernini (1990: 121), where it is also observed that replies to interrogative utterances seem to be more basic, or more prototypical than replies to other kinds of sentences; in fact the short answer forms used in reply to interrogative utterances are also used for short answers to statements and commands. The reverse is not true: no short answer forms used mainly with the latter two types of expression are also used with replies to interrogatives. Furthermore 'NO' seems to be more widely diffused and 'stronger' than 'YES': in English the distribution of *yes* is more limited than that of *no* and alternates, for example, with *so* when dependent on a 'verbum putandi'; cf. It. *penso di sì* vs. Eng. *I think so*; It. *tu no, ma io sì* vs. Ger. *du nicht, aber ich schon* /***ja*, lit. 'I no/not, but you yes' for 'I do, you don't'. After all, as is well known, *sì* historically comes from the affirmative formula *sic est*, as *oui* comes from *oïl* < *hoc illi* and Occit. *o(c)* from *hoc est*. The linguistic tradition of *no(n)* is much more stable than its affirmative counterpart.

The expressions 'yes', 'no' are also called 'prosentences', in that they represent an entire sentence with the same propositional content as the utterance in the preceding context. In ex. (1): B: *No* (≡'I haven't seen John'/ 'Non ho visto Giovanni'). There are however languages such as the Celtic ones which while they involve an ellipsed sentence do not omit the Vb (cf. also example (3) below):

(2)   Welsh
         A. *A   wyt   ti   wedi gweld Siôn?* - B: *Nag   ydwyf*
            INT are:2SG you after see   John   NEG am

Short answers to interrogative utterances seem to be a property of all known languages and their origin may be seen in the "grammaticization of a cultural prohibition against undue prolixity" (Sadock–Zwicky 1985: 191).[1] Taken all together the languages of Europe also confirm the validity of this generalisation, in that none of them has forms of reply that obligatorily require all the lexical material and the complete sentence structure of the question to be repeated (obviously with due modification of the deixis to reflect the alternation of speaker and hearer roles). Not all the languages of Europe, however, have recourse to the same devices for reducing the negative reply.

The parameter of typological comparison is represented in this regard by the strategies used to construct short answers, of which there are essentially two options: ellipsed sentences and the use of proforms, specifically prosentences of the Italian type *no* (here labelled *NO*).

The languages of Europe which make exclusive use of ellipsed sentences[2] are in a clear minority and from the areal point of view are situated on the fringes of the European linguistic territory. The languages in question are Irish and Scottish Gaelic (in fact not included in our questionnaire)[3] to the (north-)west, and Estonian and Finnish to the north-east. Cf.:

(3)   Irish
        An   bhfaca   tú   Seán? - Ní   fhacas
        INT   see:PRET:3SG   you John   NEG   saw:1SG

(4)   Scottish Gaelic (Mackinnon 1971: 16)
        An   robh   thu   sgìth? - (Bha)/   Cha   robh
        INT   was:3SG   you   tired   was:3SG   NEG   was:3SG
        'Were you tired? — Yes / No'

(5)   Estonian
        Kas   sa   ol-e-d   Johni näi-nut? - Ei   ole
        INT   you   be-PRES-2SG   John   see-APP   NEG   be

(6)   Finnish
        Ole-t-ko   näh-nyt   Jukkaa? - E-n   (ole)
        be-2SG-INT   see-APP   John:PART NEG-1SG   be

As can easily be observed from examples (3–6), in Irish (and Scottish Gaelic) as well as in Estonian,[4] the non-ellipsed element in the reply sentence is the conjugated verb (be it full or auxiliary), accompanied by the negation (in the case of negative replies: cf. Eng. *I didn't*; in the case of an affirmative reply, not relevant here, the verb is instead used on its own: Eng. *I did*). Essentially the same picture emerges in Finnish, with the difference that negation here, as we have already had cause to note (see 3.4.), is codified by a specific auxiliary which, being the conjugated verbal form, obviously appears in the reply. The type illustrated in examples (3–6) may also be defined as an echo reply, in that the reply consists in the repetition of the conjugated verb of the question (cf. Sadock–Zwicky 1985: 109). In Finnish the negative verb does not appear in the question, but one has to take into account that the inflectional categories of the verb are expressed in it. Furthermore, as far as the system of short answers is concerned, the use of the negative verb (optionally accompanied by the main verb), corresponds structurally to the use of the conjugated verb (main or auxiliary) of the question in the affirmative reply.[5] We may thus conclude that Finnish belongs to the same category as Irish, Scottish Gaelic and Estonian.

The languages of Europe that make use of prosentences are in the majority, and are precisely the following:

Basque;
Breton;[6]
Portuguese (but cf. below), Spanish, Catalan, French, Provençal, Italian, Rhaeto-Romansh, Friulian, Rumanian;
German, Dutch, Frisian, Danish, Swedish, Norwegian, Icelandic, English (but cf. below);
Albanian;
Modern Greek (but cf. below);
Latvian, Lithuanian;
Slovenian, Serbo-Croatian, Macedonian, Bulgarian, Czech, Slovak, Polish, Belorussian, Ukrainian, Russian;
Hungarian;
Maltese.

A sub-group of these languages has the same morpheme for expressing (prosody apart) the short negative answer to questions and sentence negation (see Q5 *John doesn't eat fish*) which will become very significant in the discussion of the replies to sentence Q2 (see 5.2.). This sub-group comprises:

Basque;
Portuguese, Spanish, Rumanian;
Polish, Czech, Slovenian, Serbo-Croatian, Macedonian, Bulgarian, Belorussian;
Latvian, Lithuanian;
Hungarian.

Alongside the two principle types there exists a third intermediate type, where ellipsis and prosentences combine in different ways. English, Portuguese, Modern Greek belong to this group; these languages use prosentences and echo-type elliptical replies in alternation or in combination.

For English see example (1), for Portuguese cf.

(7)   a. *Viste o João? − Não.*
            'Have you seen John? − No'
         b. *Tem lume? − Tenho (sim) / Não tenho*[7]
            'Have you got a light? − Yes / No'

According to data supplied by Joseph – Philippaki Warburton (1987: 13 – 14), in Modern Greek a reply may be made using the prosentence *ókhi* 'no' (and *naí* 'yes' in the affirmative reply) or by repeating the verb in the question if this is intransitive or transitive accompanied by an indefinite object; a transitive verb must be preceded by an appropriate personal pronoun if accompanied by a definite object, cf.

(8)   a. *Méneis edó péra? – Ókhi/Naí; Dén ménō/Ménō*
          'Do you live around here? – No / Yes'
       b. *Diabázeis pollá biblía? – Dén diabázō/Diabázō*
          'Do you read many books? – No / Yes'
       c. *Ébales tó biblío stó trapézi? – To ébala*
          'Have you put the book on the table? – Yes' (lit. 'I put it')

The last of the languages to have both types is Welsh, which again is a case unto itself, in that the prosentence is limited to replies to questions in which the verb is conjugated in the synthetic past, cf.

(9)   a. *A   wel-aist   ti   John? - Naddo/ Do*
          INT see-PRET-2SG you John   no   yes
       b. *A   wyt ti   wedi gweld John? - Nag   ydyf/   Ydyf*
          INT are you after see   John   NEG   am:1SG am:1SG

Note that the negative reply in (9b) does not involve the discontinuous construction of the negation, usual in non elliptical sentences – at least for some varieties, for example

(10)   *D-ydy   John ddim   yn bwyta pysgod*[8]
         NEG-is John NEG   in   eat   fish
         'John doesn't eat fish' [Q5]

5.2. Sentences Q2 and Q34: anaphoric holophrastic negation ['NEG$_{HOL}$']

The sentence Q2, that is

(11)   Eng. *John eats fish, but his companions do not*
          It. *Giovanni mangia pesce, i suoi compagni no*

serves, in this sort of contrastive context, to highlight the negative representation, in the second part of the conjunction, of what is affirmed in the first part.

As can be seen, Italian represents it anaphorically by means of a prosentence (therefore a holophrastic form) with respect to which the NP functions as a topical element.[9]

The different constructions that the languages of Europe adopt to express this type of anaphoric holophrastic negation may be ordered along a *continuum* according to the use made of prosentences or of other means of expression.

(A) At one end of the *continuum* may be situated the languages that have the same form for the holophrastic negative reply to yes/no questions (:Q1), that is 'NO', and for the standard sentential reply (:Q5, *John doesn't eat fish*), that is 'NEG$_{PRED}$', and which use this form, accompanied by an NP, also in Q2 (:NEG$_{HOL}$'). With reference to the construction illustrated in the examples, this type may be summarily defined as 'NO' = 'NEG$_{HOL}$' = 'NEG$_{PRED}$', or *NO* at the level of the expression. Cf.:

(12)   Spanish
     a. *Has visto a Juan? – No.*   (Q1)
     b. *Juan come pescado, sus compañeros no.* (Q2)
     c. *Juan no come el pescado.*   (Q5)

(13)   Basque
     a. *Ikus-i   duzu   Jon? - Ez.*
       see-PFP AUX John NEG
     b. *Jon-ek   arrain-a   ja-ten   du   baina har-en*
       Jon-ERG fish-DET eat-PRP AUX but   that-GEN
       lagun-e-k   *ez.*
       companion-DET-ERG NEG
     c. *Jon-ek   ez   du   arrain-ik   ja-ten*
       Jon-ERG NEG AUX fish-PARTC eat-PRP

(14)   Czech
     a. *Viděl jsi Jana? – Ne.*
     b. *Jan jí ryby, jeho společníci ne.*
     c. *Jan nejí rybu.*

(15)   Hungarian
     a. *Láttad   John-t? -   Nem.*
       saw:2SG John-ACC NEG
     b. *John   hal-at   eszik, de   társ-ai   nem*[10]
       John fish-ACC eats   but companion-3PL NEG
     c. *John   nem   eszik   hal-at*
       John NEG eats   fish-ACC

As far as these languages are concerned it is of course necessary to go more deeply into the question of whether in *b* we are dealing with a real prosentence or a strategy of ellipsis that causes only the negation to remain on the surface. Prosodic factors are probably an indication that the negative morpheme in both *a* and *b* has a certain autonomy: it does in fact have its own stress in the case of holophrastic replies but in the case of sentence negation often it does not.

In written texts this is clear for languages such as Czech (example 14), where the sentence negation morpheme is usually written with the verb in a single word; not to mention languages such as Belorussian and Lithuanian, which in Q2 separate the negative morpheme with a hyphen, cf.

(16)   Belorussian
        Džovanni esc' rybu, a jago sjabry − ne.

(17)   Lithuanian
        Jonas valgo žuvį, o jo draugai − ne

The following belong to this group:

> Basque;
> Portuguese, Spanish, Friulian, Rumanian;
> Czech, Polish, Slovenian, Serbo-Croatian, Bulgarian, Belorussian;
> Latvian, Lithuanian;
> Hungarian.

From an areal point of view, the Iberian peninsula (excluding Catalonia) and central-eastern Europe with partial exclusion of the Balkans (Bulgarian but not Macedonian) with the Slovak enclave and the exclusion, in the extreme east, of Russian, form tightly-knit zones.

(B) Differing from this extreme type are several languages that employ a morpheme for the holophrastic negative reply to questions (:'NO' of Q1) which differs from that used for sentence negation ('NEG_PRED'), and which is also used in the case of Q2. In these languages, that is, we have 'NO' = 'NEG_HOL' ≠ 'NEG_PRED'. Italian and also Russian, Modern Greek, Albanian and Maltese behave in this way. Cf.:

(18)   Russian
        a. *Ty videl Ivana? − Net.*
        b. *Ivan est rybu, ego tovarišči net.*
        c. *Ivan ne est rybu.*

(19)   Modern Greek
        a. *Eídes tón Giánnē? − Ókhi.*

b. *Ho Giánnēs tróei psária, allá hoi phíloi tou ókhi.*
c. *Ho Giánnēs dén tróei psária.*

(20)   Albanian
a. *A e pe Gjonin? − Jo.*
b. *Gjoni e ha peshkun, por shokët e tij jo.*
c. *Gjoni s'ha peshk.*

(21)   Maltese

a. *Rajt-u*   *'l/*   *(li-l)*   *Ġanni? - Le.*
saw:2SG-3SG   ART   to-ART   John   No

b. *Ġanni jiekol ħut, sħabu*   *le*
John   eats   fish   companions-3SG   no

c. *Ġanni ma*   *jiekol-x*   *ħut.*
John   NEG   eats-NEG   fish

These languages, some of which, like Italian for example, have developed
prosentences in the full meaning of the term, are relatively at the fringes of the
European context and are geographically close to languages of type (A), of
which they are variants.

(C) A third type, which represents a further deviation with respect to type
(A), includes German, Dutch and Frisian, which have separate morphemes for
sentence negation (Q5) and for replies to yes/no questions (Q1), but which use
the same morpheme as that for sentence negation for 'NEG$_{HOL}$' (Q2), that is,
a strategy of ellipsis centred on the negation: 'NO' ≠ 'NEG$_{HOL}$' = 'NEG$_{PRED}$'.
Cf.

(22)   German
a. *Hast du Hans gesehen? − Nein.*
b. *Hans ißt Fisch, seine Freunde nicht.*
c. *Hans ißt diesen Fisch nicht.*[11]

(23)   Dutch
a. *Heb je Jan gezien? − Nee.*
b. *Jan eet (wel) vis, maar zijn vrienden niet.*[12]
c. *Jan eet die vis niet.*

(24)   Frisian
a. *Hawwe jo Jan sjoen? − Nee.*
b. *Jan yt fisk, mar syn maten net.*
c. *Jan yt net fisk.*

Rhaeto-Romansh falls between (B) and (C), in that in the construction concerned it may insert either a negative prosentence or other negation morphemes,
cf.

(25)   Rhaeto-Rom. (Vallader)
            Jon mangia pesch, seis cumpogns brich / nüglia // na.

Na is the negative prosentence (the preverbal morpheme of sentence negation
is *nu(n)*); *brich* is the postverbal morpheme of negation reinforcement, comparable to the Italian *mica* and is obligatory in other varieties of Rhaeto-Romansh
(cf. chapter 1); *nüglia* is also the negative quantifier 'nothing'.

(D) A fourth type, linked to that described in (C), is represented typically by
English, which replies to yes/no questions with a prosentence and also with a
type of echo short answer centred around an auxiliary or a pro-verb. This construction is used in *b* as well as in *c.* Cf.

(26)   English
            a. *Have you seen John? — (No,) I haven't.*
            b. *John eats fish, but his companions do not.*
            c. *John doesn't eat fish.*[13]

    Welsh and Breton, which have short answers codified by prosentences and
elliptical constructions, as already seen, may be included in this type (see respectively example (9) and note 6). Cf.:

(27)   Welsh
            Y   *mae John   yn bwyta pysgod ond   nid   yw ei   gyfeillion*
            DECL is John in eat   fish   but NEG   is of.him friends
            ddim
            NEG

(28)   Breton
            Yann a   zebr pesked, e   geneiled   ne   reont
            John PTCL eats fish   of.him companions NEG do:3PL
            ket
            NEG
            'John eats fish, his companions do not'

Finnish may also be included in this type, although as has been seen (cf. example
(6)), it does not have a prosentence but a negative verb: cf.

(29)   *Jukka syö kalaa,   mutta hänen ystävänsä   ei-vät.*[14]
            John eats fish:PART but of.him companions NEG-3PL

    (E) A fifth type on our *continuum* is characterised by the presence of a negative
prosentence and by the use of constructions centred around an auxiliary (or
even a pro-verb) with an anaphoric pronoun for the construction in question.
This is the situation typified by Swedish, cf.

(30)   a. *Har du sett John? − Nej.*

      b. *John äter fisk, men det gör   inte   hans kamrater.*[15]
        John eats fish but that do:3PL NEG his   companions

      c. *John äter inte fisk.*

This is common, however, to all the northern Germanic languages, cf.:

(31)   Danish

      a. *Har du set Hans? − Nej.*

      b. *Hans spiser fisk, men det gør hans venner ikke.*

      c. *Hans spiser ikke fisk.*

(32)   Norwegian (Bokmål)

      a. *Har du sett John? − Nei.*

      b. *John spiser fisk, men det gjør ikke vennene hans.*

      c. *John spiser ikke fisk.*

(33)   Icelandic

      a. *Hefurðu séð Jón? − Nei.*

      b. *Jón borðar fisk en félagar hans gera það ekki.*

      c. *Jón borðar ekki fisk.*

Examples (30a) − (33a) of the northern languages behave like the corresponding ones of groups (A), (B) and (C), that is, like a prosentence and not like (D) − while in the cases of Q2 and Q5 they coincide with those of (C) (that is, 'NEG$_{HOL}$' = 'NEG$_{PRED}$') and also with (D) as far as the use of a (semi)auxiliary Vb is concerned. This indeed demonstrates the existence of the *continuum*.

In all these examples what is asserted in the first half of the conjunction (by asyndeton or with an explicit adversative conjunct) is represented in the second half by a pro-verb similar to the Swedish type *göra* 'to do' and by a pronoun like the Swedish *det* 'that, it'. As for (D), this type is characterised by the greater explicitness of the proforms it uses. Note, however, that the informants of all these languages, except for Swedish, also suggested as a short answer to Q1 an elliptical construction of the main verb but with a demonstrative pronoun, such as in the following Icelandic example:

(34)   *Hefurðu séð Jón? − Nei, það hef ég ekki / ég hef það ekki.*[16]
      'Have you seen John? − No' (lit. 'that have I not / I have that not')

(F) The other extreme of our *continuum* should be represented by a rendering of the sentence in question with the maximum of lexical explicitness, that is, repeating the main verbal lexeme and any complements that may be required by it. Only Irish which, as will be remembered, has no proforms whatsoever, conforms to this type, cf.

(35)   *Itheann Séan iasc ach ní itheann a   chomrádaithe iasc*
         eats   John fish but not eats   POSS:3SG companions fish

The *continuum* of strategies that we have proposed is based on the means of expression used for the reproduction of the second half of the sentence. These range from a minimum of explicitness (use of prosentences or similar, types (A), (B)) to a maximum of explicitness in the sense that they repeat the lexical material of the first part (type (F)), passing through elliptical constructions (types (C),(D)) or they use proforms in addition to ellipsis (type (E)). The constructions under consideration are of course correlated with the presence/absence of an element having the value of a negative prosentence. This correlation is greatest in cases such as Italian and less so, for example, in the Germanic languages.

From the areal point of view, in the realisation of Q2 the European linguistic territory divides into two macro-areas according to the use of prosentences (or the impossibility of distinguishing negation morphemes, i. e. 'NEGPRED', and prosentences, i. e. 'NO') or the use of other means. The first comprises the whole of southern and eastern Europe and links the Romance languages, Maltese, Albanian, Greek, Hungarian, and the Slavic and Baltic languages; the second comprises the Germanic languages and the Celtic and Balto-Finnic languages. What is interesting is the gradual proceeding in a roughly south-north direction from less explicit to more explicit constructions, with the intermediate role held by western Germanic (or rather by only German, Dutch and Frisian) that, in this case, act as a hinge between the use of prosentences (e.g. in Italian) and the use of more explicit constructions which combine ellipsis and the use of pro-forms other than prosentences we find in the other Germanic languages.[17]

Interesting in this regard is the anomolous position of Catalan, French and Provençal on the one hand and Slovak and Macedonian on the other, which, while having prosentential elements (whether true and proper prosentences as in French, Provençal, Slovak, or common morphemes for negative replies and sentence negation as in Catalan and Macedonian), tend to render the construction in question with the maximum of explicitness or call upon other constructions, cf.

(36)   Cat. *Joan menja peix, però els seus companys no en mangen (pas).*

(37)   Fr. *Jean mange du poisson, pas ses compagnons / ses compagnons n'en mangent pas / ses amis, non.*[18]

(38)   Prov. *Jan manjo de peissoun, si coumpan n'en manjon pas.*[19]

(39) Slovk. *Ján je rybu, ale jeho priatelia nie / jeho priatelia nejedia.*[20]

(40)   Mac. *Jovan jade riba, no negoviot sopatnik ne jade.*

One could hazard an interpretation of this anomalous behaviour, at least as far as the Romance languages in this group are concerned, by calling upon the development of postverbal negations and the possibility of having reduced contexts when prosentences are used, as in the Germanic languages.[21]

A very different picture emerges from the replies to sentence Q34, which elicits the possibility of employing the same construction as Q2 in the second expression of comparison, cf.

(41)   = Q34

Eng.   *In the contest of wits, Ulysses — more often than not — came out the winner.*

It   *Nelle gare di astuzia Ulisse era più spesso vincitore che no.*

We are dealing here with a complex construction, where the prosentence is used in a comparative elliptical context: its label is 'QUAM NON'. In fact many replies avoided this use, resorting to alternative strategies to express the same content.

The following languages reply to this construction with a prosentence (that is, with *NO*):

Portuguese, Spanish, Italian;
Belorussian;
Lithuanian;
Hungarian;
Albanian;
Maltese.

As may be noted, the construction is not represented in Germanic, Celtic and Balto-Finnic; but even in the other linguistic groups few languages allow it (for example, in Romance, Catalan, French, Provençal, Rhaeto-Romansh, Friulian, Sardinian and Rumanian do not make use of it). The languages in italics on the list have only one form for holophrastic negation Q1 and Q2 as well as for sentence negation (for example Port. *não*; Sp. *no*; Bel., Lith. *ne*; Hung. *nem*); but this doesn't really seem to favour the use of a prosentence even in Q34, as is shown by comparison with the other languages that have indeed the same form for holophrastic negation as for sentence negation, but which translate Q34 'freely': see, for example, Cat... *més sovint que rarament* ... 'more often than rarely'; Rum. ... *mai multe ori* 'most of the time'; Dan. ... *var det som oftest Odysseus, der vandt* ' ... it was more often Ulysses who won'; Pol. ... *częściej niż rzadziej* 'more often than more rarely', etc. The same goes for languages such as Rhaeto-Romansh and Russian, which while having a prosentence distinct from the 'NEG$_{PRED}$' morpheme, unlike other languages on the list with the same characteristic, are not able to render Q34. Cf. Bel. *U spabornictvax na xitrasc' Ulis čascej byŭ peramožcam, čym ne* ' ..., than not', but Czech *V soutěži chytrosti Odysseus obvykle zvítězil* ' ... usually won'; Rhaeto-Rom. ... *dapü co quai ch'el perdeiva* (lit. ' ... more than what he lost'). Cf. also the already cited Cat. *més sovint que rarament*, Fr. *assez souvent* 'very often', Russian *čašče pobeždal, čem proigryval* 'more often won than lost' and so on.

For this construction English and Dutch use the negative sentence particle, that is, respectively *not* (*more often than not*) and *niet* (*vaker wel dan niet*), a solution which ties in with a strategy of ellipsis based on sentence negation.

The context where the negation in Q34 is used turns out therefore to be particularly 'marked' and consequently immune to reductionist codifications (prosentence or ellipsis) even in those languages that do have them.

5.3. Sentences Q3, Q4: negative coordination

Q3 (a) *John neither speaks* (b) *nor moves*
    (a) *Giovanni non parla* (b) *né si muove*

exemplifies the behaviour of NEG in coordinate sentences [(a) and (b)], while

Q4 (a) *Neither John*   (b) *nor his companions wanted to leave*
    (a) *Né Giovanni*   (b) *né i suoi compagni volevano andarsene*

deals with the behaviour of NEG in nominal constituents [(a) and (b)] coordinated in the same sentence: Q3 will thus be 'NEC ... NEC$_S$', while Q4 will be 'NEC ... NEC$_{NP}$'. The Italian will have the label *NEC1 ... NEC1* and the English *NEC1 ... NEC2*: in Italian the two negative morphemes in fact coincide, but not in English; furthermore, neither in Italian nor English do the morphemes in either the first or the second negative coordinate coincide with that of Q1 (: $NO \neq NEC1 ... NEC1/2$).

A distinction may be made between the languages that use the same morph in Q3a as in the simple negative declarative sentence of Q5 *Giovanni non mangia pesce* ('NEG$_{PRED}$') such as Italian (: Q3a *Giovanni non parla*) and those that don't, such as English (: Q3a *John neither speaks* vs. Q5 *John doesn't eat fish*). It may be said that in a certain sense the negative declarative status of Q3a prevails in the first case, while in the second the negative coordination prevails: contrast It.

non...né of Q3 with. *né ... né* of Q4; in Q4 the negation has the two NP coordinates in its scope. Belonging to the first group [: Q3a = Q5] are, for example, Portuguese (: Q3 *não ... nem*, Q5 *não*), Spanish (: Q3 *no ...ni*, Q5 *no*), Rumanian (: Q3 *nu ...nici nu*, Q5 *nu*), Czech and Slovak (: Q3 *ne ... ani ne*, Q5 *ne*). Irish (: Q3 *ní ... ná ní*, Q5 *ní*), Armenian (: Q3 *či ... oč al*, Q5 *či*) etc. The second group [: Q3 = Q4 ≠ Q5] comprises Catalan (: Q3 *ni ...ni*, Q5 *no*), Provençal (: Q3 *ni ... ni*, Q5 *pas*),[22] the Scandinavian languages − see for example Norw. Q3 *verken ... eller*, Q5 *ikke* − and lastly those languages also which reinforce the negation in Q3 such as Slovenian and Serbo-Croatian (: Q3 *niti ne ... niti (ne)*, Q5 *ne*).[23] The fact that the second negative morph (i. e. that of Q3b, the more typical part of the negative coordinate) coincides with that of Q5 seems to be more significant, since in this case Q3b in some way loses its negative coordinate character and coincides with the negative sentence 'tout court' (as if in Italian we were to have Q3 *non* ..., Q3b *e non* ..., and in English Q3a *doesn't* ..., Q3b *and doesn't* ...: cf. the last part of this section).[24]

This is the case with Basque, which generalises the morph *ez* 'no(t)' to the entire group of sentences examined so far:

(42)   a. = Q3 *Jon   ez   da   ez   mintzatzen ez   mugitzen*
                J.(ABS) NEG AUX NEG speaking   NEG moving
        b. = Q5 *Jon-ek   ez   du   arrain-ik   jaten*
                J.-ERG   NEG AUX fish-PART eating

Behaving in the same way as Basque are Sardinian, Rhaeto-Romansh, Friulian, Russian, Belorussian (with the solution of the type *né* [= 'NEC1/2'] *e no(n)*),[25]

(43)   = Q3 Sard.   *Ǵuanne non faèḍḍaḍ e non si mòveḍe*
                 Rhaeto-Rom.   *Jon nu discuorra a nu's moua*
                 Frl.   *Giani nol ciacare e nol si môf*
                 Rus.   *Ivan ne govorit i ne dvigaetsja*
                 Bel.   *I. ne gavoryc' i ne ruxaecca*

and

(44)   = Q5 Sard.   *Ǵ. non mandiga ppiske*
                 Rhaeto-Rom.   *J. nu mangia pesch*
                 Frl.   *G. nol mange pes*
                 Rus.   *I. ne est rybu*
                 Bel.   *I. ne esc' rybu*

Amongst the Celtic languages, Irish (but not Welsh or Breton) has a coincidence of NEG (although reinforced) in Q3 and Q5:

(45) = Q3 *Ní labhraíonn Seán ná* ('nor') *ní chorraíon sé*

(46) = Q5 *Ní itheann Seán iasc*

Rumanian and Hungarian behave in the same way:

(47)   a. Rum. *Ion nu vorbeşte, nici nu   se   mişcă*
                          nor NEG REFL moves

        b. Hun. *János se   nem   beszél, se   nem   mozdul*
                 Janos nor NEG speaks nor NEG moves

The same construction is found in the Slavic languages, which in general –
as is known – have an abundance of NEG markers:

(48)   = Q3   Pol. *Jan (ani) nie mówi, ani się nie rusza*

with *ani* 'nor' also repeated before *nie* 'no(t)'; literally therefore 'nor not'. The
same is also found in:

(49)   Czech   *Ján nemluví, ani se nekylbe*
        Slovak   *Ján ani nehovorí ani sa nehylbe*
        Slovenian *Jan niti =* ('nor') *ne govori, niti se ne premika*

Differing from Croatian, which follows the same pattern as Slovenian (: ...
niti ne govori, niti se (ne) kreće), we have

(50)   Serb *Jovan niti govori niti se pomera*
        Mac. *Jovan niti zboruva niti se mrda*
        Bulg. *Dž. nito govori, nito se dviži*

without repetition of NEG on the verb (and thus with Q3b ≠ Q5!).

For *NOT* of 'NEGPRED' in Q5 the Slavic languages have: Pol. *nie*, Czech,
Slovak, Slovenian, Serbo-Cr., Mac., Bulg., Bel., Rus. *ne*. Rumanian has *nu*, Hungarian *nem*.

There are thus languages which have the same negative morph (sometimes
preceded by a reinforcing element, as in Rum. ...*nici nu*) for Q3b as for Q5, and
others that do not. At this point, a parameter of cross-linguistic variation may
be introduced. (For a general discussion of parameters see chapter 10).

The languages in which the NEG of Q3b and the NEG of Q5 are the same
constitute a minority in our 'corpus': they are those that normally resort to the
strategy of coordination with 'and not' (in itself possible in other languages [cf.
It. *non ... e non*: see above], but not given as a normal construction by our
informants): Basque, Sardinian, Rhaeto-Romansh, Friulian, Russian, Belorussian,
Polish, Czech, Slovak, and also Irish, Rumanian, Hungarian, Slovenian, which
reinforce negation (for example: Rum. ... *nici nu*; cf. above): see examples (42)-

(49). Consequently, the languages which have the same morph for *NEC* of Q3b and *NOT* of Q5, tend to have different strategies for 'NEC...NEC$_S$' of Q3 and for 'NEC...NEC$_{NP//PP}$' of Q4 (see the German example in note 25): cf. for example Sardinian

(51)   = Q4 *Nè   Ǵuanne,   nè   sos   kumpandzos   suos   sike   ǵerian*
            Nor John   nor the companions his   REFL wanted
            andare
            go:INF

vs. *non ... e non* of Q3 (cf. example (43)).

But the majority of the European languages prefer to use the same morph as Q4b for Q3b (It. *né*, Eng. *nor*) — and more generally tend to have the same constructions for Q3 and Q4 (Eng. Q3 and Q4 *neither ... nor*; Greek Q3 and Q4 *oúte ... oúte*; Swed. Q3 and Q4 *varken ... eller*; Lith. Q3 and Q4 *nei ... nei*); cf. also the Finnic languages which introduce a negative coordinating suffix (Finn. *ka/-kä*):

(52)   Estonian
            = Q3 *Juhan   ei   räägi   ega   liigu*
            John   NEG speak   nor [< *ei-ga*] move
            like Q4 *Ei   Juhan   ega   ta   kaaslased   tahtnud   lahkud*
            NEG John   nor 3SG companions want:APP   go
            but Q5 *Juhan   ei   söö   kala*
            John   NEG eat   fish

(53)   Finnish
            = Q3 *Jukka   ei   puhu   ei-kä   liiku*
            John   NEG-3SG speak   NEG:3SG-CONJ$_{NEG}$ move
            like Q4 *Ei   Jukka   e-ivät-kä   hänen*
            NEG:3SG John   NEG-3PL-CONJ$_{NEG}$ 3SG:GEN
            ystävä-nsä-kään   halunneet   lähteä
            companions-3SG-not.even want:APP:PL   go
            but Q5 *Jukka   ei   syö   kalaa*
            John   NEG:3SG eat   fish-PART

(54)   Lapp.
            = Q3 *Jovnna   ii   hála (huma)   ii-ge   lihkat*
            John   NEG:3SG speak   NEG:3SG-CONJ$_{NEG}$ move
            like Q4 *Ii   Jovnna eai-ge   su*
            NEG:3SG John   NEG:3PL-CONJ$_{NEG}$ 3SG
            ustibat   vuolgge gosage
            companions go   anywhere

> but Q5 *Jovnna ii   bora guoli*
> John   NEG:3SG eat   fish

Languages in which the morphs Q3b = Q5 are an exception (but not, of course, Basque which — as already said — has a generalised negative morph *ez*):

(55)   = Q4
> Hung. *Sem János, sem társai   nem   akartak*
> Nor John nor companions:3SG NEG wanted
> *elindulni*
> leave:INF
> (with *sem ... sem* [+ *nem*] vs. *se nem ... se nem* for Q3);
> Russ. *Ni   Ivan, ni   ego   tovarišči   ne   choteli*
> Bel. *Ni   Ivan, ni   jago   siabry   ne   chaceli*
> Nor John nor 3SG:GEN companions NEG wanted
> *uchodit';*
> *ŭchadzic'*
> leave:INF
> (vs. *ne ... i ne* for Q3);
> Serbo-Cr. *Ni   Jovan ni   niegovi drugovi   nisu   hteli*
> Nor John nor his   companions NEG wanted
> *da   odu*
> that leave:SJNT:3SG/PL
> (vs. *niti (ne) ... niti (ne)* for Q3);
> Mac. *Ni   Jovan ni   negoviot sopatnik   ne   sakaa   da*
> nor John nor his   companion NEG wanted:3SG that
> *si   odat*
> REFL left:3PL
> (vs. *niti ... niti* for Q3);
> Rhaeto-Rom. *Ne Jon   ne   seis cumpogns   nu*
> Nor John nor his companions NEG
> *leivan   ir   davent*
> wanted:3PL go away
> (vs. *nu...e nu* for Q3);
> Frl. *No   orevin partì nè Giani nè il   so*
> NEG wanted leave nor John nor ART his
> *compain*
> companion
> 'They didn't want ... etc.'
> (vs. *no(-l) ... e no(-l)* for Q3);

Sard. *Nḕ Ĝuanne, nḕ sos kumpandzos suos sike gerian andare*
(vs. *non ... e non* for Q3)
(For German see note 25).

Rumanian has *nici ... și nici nu* in Q4 and *nu ... nici nu* in Q3 (cf. (47)). Notice furthermore the behaviour of Q4 in:

(56) Pol. *Ani Jan jego współtowarzysze nie chcieli wyjść*

and then *(ani) nie ... ani nie* in Q3,

(57) Slovak *Ani Ján ani jeho priatelia nechceli odísť*

and here also *ani ne- ... ani ne-* in Q3,

(58) Czech *Ani Ján, ani jeho společníci neměli cestu k útěku,*

with *ne- ... ani ne-* in Q3.

We are dealing here with those languages which display reinforcement of coordinated NEG of the type 'nor not' (see above) and thus have either the morph for 'NEC' or that for 'NEGᴘʀᴇᴅ': such languages in a sense are situated halfway between those with Q3b = Q5 (and Q3 ≠ Q4) and those with Q3b ≠ Q5 (and Q3 = Q4). What emerges from these observations is the centrality of this parameter drawn to distinguish between the disjunctive strategy of the type 'neither ... nor', typical particularly of Q4 NPs, and coordinated strategies of the type 'not ... and not'.

We postpone until chapter 10 a more detailed examination of the distribution of the languages with respect to the parameters, meanwhile by way of drawing together the various threads of what has been dealt with in this section we may sum up the situation as follows (with * indicating the languages which have forms of reinforcement of NEG in the coordination, as usual of the Rum. type *...nici nu*).[26]

i. Q3b = Q5
Basque, French, Sardinian, Rhaeto-Romansh, Friulian, Frisian, German, *Hungarian, Latvian, Belorussian, Russian, Albanian.

ii. Q3b ≠ Q5
*Irish, Scottish Gaelic, *Welsh, *Breton, Portuguese, Spanish, Catalan, Provençal, French, Italian, *Rumanian, Icelandic, Norwegian, Swedish, Danish, English, Dutch, *Polish, *Czech, *Slovak, *Slovenian, *Croatian, Serbian, Macedonian, Bulgarian, Latvian, Lithuanian, *Lapp, *Finnish, Estonian, *Hungarian, Greek, Turkish, Maltese, Armenian, Georgian.

iii. Q3a = Q5
Irish, Welsh, Breton, Basque, Portuguese, Spanish, French (cf. note 25), Sardinian, Italian, Friulian, Rhaeto-Romansh, Rumanian, Greek, (*)Polish, Slovak, *Slovenian, *Serbian and

Croatian, Lapp, Finnish, Estonian, *Hungarian, Armenian, Maltese,[27] German (cf. note 25).

iv. Q3a ≠ Q5
Catalan, Provençal, Icelandic, Danish, Norwegian, Swedish, English, Frisian, Dutch, German, Czech, Bulgarian, Macedonian, Albanian, Lithuanian, Georgian.

v. Q3 ≠ Q4
Breton, Welsh, Frisian, Portuguese, Spanish, Sardinian, Italian, Provençal, Rhaeto-Romansh, Friulian, German (cf. note 25), Hungarian, Macedonian, Serbian and Croatian, Belorussian, (and also Turkish).

vi. Q3 = Q4
Basque, English, Dutch, Icelandic, Danish, Norwegian, Swedish, *Catalan, French, Lithuanian, Estonian, Latvian, Finnish, Lapp, Bulgarian, *Polish, *Czech, *Slovak, *Slovenian, Albanian, Greek, *Rumanian, Maltese, Armenian, Georgian.

i. and ii., iii. and iv., v. and vi. are of course mutually exclusive.

5.4. Sentences Q6, Q7: phrasal negation

Q6	a *John doesn't eat fish,*	b *but he does eat meat*
	a *Giovanni non mangia pesce,*	b *ma carne*
Q7	a *John and Mary met not at school,*	b *but at a party*
	a *Giovanni e Maria si incontrarono non a scuola,*	b *ma a una festa*

examine the behaviour of contrastive negation which has in its scope an Object and, respectively, a Prepositional Phrase. Employing the Latin expression we call it 'NON … SED$_{OBJ}$' and, respectiveluy 'NON … SED$_{PP}$'.

The difference in German between *aber* and *sondern* is well-known:

(59)   *Für ganz einsam hielt er sich, aber (**sondern) er war belauscht*
        'He believed himself all alone, but he was watched'

against

Q6   *Hans ißt nicht Fisch, sondern (**aber) Fleisch.*

We have used the label *ABER* for languages such as Italian and English, *SONDERN* for languages such as German and Spanish: consequently in Q6 Italian will have *NOT1 … ABER*, and German *NOT1 … SONDERN*.

Apart from this opposition, there are very few languages that deal with Q6 in a different way to Q7.[28] The absence of a verb in Q7 does not seem to be what determines 'NON … SED'; and in almost all cases Q6a behaves like Q5, that is, as 'NEGₚᵣₑᴅ'. Take for instance the Italian example *Giovanni non mangia pesce, ma carne*: in the second conjunct of Q6, which consists of an OBJ, the languages situated geographically towards the Atlantic, that is, Basque, Breton, Welsh, Irish and English, repeat the finite Vb (or substitute it with a pro-verb), confirming a certain propensity for explicit constructions (cf. 5.2., 5.3.). Observe the case of Basque:

(60)   *Jon-ek   arrain-ik   ez   du   jaten,   baina*
        J.-ERG fish-PART NEG AUX:3SG.ABS:3SG.ERG eating but
        haragi-a   jaten   du
        meat-DET(ABS) eating AUX (as above),

or without repetition of the verbal complex in the second part

        Jonek arrainik ez du jaten, baina haragia bai ['yes', prosentence!]

The first variant of Q6 in Welsh makes use of NEG incorporated into the Vb:

(61)   a. *D-ydy   Siôn   ddim   yn bwyta pysgod, ond mae o 'n   bwyta   cig*
           NEG-is John NEG   in eat   fish   but is   he in eat   meat

with *dydy* (< *nid ydyw* 'it isn't'), exactly as in Q5.

The construction which is possible in Q5 is also repeated in the first part (Q6a) of the other two variants of Q6:

        b. *Nid   yw   S.   yn bwyta pysgod, ond mae 'n bwyta cig*
           NEG is J.   in eat   fish   but is   in eat   meat

and

           Ni   fwyty   S.   bysgod, ond bwyta gig
           NEG eats J.   fish   but eats   meat

The construction in (61a) is also possible in Q7 when a sort of 'auxiliary' appears:

(62)   a. *Ddar(f)u   S.   a   Mair gyfarfod ddim   yn yr   ysgol   ond*
           happened→NEG J. and M.   meet   NEG in the school but
           mewn parti
           in   party

Otherwise NEG quite clearly has scope over the PP, as in English …*met not at school, but at a party* next to the form with a negative AUX *didn't meet at school, but at a party*. Cf.:

b. *Nid   yn yr   ysgol   y   cyfarfu S. a   M., ond mewn parti*
   NEG in the school DECL met   J. and M. but in   party

or

Cyfarfu S. a   M., nid   yn yr   ysgol,   ond mewn parti
met   J. and M. NEG in the school, but in   party

In conclusion, opposition between Q6 and Q7 does not appear even in Welsh (or in English). An interesting case presents itself in Russian:

(63)   *Ivan est   ne   rybu, a   mjaso*
        J.   eats not fish   but meat

which differs from Q5 (: *Ivan ne est rybu*) and exactly parallels Q7:

(64)   *Ivan i   Marija vstretilis' ne   v   škole,   a   na prazdnike*
        J.   and M.   met   not at school but at party

The order of (63) is also possible in Italian and other languages (for example Rumanian, Armenian, variants of which are given as 'more literary') with an emphatically accentuated contrast between the two Objects 'fish' and 'meat'. Though this appears to be rather dubious in English (: ??*John eats not fish but meat*).

The phenomenon of so-called 'NEG-raising' ('NEG-Anhebung'), which we will have to go into in greater detail when we deal with sentence Q36 (a and b) (cf. chapter 9), is found in the unemphatic construction of Q6, *Giovanni non mangia pesce ma carne* vs. the emphatic *Giovanni mangia non pesce ma carne*. The truth content of *Giovanni non mangia pesce ma carne* and also of *Giovanni e Maria non si incontrarono a scuola ma a una festa* 'John and Mary didn't meet at school but at a party' is undoubtedly the same as that of, respectively, *Giovanni mangia non pesce ma carne* 'John eats not fish but meat' and *Giovanni e Maria si incontrarono non a scuola ma a una festa* 'John and Mary met not at school but at a party': the fact is that John *doesn't* eat fish and that he *does* eat meat; John and Mary *didn't* meet at school (but they *did* meet somewhere else). The difference between the two types of sentences is pragmatic: in the case of NEG preposed to the NP or the PP (: ...*met not at* ...) the factual reality that the two have met is immediately and explicitly declared; in the case instead of preverbal NEG (: ... *didn't meet* ...) the sentence could in theory end after *at school* and maintain a sense of completion; one has to wait for the *but* to know that the sentence continues. On the other hand *Giovanni e Maria si incontrarono non a scuola* 'John and Mary met not at school' is clearly an incomplete sentence: it is obvious that Q7 focuses on the contrast between *scuola* 'school' and *festa* 'party', more than the sentence with so-called 'NEG-raising' does, even taking into account a complex play of presuppositions: 'It is not at school (as one might believe/is commonly believed) that John and Mary met, but...'.

In our replies to the questionnaire 'NEG-raising' in Q7 is found to occur in the following languages.[29]

Basque, Portuguese, Spanish, French (however with the alternative reply without 'raising' as well: *non pas à l'école, mais à un party*), Sardinian, Friulian, Rumanian, Polish (with alternative), Slovenian, Slovak, Serbo-Croatian (with alternative), Greek, Albanian, Latvian (with alternative).

The languages with postverbal NEG such as the Scandinavian ones are ambiguous in the written reply, which does not indicate the intonational segmentation of the sentence: Ice. *Jón og Maria hittust ekki í skólanum heldur í partii*. The same also goes for Welsh in the variant *Ddar(f)u Siôn a Mair gyfarfod ddim yn yr ysgol ond mewn parti*: lit. 'NEG:it.happened J. and M. meet NEG at school but at a party' (cf. *Dydy* in Q6 ('NEG-is'), *John ddim yn bwyta* ('in eat') *pysgod!*).

Finnish, Lapp, which have a negative verb, do not of course pose this type of problem since NEG is anyway on the verb.

5.5. Sentence Q5: the simple negative sentence

The simple negative declarative

Q5   *John doesn't eat fish*
          Giovanni non mangia pesce

has already been repeatedly discussed in dealing with other types of sentences such as the coordinated negative 'NEC ... NEC', sentential (Q3: *John neither speaks nor moves*) as well as phrasal (Q4: *Neither John nor his companions wanted to leave*): see 5.3. The same can be said for sentence Q6 (*John doesn't eat fish, but he does eat meat*) whose first conjunct is the same as Q5; and also for Q7 (*John and Mary met not at school but at a party*) which — we have seen, cf. 5.4. — may in some languages may be treated in the same way as *John and Mary didn't meet at school but at a party*.

As already stated in the introduction to this volume, this type of sentence is universally possible: *it must* be universally possible for every natural language to negate the truth of an utterance, even if the strategies employed in the various languages may be more or less divergent. There are languages such as Swahili which have different paradigms for the affirmative and the negative (cf. 0.2.);

there also exist languages such as Welsh which have markers for the positive sentence as well as for the negative [and also for the interrogative]:

(65)   *YR   ydyt   ti   'n   siarad*
        PTCL   are   you   in   speak
        'you speak'

vs.

(66)   *NID ydyt ti 'n siarad*
        'you don't speak' (see Danielsen 1977: 137),

(67)   *A ydyt ti'n siarad*
        'are you speaking?' (with *a* = interrogative PTCL)]

In the Dravidian languages every verb — active, passive, 'neutral' or causative — may be conjugated in the negative: the agglutinating NEG morpheme is generally *-a-* (pres./fut. *-p-a-*; pret. *-t-a*); in Tamil, however, *-ā-* "en contact avec la voyelle désinentielle s'est amui; le résultat est que le verbe négatif ne se caractérise par rapport au positif que par l'absence du suffix temporel: *kāṇ-b-ēn* 'je verrai', *kāṇ-ḍ-ēn* 'j'ai vu', mais *kāṇ-ēn* 'je ne vois, verrai, vis pas' " [in contact with the desinential vowel is dropped; the result is that the negative verb is not characterised in relation to the positive verb but by the absence of the temporal suffix: *kāṇ-b-ēn* 'I will see', *kāṇ-ḍ-ēn* 'I saw', but *kāṇ-ēn* 'I do/will/did not see'] (Bloch 1946: 51). In Kannada the verbal form carries with it tense markers: from *māḍu* 'to do' we have *māḍutt-ēne* (1SG.PRES), *māḍid-e(nu)* (1SG.PRET.), *māḍuv-e(nu)* (1SG.FUT), but the negative 'mood' is simply *māḍ-e(nu)* (vs. for example a 'potential' *māḍi-yēnu,* or an imperative *māḍuve*). The negative forms are thus morphologically less marked than the positive ones. (These negative forms are, however, very little used and a much more frequent way of expressing NEG is to add a negative morph (*illa, alla*) to the gerund or to the infinitive : see Jensen (1969: 98, 114 ff.)). In any case the opposition between affirmation and negation is always clearly expressed. Far more frequent, however, is the tendency to mark the negation with an explicit NEG morph — as in fact is the case even in Kannada. The negative sentence in such a case will count an extra morphosyntactic unit in addition to the corresponding positive one: *Giovanni* non *mangia pesce* vs. *Giovanni mangia pesce* 'John *doesn't* eat fish' vs. 'John eats fish', Georg. *Žoni ar čams t'evzs* vs. *Žoni čams t'evzs,* Finn. *Jukka ei syö kalaa* vs. *Jukka syö kalaa.* This structure corresponds to the semantic function of the negative sentence, such as defined above (0.2.; cf. also 3.2.): the meaning of a negative sentence does not refer to a state of affairs but rather expresses a judgement on it (like one of its modalities). The vast majority of European languages behave exactly in this way and choose to add to the verb one or more negative markers. Only the Finnic group (Lapp, Finnish, Estonian) use a negative verb, as do, outside of Europe, for example, Maori in New Zealand and Comox in British Columbia (see for example Finn.:

(68)   a. *Jukka ei   syö kalaa*
           John NEG:3SG eat fish

cf.

        b. *Jukka syö kalaa*
           John eats fish).

Amongst all the other European languages, the one that comes closest to this is English, which does indeed have an explicit NEG marker *not/-n't* but which nonetheless adopts a verb (*does*: AUX, or other auxiliary). However, in 3.4. we have seen that there is a growing tendency to transform these verbs or negative auxiliaries into invariable NEG markers, as in the case of Estonian. In terms of a 'natural morphology' it seems indeed to be the invariable marker which is the preferred strategy: based on what has just been observed concerning the negative modality which is added to the positive sentence, such a strategy comes closer to the ideal schematic 1:1 relationship between morph and function. (The passage from NEG2 to NEG3 [> NEG1] illustrated in the diachronic part of this book (see chapter 3) may also be viewed from this perspective).

Returning to the corpus of our languages, special mention must be made of Frisian, Dutch and German, which have the possibility of transposing the NEG marker onto an adjectival form: see, for example, Fris.

(69)   a. *Jan   yt   gijn fisk*
           John eats no fish

alongside

        b. *Jan   yt   net   fisk*
           John eats NEG fish

The conditions governing this alternation are extremely subtle and depend on pragmatic rather than grammatical factors. Our German informant gives, for example, for Q5 only the variant *Hans ißt keinen Fisch*, but for the contrastive text in Q6 also accepts *Hans ißt nicht Fisch, sondern Fleisch* next to *...keinen Fisch*. For our typological research it will be sufficient to note the possibility that in Q5 a form of negative adjective appears ('no-one') as an alternative to the NEG marker − which in these three Germanic languages is the same as for Q2 (namely Fris. *net*, Dut. *niet*, Ger. *nicht*: see 8.4.).

Q5 carries the label 'NEG$_{PRED}$' and languages such as Italian and Greek (*ho Giánnēs dén tróei psári*) will be marked as *NOT1* for Q5, while Spanish (*Juan no come el pescado*) and Lithuanian (*Jonas nevalgo žuvies*) for example will instead be marked as *NO*, the same form of negation as appears in Q1 (Sp. *¿Has visto a Juan? No*, Lith. *Ar matei Joną? Ne*). (On the parameters involved in Q5, see chapter 10).

5.6. Sentences Q37, Q38: the negative imperative

An important point to which we have already alluded in the Foreword to Part II, is that of the difference between the declarative negative sentence Q5 and the prohibitive sentence, represented in our questionnaire by

Q37a   *Do not cross, John!*
            Giovanni, non attraversare!

and

Q38a   *Do not cross, my children!*
            Bambini, non attraversate!

The negative declarative sentence expresses a factual reality, a real state of affairs expressed negatively (: *John doesn't eat fish*); the prohibitive sentence doesn't express a real state of affairs but rather an interdiction on doing something; it therefore averts the realisation of a state of affairs and is thus by its nature linked to imperative modality, which most usually is realised by a different verbal form to that associated with reality (imperative, subjunctive, optative).

For Q37a, Q38a ('NEG$_{PROHIB}$') many languages use the same NEG morph as they do for Q5 ('NEG$_{PRED}$'); others instead use different morphs. Given the centrality of the (simple) negative declarative sentence in every language's system, it would be interesting to establish a parameter of coincidence or non-coincidence of the 'NEG$_{PRED}$' morph with that of 'NEG$_{PROHIB}$' (cf. chapter 10).

In the following languages the morphs of Q5 and Q37 coincide:

Basque;
Portuguese, Spanish, Catalan, Provençal, French, Italian, Rhaeto-Romansh, Friulian, Sardinian, Rumanian;
Icelandic, Norwegian, Swedish, Danish, English, Dutch, Frisian, German;
Lithuanian, Latvian;
Russian, Ukrainian, Belorussian, Polish, Czech, Slovak, Slovenian, Serbo-Croatian, Macedonian, Bulgarian;
Finnish, Lapp.[30]

The following European languages instead make use of a distinct negative marker for the prohibitive – a distinction that though relatively rare in Europe, is extremely widespread in the rest of the world (cf. Croft 1991: 14):

Gaelic, Irish, Welsh, Breton;
Estonian,[31] Hungarian;
Bulgarian;
Albanian;
Greek;
Maltese;
Armenian;
Georgian.

As far as Breton is concerned (Q5 *ne*+Vb+*ket* vs. Q37a *na*+Vb+*ket*) our informant has given for Q37a and Q38a not only

(70)   a. *Na dreuz ket, Yann*
       b. *Na drauzit ket, ma bugale!*

but also the following variants:

(71)   a. *Arabad treuzi, Yann*
       b. *Arabad treuzi, ma bugale.*
          'It is forbidden to cross, etc.'

where *arabad* is, perhaps, an adverb which is used before an infinitive, to form negative imperatives (Press 1986: 319).

This is a strategy which uses alternative and different lexical means to express 'NEG$_{PROHIB}$', for example in Latin (cf. Croft 1991: 15):

(72)   *Noli*   *me*   *tangere*
       not.want:IMPER   me   touch
       'Don't touch me!'

and in Welsh:

(73)   *Peidiwch* *â*   *siarad*
       stop   with   speak
       'Don't speak'[32]

Bulgarian is a different case, having two possible grammatical strategies for Q37 and Q38a:

(74)   a. *Ivan nedej*   *da*   *presičaš!*
          John NEG:IMPER:2SG   CONJ   cross:IND:2SG
       b. ... *ne*   *presičaj!*
             NEG   cross:IMPER:2SG

(75)   a. *Deca,   nedejte   da   presičate!*
          children NEG:IMPER:2PL CONJ cross:IND:2PL

        b. ... *ne   presičajte!*
               NEG   cross:IMPER:2PL

The fact that there are many languages in which the NEG of Q37a coincides with the NEG of Q5 should not lead to thinking that the distinction between 'NEG$_{PRED}$' and 'NEG$_{PROHIB}$' is not very clear. Other means, generally centred on the verb morphology, are sufficient to indicate the difference. Cf., for example, in Italian

(76)   *Non attraversare* (imperative) vs.

        (Tu) non attraversi (declarative)

or in English

(77)   *Do not cross* (imperative) vs.

        You do not cross (declarative)

On the other hand, a language such as Modern Greek, which often does not distinguish indicative from subjunctive in the morphology, relies on the contrast between *dén* and *mén* to mark the difference:

(78)   a. *(Su) dén trós psári*
           '(You) don't eat fish'
        b. *Mén trós psári!*
           'Don't eat fish!'

In some languages, such as French, only the intonation distinguishes the declarative from the prohibitive (at least in some forms of the verbal inflection):

(79)   a. *Jean ne traverse pas*
           'John doesn't cross'
        b. *Jean, ne traverse pas*
           'John, don't cross!'

Note in general the following scale of the formal means for expressing prohibition:

        a) only intonation: see example (79a) vs. (79b);

        b) morphosyntax: see example (77);

        c) different negative morphs: see example (78);

        d) verbal morphology: see example (76);

        e) lexical: see examples (72), (73).

The means listed in c) and d) may also accumulate, as is the case in Latin. Cf.

(80)   a. *Ne cantes*
          NEG sing:SJNT:2SG
          'Do not sing!'
       b. *Non cantas*
          NEG sing:IND:2SG
          'You do not sing'.

6. Quantifier systems

6.1. Introduction

Chapters 6, 7 and 8 are given over to dealing with negative quantifiers such as *no-one, nothing, never*. Amongst the world's languages these are not universally lexicalised, yet they are characteristic of the overwhelming majority of European languages, as we shall see in the course of the chapter. In this chapter, but not only here, the discussion will of necessity also involve existential quantifiers, specific (such as *somebody*) and generic, which, with negative quantifiers, enter into a complex interplay of oppositions on the paradigmatic level and of compatibilities on the syntagmatic level.[1]

In general terms, the behaviour of quantifiers in negative sentences may, according to the nature of the quantifier involved and whether the negation morpheme is present or absent, be arranged into the following four types:

(i) negation and existential quantifier, cf. Hindi (Bhatia 1978: 62):

koī	*nahī̃*	*āyā*	*thā*

someone NEG come was

'No-one came'

(ii) negation and generic quantifier, cf. English *John did not see anybody*;

(iii) negation and negative quantifier, cf. Italian *Giovanni non vide nessuno* 'John didn't see anyone';

(iv) negative quantifier (without negation), cf. German *Hans hat niemanden gesehen* 'Hans has seen no-one'.

These four types are also recognised by Kahrel (in prep.)[2] and with slight variations date back to a proposal by Dahl (1979: 105, note 1). On the basis of the possibility of converting a positive declarative sentence containing a quantifier into a negative, Dahl had actually established three main types, the last of which consisted of two subtypes.[3] In the negative conversions of the sentences in question we find:

(a) the same quantifier as that present in the positive sentence with the addition of a negative morpheme (cf. type (i));

(b) substitution of the quantifier (cf. type (iv))

(c) substitution of the quantifier with the addition of a negative morpheme, with two realisations:

  − the quantifier has an inherent negative interpretation (cf. type (iii));
  − the quantifier doesn't have an inherent negative interpretation (cf. type (ii)).

Payne (1985: 236−238) instead identifies types (iv) and (iii) illustrated above as the main ones and assigns type (ii) the secondary function of expressing existential quantification in the scope of another negative element, including not only constructions of type (ii) but also those of the English type *Nobody saw anything*. Payne makes no mention of the constructions included in type (i).

The proposals made so far take into account the semantic level (the value of the quantifier in question) as well as the syntactic, taking as the parameter the cooccurence with sentence negation. This, however, is only one aspect of the syntactic behaviour of quantifiers in negative sentences, allowing very general regularities to be established, as are those summed up in the four types illustrated. Here we are attempting to arrive at a 'tightly knit' typology, starting with a characterisation of the oppositions between negative and non-negative quantifiers (Chapter 6) in the languages of Europe, then proceeding to examine the inventories of quantifiers present within them and their distribution over grammatical categories (Chapter7) and lastly to consider the problems raised by their syntactic behaviour (Chapter 8).[4]

6.2. "Tertia comparationis": semantic value and grammatical categories

The basis for comparing quantifier systems is their value on the semantic level, which allows firstly a distinction to be made between, for example, languages which have inherently negative quantifiers, such as It. *nessuno* 'no-one', *niente* 'nothing', *mai* 'never', and languages which don't. Secondly, comparison of different behaviours on the syntactic level invokes the different grammatical categories across which the relevant quantifiers are distributed in individual languages. In Italian, for example, *niente* is an indefinite pronoun, *nessuno* a pronoun and an adjective (*Non è venuto nessuno* 'noboby came' vs *Nessun dubbio* 'no doubt'), *mai* an adverb.

6.2.1. Types of quantifiers

On a strictly semantic level, the *tertium comparationis* with respect to which each of the variations found in the values of the quantifiers of individual languages is measured, is constituted by three focal values represented respectively by:

(i) existential negative, with presupposition of non-existence, such as Lat. *nemo*, Eng. *nobody*, It. *nessuno*,[5] as appears, for example, in elliptical replies, cf.: *Chi hai visto? – Nessuno* 'Who did you see? – Noboby' (that is, 'There does not exist an *x* such that I have seen *x*', which implies '*x* does not exist');

(ii) specific existential with presupposition of existence, such as Lat. *quidam*, Eng. *someone*, It. *qualcuno*, even in negative contexts, cf. *Giovanni non vide qualcosa*, lit. 'John didn't see something' ⊃ 'there exists something that John didn't see';
(iii) generic and neutral existential without presupposition of existence, such as Eng. *anyone*, which corresponds to the behaviour of negative polarity items (NPIs), as is well-known from English.

Amongst the languages of Europe this tripartition is well represented only in English where generic quantifiers (cf. *anyone can buy a ticket*, or the following example taken from Horn (1989: 181): "[...] some proposition that was directly inserted into the discourse model (by *someone's* − *anyone's* − previous assertion) [...]") are used as negative polarity items. Therefore they appear in contexts not entirely factual, such as questions.[6] Cf., in our questionnaire, the sentences:

(1)   Q12 Have you seen *anything*?
           Q15 Didn't you see *anyone*?

as compared to the Italian

(2)   Q12 Hai visto *qualcosa*?
           Q15 (Non) hai visto *nessuno*?

Under negation, English quantifiers receive an interpretation of non-existence and therefore their use constitutes an alternative to negative quantifiers, which do not require other negative elements in the same sentence, cf.

(3)   Q19 John did*n't* have *anything*, he did*n't* know *anybody* vs
           John had *nothing*, he knew *nobody*.

For these reasons English quantifiers lend themselves well to providing useful acronyms with which to gloss the values of quantifiers in the other languages of Europe, allowing a quick comparison of them. They will therefore be indicated with:

N (for *no-*) negative quantifiers (as above in (i));
S (for *some-*) existential quantifiers with presuppositions of existence (as above in (ii));
A (for *any-*) generic existential quantifiers with the characteristics of negative polarity items (as above in (iii)).[7]

6.2.2. Grammatical categories

The distribution of quantifiers, intrinsically negative or otherwise, across the various grammatical categories is a criterion relevant to cross-linguistic comparison, both in the inventories of quantifier systems and their internal structure in individual languages, and in the syntactic behaviour of the quantifiers themselves.

The relevant categories in the languages of Europe, and presumably in general, are the following:

- substantive (noun) or, using the more current terminology which we adopt here, pronoun, as in the case of *nothing*, It. *niente*;[8]
- determiner, or following a terminological use current in traditional grammars, adjective, such as in It. *nessuno* before nouns;
- adverb, as *never*, It. *mai*, and *nowhere*.

The inventories of the various types of quantifiers, as will be seen, do not necessarily match up neither cross-linguistically nor within a given language. In the first case, PPs in adverbial function come to mind; e.g. It. *in nessun luogo, da nessuna parte* correspond to the adverbs *nowhere* in English, *nirgends* in German with the value N. In the second case what comes to mind, in Italian, is the function that *nessuno* has within the N-paradigm as both pronoun and adjective, as opposed to *qualcuno* (only pronoun) and *qualche* (only adjective) within the S-paradigm, or even the negative adverb *mai* as opposed to *qualche volta* 'sometimes'.

6.3. Characterisation of the value of quantifiers

The presence of negative quantifiers of the Italian type *nessuno* 'nobody', *niente* 'nothing', *mai* 'never' in opposition to existential quantifiers such as the Italian *qualcuno* 'someone', *qualcosa* 'something', *qualche volta* 'sometimes' is a typical European characteristic, shared by the vast majority of the languages spoken in Europe.[9] The feature N is not, however, uniformly distributed across the languages of Europe nor within its individual languages, and the characterisation both of types of opposition systems for the values N, S and A, and of their distribution within the quantifier paradigms presents interesting problems.

6.3.1. The quantifiers N vs. A/S

For the majority of the languages of Europe an immediate distinction may be made between quantifiers of type N on the one hand and those of type S or A on the other. This is particularly evident in those languages in which quantifiers with the value N display incorporation of the negation, such as Eng. *never* (vs. *ever*), or those equipped with clear-cut paradigmatic oppositions, such as Sp. *nada* 'nothing' vs *algo* 'something'.[10]

In cases which do not , however, allow the same immediate assignment of the value N or S/A to a quantifier, such as the Celtic languages discussed further on, the context which permits an unambiguous characterisation of a quantifier with the value N as opposed to the values A and S is that constituted by elliptical replies, whether to polar questions or to partial questions. In these contexts the occurrence of quantifiers with the value N, compatible with the negative polarity prosentence in the languages that possess this, constitutes a negative reply, as in the following examples:

(4)   a. Have you seen anyone? − (No,) *nobody.*
       b. Who did you see? − *Nobody.*

(5)   a. As-tu vu quelqu'un? − (Non,) *personne.*
       b. Qui as-tu vu? − *Personne.*

On the other hand, the occurrence of items with the value S, incompatible with the negative polarity prosentence in the languages that possess this, constitutes a positive reply, cf.

(6)   a. Did you see anyone? − (Yes,) *someone.*/**No, *someone.*
       b. Who did you see? − *Someone.*

(7)   a. As-tu vu du monde? − (Oui,) *quelqu'un*/**Non, *quelqu'un.*
       b. Qui as-tu vu? − *Quelqu'un.*

From a more general methodological point of view, contexts of this sort lend themselves well as control tests to correctly characterise the value of the quantifier in different languages.[11] In fact one may thus distinguish intrinsically negative quantifiers, which can constitute elliptical negative replies, from A or S quantifiers, for which the presence of a negative operator is necessary to obtain a negative interpretation, as in the following examples:[12]

(8)   Basque
      a. *Ikus-i*   *duzu*   *inor?*
          see-PFP AUX:PRES:3SG.ABS:2SG.ERG [A/+anim](ABS)
          Ez,   *inor*   *ez*
          NEG [A/+anim](ABS) NEG
          'Did you see anyone? − No, nobody'
      b. *Ikus-i*   *duzu*   *ezer?*
          see-PFP AUX:PRES:3SG.ABS:2SG.ERG [A/−anim](ABS)
          Ez,   *ezer*   *ez*
          NEG [A/−anim](ABS) NEG
          'Have you seen anything? − No, nothing'

In (8a,b) the elliptical reply is constituted by the pronouns *inor* and *ezer* respectively, accompanied by the negative morpheme *ez*.[13]

Amongst the European languages under examination, Finnish and Lapp behave in the same way as Basque in this context, cf.

(9)   Finnish
   a. *Näit-kö   ketään? –*   *E-n   ketään.*
      saw:2SG-INT [A/+anim]:PART NEG-1SG [A/+anim]:PART
      Did you seen anyone? – No, nobody'
   b. *Olet-ko   näh-nyt   mitään? –*   *E-n*
      be:2SG-INT see-APFP [A/–anim]:PART NEG-1SG
      mitään.[14]
      [A/–anim]:PART
      'Have you seen anything? – No, nothing'

(10)   Lapp
   a. *Oidnet   go   ovttage? –*   *I-n   ovttage*
      saw:2SG INT [A/+anim]:ACC NEG-1SG [A/+anim]:ACC
      'Did you see anyone? – No, nobody'
   b. *Leat   go   oaidnán   maidige? –*   *I-n,*
      be:PERF:2SG INT see:APFP [A/–anim]:ACC NEG-1SG
      i-n   maidige
      NEG-1SG [A/–anim]:ACC
      'Have you seen anything? – No, nothing'

In these two Finno-Ugric languages the elliptical reply also consists of a non-N type pronoun, and more specifically an A type, that is, Finn. *kukaan, mikään* (in the respective partitive forms *ketään, mitään*) and Lapp *oktage, mihkige* (in the respective accusative forms *ovttage, maidige*) accompanied by the negative operator, which in these languages is constituted by the negative auxiliary. The Lapp example (10b) is, in this regard, particularly interesting, because it seems to allow the negative reply to be expressed by the auxiliary *in* alone; the elliptical reply in which the pronoun appears has, in its turn, to be accompanied by the auxiliary (that is, *In/In maidige*, but not ** *Maidige* or **In, maidige*).[15]

As far as these two pronominal quantifiers are concerned, the vast majority of the languages of Europe fall within the category N. The complete list of these languages, subdivided according to genetic affiliation, is as follows:

CELTIC: Welsh, Breton;
ROMANCE: Portuguese, Spanish, Catalan, Provençal, French, Italian, Friulian, Rhaeto-Romansh, Sardinian, Rumanian;
GERMANIC: Icelandic, Norwegian, Swedish, English[16], literary Frisian[17], Dutch, German;

SLAVIC: Polish, Czech, Slovak, Slovenian, Serbo-Croatian, Macedonian, Bulgarian, Belorussian, Ukrainian, Russian;
BALTIC: Latvian, Lithuanian;
FINNO-UGRIC: Hungarian;
SEMITIC: Maltese;
Greek;
Albanian.

The non-N languages are Basque, Finnish, and Lapp (see examples above). These languages have elliptical replies allowing only the use of a type A pronoun accompanied by the standard negation, that is, an independent particle for Basque and the negative auxiliary for the Finno-Ugric languages.

6.3.2. Problematic cases

6.3.2.1. English

Amongst the problematic cases, we need first of all to justify the inclusion of English in the N languages, despite the presence of two quantifier paradigms, N and A, in complementary distribution in negative sentences (see example 3). From the point of view adopted here, English is an N not a non-N language, because the A quantifiers are excluded from elliptical replies, cf.

(11)   Did you see anyone? — *Nobody*
                 Anybody/Not anybody
                 **I didn't anybody

It is of course possible to reply to the question in example (11) with a complete negative sentence containing the A pronoun, cf. *I didn't see anybody.*

6.3.2.2. Danish

Not included in the above list, Danish constitutes the second problematic case. In the questionnaire Danish gives the elliptical reply *ingen* 'no-one' to the question posed by the Cyclops Polyphemus,[18] cf.

(12)   *Hvad er dit navn? — spurgte Polyfem.*
                 'What's your name? — asked Polyphemus'
                 Ingen — Svarede Odysseus.
                 'No-one — replied Ulysses'

In the other contexts of elliptical replies included in the questionnaire, we have behaviours differing according to the two types of pronouns under examination. Against Eng. *nothing* there are:

(a) elliptical replies with the N items *intet/ingenting*;
(b) elliptical replies with non-N pronoun accompanied by a sentence negation particle *ikke*, that is, *ikke noget* (lit. 'not something');
(c) full replies with both types of pronoun. Cf.:

(13)   *Hvad kan du se? — spurgte Hans.*
         'What can you see? — asked John'
         Ingenting/Intet/Ikke noget — svarede hans ven.
         'Nothing — replied his friend'

(14)   *Har du set noget? — Nej, jeg har ingenting set/Nej, jeg har ikke set noget.*
         'Have you seen anything? — No, nothing'

Against Eng. *nobody* we have instead only instances of the full reply with the non-N pronoun, cf.

(15)   *Så du nogen? — Nej, jeg så ikke nogen.*
         'Did you see anyone? — No, nobody'

Danish behaves in some ways like an N language (elliptical replies with only the pronouns *ingen, intet/ingenting*), yet in other ways like a typical non-N language (elliptical replies of the type *ikke noget*). The elliptical constructions, however, seem to find less favour than a full reply, as examples (14) and (15) show.[19] We may therefore conclude that Danish is an intermediate case between the N and the non-N languages, although closer to the former than to the latter. Supporting this is the marginality of replies with a non-N quantifier plus standard negation with respect to full replies, a situation which recalls the constraints imposed on quantifiers of the A paradigm in English. In short, the distribution of the replies in the questionnaire shows how 'nobody' is further than 'nothing' from type N, across the paradigm of quantifiers.[20]

6.3.2.3. Estonian

The third problematic case is constituted by Estonian, which, with respect to the non-N languages, in some ways reflects the position that Danish occupies with respect to the N languages. Against Eng. *nobody* and *nothing*, Estonian replies respectively with the indefinite pronouns *keegi* and *miski*, usually considered S items,[21] preceded by the particle *mitte*, a non sentential negative operator.[22] Cf.

(16)   *Kas sa   nägid kedagi? —   Ei,   mitte   kedagi.*
         INT you saw   [S/+anim]:PART NEG NEG [S/+anim]:PART
         'Did you see anyone? — No, nobody'

(17)   *Kas   sa   oled   midagi   näinud? – Ei,*
        INT you be:PRES:2SG [S/−anim]:PART seen   NEG
        mitte   midagi
        NEG [S/−anim]:PART
        'Have you seen anything? – No, nothing'

Note that *mitte kedagi, mitte midagi* on their own may constitute elliptical replies and are therefore considered to be similar to the N items characteristic of the other European languages.[23] On the other hand, their formation may not be considered on the same level as the incorporation of negation which has occured in the Romance, Germanic and Slavic languages. In fact, in other types of construction, *keegi* and *miski* interact with the negative sentence operator and behave in a similar way to the A items in Finnish, cf.

(18)   Q11 *keegi   ei   tulnud*
           [S/+anim]:NOM NEG come
           'Nobody came'

Estonian therefore represents the case of a non-N language which has moved away from the prototypical non-N instances in the direction of the N prototype; it has developped a formation that corresponds functionally (and maybe also morphologically) to the N pronouns used for elliptical replies and for resolving ambiguities and/or for the purpose of emphasis. In the following example:

(19)   Q17 *Keegi   ei   näinud mitte   midagi*
           [S/+anim]:NOM NEG seen   NEG [S/−anim]:PART
           'Someone didn't see anything'

mitte midagi is unquestionably equivalent to 'nothing' and is opposed only to *midagi* which should be understood as 'something', cf.

(20)   Q18 *Keegi   ei   näinud midagi*
           [S/+anim]:NOM NEG seen   [S/−anim]:PART
           'Someone didn't see something'

In the following example, however, according to our informant *mitte midagi* emphasises the complete lack of goods on John's part, cf.

(21)   Q19 *John-il   p-olnud   (mitte) midagi*
           John-ADESS NEG-been NEG [S/−anim]:PART
           'John had nothing'

6.3.2.4. Irish

Irish does not fit in with our characterisation because it does not allow any type of elliptical reply (see also 5.1. and 5.2. regarding short answers of the Italian type *no*). In those contexts of our questionnaire intended to elicit elliptical replies with negative pronouns, Irish gives the following responses:

(22)   *An   bhfaca   tú   duine   ar bith?* − *Ní   fhacas,   ní*
INT saw:3SG you person on world NEG saw:1SG NEG
fhaca   mé duine   ar bith.
saw:3SG I   person on world
'Did you see anyone? − No, nobody'

(23)   *An   bhfaca   tú   rud   ar bith?* − *Ní   fhacas,   ní*
INT saw:3SG you thing on world NEG saw:1SG NEG
fhaca   mé rud   ar bith.
saw:3SG I   thing on world
'Have you seen anything? − No, nothing'

The transparent locutions used in these examples, that is *duine ar bith* (lit. 'person on world') and *rud ar bith* (lit. 'thing on world') have a non-N value, in that they are found in both the positive question and the negative reply.[24] Rather than pronouns true and proper, they may instead be considered negative polarity items (NPIs) all the more so for their etymological transparency. However, in contexts particularly susceptible to ellipsis such as those under consideration even Irish seems to be giving way in the direction of type N. This is revealed in the following replies, where other NPIs appear, that is, *aon duine*, lit. 'a person' (example 24), and *dada* (see example 25; glossed 'iota, jot, a whit, tittle' by Ó Dónaill (1977, s.v.), with obvious N value. Cf.

(24)   Q8 *Cé-n   t-ainm a-tá   or-t?* −   a   dúirt Polaiféamas*
what-ART name REL-is on-2SG REL said Polyphemus
Aon duine −   a   dúirt Uiliséas.*
a   person REL said Ulysses
'What's your name? − asked Polyphemus.
No-one − replied Ulysses'

(25)   Q10 *Céard a   fheiceann tú?* −   a   dúirt Seán.*
What REL see:3SG you   REL said John
Dada −   a   dúirt a   chomrádaí*
thing   REL said 3SG:M:POSS companion
'What can you see? − asked John.
Nothing − replied his companion'

6.3.3. S quantifiers vs. A quantifiers

Although a characterisation of quantifiers with the value S may be readily made in the vast majority of the languages of Europe (see 6.3.1, at the beginning) it is worth while pausing a moment on the question of how to unambiguously characterise items with the value S, and also A. As has already been pointed out (cf. 6.3.1 again) this is relevant from a general methodological point of view and, as far as our aim of typological comparison is concerned, it is also important when applied to some not too clear cases which will be discussed presently.

With respect to N items, characterisation of the value S or A of a quantifier is a more complex operation, which must take into account various types of context which on the pragmatic level favour one or other of the two interpretations. In order to obtain a rigorous classification we will examine two contexts:

(i) positive, including elliptical, replies
(ii) positive and negative interrogatives.

Both contexts are included in our questionnaire under the following entries:

(26) Q12 Have you seen *anything?* − No, nothing.
           Hai visto *qualcosa?* − No, *niente*
      Q13 Haven't you seen *anything?* − Yes, I have seen *something.*[25]
           (Non) hai visto *niente?* − Sì, *qualcosa.*
      Q14 Did you see *anyone?* − No, *nobody.*
           Hai visto *qualcuno?* − No, *nessuno.*
      Q15 Didn't you see *anyone?* − Yes, I did see *someone.*
           (Non) hai visto *nessuno?* − Sì, *qualcuno.*

The reply in Q13 and Q15 is factual, has positive polarity, and constitutes a favourable context for quantifiers of the S type. The interrogative, on the other hand, whether neutral (positive polarity) or orientated (negative polarity), because of its non-factual nature represents a different type of context, as the use of the English pronouns *anyone, anything* in (26) shows. In these contexts the optional nature of the sentence negation morpheme *non* in Italian, is such that the pronouns *qualcuno/qualcosa* and *nessuno/niente* are functionally equivalent.

With respect to A items, S quantifiers also stand out for the fact that in negative contexts, despite being in the scope of the negative operator, they maintain their existential value. In our questionnaire the following entry fits this pattern:

(27)   Q18 *Somebody* didn't see *something*[26]
            Qualcuno non vide *qualcosa*

The two versions of (27) may be paraphrased as follows:

(28)   'There is something that someone didn't see'
            (or: 'there exists a thing x such that y didn't see x')

and serve as a third context on the basis of which the initial assignment of the values S and A may be submitted to further controls.

To characterise the values S and A of the quantifiers it will be necessary above all to note the distribution of the items in opposition that the individual languages display in the four contexts provided by the entries Q12−15 in the questionnaire, that is:

(29) (i)   negative reply;   (ii)   positive reply;
      (iii) positive interrogative;   (iv)   negative interrogative.[27]

Furthermore, the distinction between N and non-N items in the context of negative elliptical replies (as in (i) above, cf. also 6.3.1.), based on the presence or otherwise of a negative operator alongside the quantifier, permits the use of this very context as a reference point from which to assign the correct value to the quantifiers concerned.

6.4. Types of quantifier oppositions

The procedure described keeps the functional level, which on the basis of the conventions adopted in 6.2.1. is indicated with the three initials N, S and A, and the level of expression, for which we will make use of the symbols x, y, z, distinct. In particular, negative elliptical replies unambiguously characterise items with an N value (see 6.3.1.); the positive replies items with an S value; the two interrogatives, positive and negative, represent instead contexts with a potential A value, as illustrated by the schema (30), which will serve as a reference for subsequent sections:

(30)   Contexts for N, S, and A values of quantifiers

	Neg.	Pos.
Reply	N	S
Question	A	A

The distribution of quantifiers in the four relevant contexts allows us to observe the types of oppositions around which the quantifier paradigms are organised. These types number seven in the languages of Europe.

6.4.1. Type: N vs S vs A

The first type has three distinct quantifier forms which are distributed within the relevant contexts according to schema (31), where NEG indicates the obligatory presence of a negative operator.

(31)   Type N vs S vs A

	Neg.	Pos.
Reply	x	y
Question	NEG z	z

By comparing (30) with (31) we see the specific values of each of the three quantifier forms as N, S and, respectively, A.

We already said that paradigms organised around three items are found in Europe only in English, which has, for example, *nobody* and *nothing* in negative replies (= x), *somebody* and *something* in positive replies (= y) and *anybody* and *anything* in questions, independently of their polarity (= z). The distribution of the three items is categoric, with no overlapping of the values of the three items involved. Examples have already been given (cf. (3), (26)).[28]

6.4.2. Type: N vs. S_1 vs. S_2

The second type to be examined also consists of oppositions between three forms, which are distributed as indicated in schema (32).

(32)   Type N vs S_1 vs S_2

	Neg.	Pos.
Reply	x	y
Question	NEG x	z

The lexeme x of the quantifier with the value N appears in oriented questions together with the standard negation. In positive contexts we have instead the opposition of an item y in replies and an item z in questions. This type is found, for example, in Russian. Cf.

(33)   a. *Ty videl kogo-nibud'? – Net, nikogo.*
            'Did you see anyone? – No, nobody'
        b. *Ty nikogo ne videl? – Da, koe-kogo.*
            'Didn't you see anyone? – Yes, someone'

The opposition of the item y in the positive reply to z in the positive question is, in this case, the consequence of a distinction of specificity within the subsystem of S items, illustrated, again in Russian, by the following examples (Berneker–Vasmer 1971: 70):

(34)   *Tam verojatno zvonit kto-nibud'*
            'There, probably, there is someone ringing'

(35)   *Kto-to mne skazal ...*
            'Someone told me ...'

In (35) *kto-to* (equivalent to *koe-kto* in (33b)) refers to someone known to the speaker, but whose identity is not relevant to the discourse (= S_1); in (34) *kto-nibud'* refers to someone unknown to the speaker (= S_2). This distinction overlaps with that between the S and A items in the contexts indicated above, in that in the positive reply in the (b) examples the choice of a specific item (the speaker knows who (s)he has seen but does not make it explicit) is obligatory, while in the context of a positive question the choice of a non specific item *kto-nibud'*, which turns out to be equivalent to items with the value A, is obvious.[29] This system of oppositions, however, is better labelled N vs. S_1 vs. S_2 and, in more general terms, is considered a peculiar case of the realisation of type N vs. S.[30]

In Europe oppositions of this type are found, apart from in Russian, in Belorussian, Ukrainian,[31] Serbo-Croatian, Slovenian and Lithuanian. Cf.

(36)   Lithuanian
    a. *Ar   matei   kąnors? — Ne, nieko.*
       INT saw:2SG someone No nobody
       'Did you see anyone? — No, nobody'
    b. *Nieko   ne-matei? —   Taip, kai ką   (mačiau).*
       nobody NEG-saw:2SG Yes   someone saw:1SG
       'Didn't you see anyone? — Yes, someone'

(37)   Belorussian
    a. *Ty štos'ci ŭbačyŭ? — Ne, ničoga.*
       'Have you seen anything? — No, nothing'
    b. *Ty ničoga ne ŭbačyŭ? — Ale, kual'ki-što.*
       'Haven't you seen anything? — Yes, something'

6.4.3. Type: N vs. S

In this type, which is more widely diffused amongst the languages of Europe, there are only two items in opposition, which are uniformly distributed between negative and interrogative contexts as illustrated by scheme (38).

(38)   Type N vs S

	Neg.	Pos.
Reply	x	y
Question	(NEG) x	y

The main opposition, which stands out in the replies, is that between the N and S items; it also arises in questions thus neutralising the value A. This type is well illustrated by Italian, which, as will be remembered, also allows the use of the item *x* without standard negation in questions (cf. (26)). Cf., by way of illustration:

(39)   Welsh
  a. *A   wyt   ti   wedi gweld rhywbeth? — Naddo, dim byd.*
     INT are you after see   something no   nothing
  b. *D-wyt   ti   ddim   wedi   gweld dim byd? — Do, r-wyf*
     NEG-are you NEG after see   nothing   yes DECL-am
     wedi   gweld rhywbeth.
     after see   something

(40)   Rumanian
  a. *Ai   văzut ceva? —   Nu, nimic.*
     have:2SG seen something no   nothing
  b. *Nu   ai   văzut nimic? — Ba da, ceva.*
     NEG have:2SG seen   nothing   yes   something

(41)   Dutch
  a. *Heb je   iets   gezien? — Nee, niets.*
     have you something seen   No   nothing
  b. *Heb je   niets   gezien? — Jawel, ik heb (wel)   iets*
     have you nothing seen   yes   I   have EMPH something
     gezien.
     seen

(42)   Macedonian
  a. *Imaš   (li)   videno nešto? —   Ne, ništo.*
     have:2SG INT seen   something no   nothing
  b. *Ne-maš   videno ništo? — Ne, imam   videno nešto.*
     NEG-have:2SG seen   nothing   no   have:1SG seen   something

(43)   Maltese
  a. *Rajt   xi ħaġa? — Le, xejn.*
     saw:2SG something no   nothing

b. *Ma   rajt   xejn? —   Iva, xi ḥaġa.*
   NEG saw:2SG nothing yes something

6.4.4. Type: N vs. SA

The fourth type is again based on an opposition of two items, but the intrinsically negative one (x in the schema (44)) is found exclusively in replies.

(44)   Type N vs SA

	Neg.	Pos.
Reply	x	y
Question	(NEG) y	y

In this type one item realises the function N, while the functions S and A are fused in the other type, as in Norwegian. Cf.

(45)   a. *Så du noen? — Nei, ingen.*
           'Did you see anyone? — No, nobody'
        b. *Så du ikke noen? — Jo, jeg så noen.*
           'Didn't you see anyone? — Yes, I saw someone'

(46)   a. *Har du sett noe? — Nei, ingenting.*
           'Have you seen anything? — No, nothing'
        b. *Har du ikke sett noe? — Jo, jeg har sett noe.*
           'Haven't you seen anything? — Yes, I've seen something'

6.4.5. Type: NA vs S

The fifth type classified here is again characterised by the opposition of two items (cf. (47)), which are distributed between four contexts in a way that mirrors the preceding type.

(47)   Type NA vs S

	Neg.	Pos.
Reply	x	y
Question	(NEG) x	x

In this type the *y* form with the value S is opposed to a form *x* which combines the values N and A. The Italian adverbs *mai* − *qualche volta* fall into this type, cf.

(48)   *(Non) ha mai visto l'uomo della fotografia? − Mai/Qualche volta.*
          'Have you (n)ever seen the man in the photograph? − Never/ Sometimes'

This type of opposition is typical of Modern Greek,[32] cf.

(49)   a. *Eídes kanéna? − Okhi, kanéna.*
             'Did you see anyone? − No, nobody'
          b. *Dén eídes kanéna? − Naí, eída kápoion.*
             'Didn't you see anyone? − Yes, I saw someone'

(50)   a. *Eídes típota? − Okhi, típota.*
             'Did you see anything? − No, nothing'
          b. *Dén eídes típota? − Naí, eída káti.*
             'Didn't you see anything? − Yes, I saw something'

6.4.6. Type: A vs. S

The sixth type now under examination, unlike the first five, is found in the languages which were defined as non-N in 6.3.1. As in the first five types we have an opposition between two forms, which are distributed as in schema (51).

(51)   Type A vs S

	Neg.	Pos.
Reply	NEG x	y
Question	NEG x	x

Functionally, however, there is an opposition between an item with the value S, which appears in positive replies, and an item with the value A, which appears in interrogatives and negative elliptical replies (in the latter case always accompanied by a negative operator).

This type is found in the more marginal of the European languages, that is, Basque, Irish (together with Scottish Gaelic), Lapp, Finnish. Note the examples reported above (8−10), (16), (17), (22), (23) and, for the opposition A-S, the following examples which are the translations of Q15 ('Didn't you see anyone? − Yes, I did see someone') and Q13 ('Haven't you seen anything? − Yes, I have seen something') respectively:

(52)   Basque[33]

a. *Ez   duzu   inor   ikusi? −   Bai,   ikusi dut*
   NEG AUX [A/+anim](ABS) seen   yes seen AUX
   norbait
   [S/+anim](ABS)

b. *Ez   duzu   ezer   ikusi? −   Bai,   ikusi dut*
   NEG AUX [A/−anim](ABS) seen   yes seen AUX
   zerbait
   [S/−anim](ABS)

(53)   Irish

a. *Nach   bhfaca   tú   duine   ar bith? −   Chonaic,   chonaic*
   NEG:INT saw:3SG you person on world   saw:3SG saw:3SG
   mé duine   éigin
   I   person [S/ADJ]

b. *Nach   bhfaca   tú   dada? −   Chonaic,   chonaic   mé*
   NEG:INT saw:3SG you [A/−anim]   saw:3SG saw:3SG I
   rud   éigin.
   thing [S/ADJ]

(54)   Finnish

a. *E-t-kö   nähnyt ketään? −   näin*
   NEG-2SG-INT   seen [A/+anim]:PART saw:1SG
   jonkun.
   [S/+anim]:GEN

b. *E-t-kö   ole nähnyt mitään? −   Olen (kyllä)*
   NEG-2SG-INT   be seen [A/−anim]:PART am   certain
   nähnyt jotain.
   seen   [S/−anim]:PART

(55)   Lapp

a. *I-t   go   oaidnán   ovttage? −   De   oidnen*
   NEG-2SG INT see:APP [A/+anim]:ACC certain saw:1SG
   muhtoma.
   [S/+anim]

b. *I-t   go   leat   oaidnán maidige? −*
   NEG-2SG INT be-PRET:2SG seen [A/−anim]:ACC
   Lean   oaidnán
   be:PRET:1SG seen

This type was probably also represented in Gothic, where, for example, the S item *sums* is in opposition to the A items *hwashun, ainshun,* which when they have the meaning 'nobody' always appear accompanied by the negative morpheme *ni*,[34] cf.

(56)   *Ni   hwashun   nimiþ þo   af   mis*
        NEG [A/+anim]:NOM takes that from me
        'Nobody takes that from me' (Joh. X, 18)

(57)   *ei   ainnohun   izwara ni   daupida*
        that [A/+anim]:ACC of.you NEG baptized:1SG
        'for I didn't baptize any of you' (Cor. I.I, 14)

The Greek original text has *oudeís* 'nobody', without negation on the verb (*oudéis aírei autén ap'emoû* for (56) and *hóti oudéna humôn ebáptisa* for (57)).

Interrogative contexts, respectively positive and negatively oriented, are attested by the following passages (in (59) *jau* implies the expectation of a negative reply [cf. Streitberg 1971 (< 1909): 72 of the glossary)).

(58)   *þata anþar ni   wait   ei ainnohun   daupidedjau*
        that other not know(1SG) if [A+anim]:ACC baptized:1SG
        'After all I don't know if I have baptized someone else' (Cor. I.I, 16)[35]

(59)   *sai,   jau   ainshun   þize   reike*
        behold perhaps.that [A/+anim]:NOM of.these princes
        galaubidedi imma aiþþau Fareisaie?
        believed   him or   of.Pharisees
        'Behold, did any of these princes believe in him or any of the Pharisees?' (Joh. VII, 48).

6.4.7. Type with only one item: AS

The last of the types found in Europe has only one item to cover all three functions N, A, S; obviously it acquires a negative value only when found within the scope of a negative operator (cf. 6.3.1).

(60)   Type with one AS item

	Neg.	Pos.
Reply	NEG x	x
Question	NEG x	x

This type is found in Danish, at least in part (cf. 6.3.2.2), and in Estonian (cf. 6.3.2.3). Cf.

(61)   Danish
  a. *Har du set* noget? — *Nej, jeg har ikke set* noget.
     have you seen x   no I have NEG seen x
     'Have you seen anything? — No, nothing'
  b. *Har du ikke set* noget? — *Jo, jeg har set* noget.
     have you NEG seen x   yes I have seen x
     'Haven't you seen anything? — Yes, I have seen something'

(62)   Estonian
  a. *Kas sa oled* midagi *näinud?* — *Ei, mitte*
     INT you be:PRET:2SG x:PART seen   NEG NEG
     midagi.
     x:PART
  b. *kas sa p-ole* midagi *näinud?* — *Jah, ma nägin*
     INT you NEG-be:PRET x:PART seen   yes I saw
     midagi.
     x:PART
     'Have you seen anything? — No, nothing'

In these cases the unique quantifier has either the value S, which corresponds to its use in positive replies, or the value A, corresponding to its use in questions and with negation.

6.5. Typology of the quantifier systems

The seven types of oppositions between quantifiers, analytically illustrated in 6.4.1.-6.4.7., may be reduced to three basic types, based on the number and value of the items in opposition:

  (i) systems with three items:
      N vs. S vs. A (cf. 6.4.1.);
  (ii) two items systems, with two main sub-types:
      a. N vs. S (cf. 6.4.2.-6.4.5.)
      b. A vs. S (cf. 6.4.6)
  (iii) one item systems, i. e. systems without any opposition between quantifiers having different values: S (cf. § 6.4.7)

These three discrete macro-types actually represent a continuum instantiated by their various manifestations between the extremes of the systems with three items and the systems with a single item. In fact the type $\langle$N vs. S_1 vs. $S_2\rangle$ (cf.

6.4.2.) belongs to macro-type (iia) because of the nature of the items in opposition, but from the point of view of its practical realisations it is equivalent, as has been seen, to macro-type (i). And the type ⟨NA vs. S⟩ (cf. 6.4.5.), while belonging to (iia), represents a crossing point towards (iib) because it has the same distribution as the functional values of this type.

The oppositions of values of these three macro-types also form the basis for possible combinations of quantifiers and negation identified at the beginning of the chapter (cf. 6.1.), as the schema (63) illustrates.

(63)   TYPE OF OPPOSITION SYNTACTIC TYPE[36]

(i)	N vs. S vs. A	a.	N
		b.	NEG N
		c.	NEG A
(iia)	N vs. S	a.	N
		b.	NEG N
(iib)	A vs. S	c.	NEG A
(iii)	S	d.	NEG S

It is necessary at this point, however, to discuss a crucial aspect, which appears not to have been brought out by other researchers. The taxonomy proposed here for quantifier systems independent of the grammatical categories by which they are realised, does not seem to necessarily characterise the entire paradigm of quantifiers of a language, in the sense that individual members of the paradigm may belong to different sub-types of the same macro-type or even to different macro-types.

An example of the first case is provided by Italian, where the pronouns *nessuno* and *niente* belong to the oppositions ⟨N vs. S⟩ (macro-type ii, sub-type a: ⟨N vs. S⟩), while the adverb *mai*, though remaining within the macro-type ii, is part of the oppositions ⟨NA vs. S⟩ (cf. 6.4.5.). An example of the second case is constituted by Norwegian, where the pronoun N *ingen* 'nobody' belongs to the type ⟨N vs. SA⟩ (or (iia), cf. 6.4.4.), but the locative adverbial *noen steder* belongs to type (iii), cf.

(64)   *John   hadde* [...] *ikke   noe   hjem   noen   steder*
        John   had   NEG   [S]   house   [S]   places
        'John didn't have a house anywhere'

On the other hand it has already been pointed out that in a language different types may be realised at the same time for the same quantifier. This has been seen for Danish, where the pronouns corresponding to Eng. *nobody, nothing* are realised either as N vs. S as in type (ii) or as S as in type (iii) (cf. 6.3.2.2.).

From all this it follows that the entire range of quantifiers in a language may be characterised by asymmetries of varying natures for each of its members, making any attempt at constructing a general typology for every quantifier system very problematic. The asymmetries within quantifier paradigms will be dealt with later in more detail (cf. 7.2., 7.4.); regarding what is pertinent to this section suffice it to note two cases of a problematic interconnection of the various types.

In Frisian the asymmetries not only cut across the paradigm but also across language varieties, as is shown by the schemas (65) and (66) of pronouns corresponding to Eng. *nobody, nothing* and to their non-negative counterparts.

(65)   Literary Frisian

	'nobody/somebody'		nothing/something'	
	Neg.	Pos.	Neg.	Pos.
Reply	nimmen	immen	neat	eat
Question	nimmen	immen	net wat/neat	eat
Type	N vs S (iia)		N vs S & N vs AS	

(66)   Colloquial Frisian

	'nobody/somebody'		nothing/something'	
	Neg.	Pos.	Neg.	Pos.
Reply	net ien	ien	neat	wat
Question	net ien	ien	net wat	wat
Type	S (iii)		N vs AS (iia)	

In this distribution it is easy to discern a diachronic drift from type (iia), that is, ⟨N vs. S⟩ to type (iii), that is, ⟨SA⟩, which, in addition to Frisian, is common to the three continental Nordic languages, although it is close to the final stage only in Danish. The oldest stage is represented by the 'nobody'-slot in literary Frisian, the most advanced by the same slot in colloquial Frisian. As for 'nothing', the original system of oppositions is barely disturbed in literary Frisian in a 'weak' sector such as that of oriented questions, while in colloquial Frisian the S item has 'invaded' every context of type A.[37] Without going into the problem of reconstructing the possible courses that processes of linguistic change of this type are forced to take, these Frisian data seem again to confirm the relative independence of the individual members of the quantifier paradigms.

A second problematic case is presented by Icelandic, which according to the grammars (for example Kress (1982: 109 and 111)), has two series of intrinsically negative pronouns for 'nobody' and 'nothing': *neinn* and *neitt, enginn* and *ekkert*. In fact the pronouns of the first series are used only in sentences that already contain a negative element.[38] They therefore more closely resemble A items, being in addition excluded from elliptical replies. For entries Q12–15 of our questionnaire we got the following answers:

(67)　　a. *Hefur-ðu   séð   eitthvað? –　　Nei, ekkert.*
　　　　　have-you seen [S/−anim] – no   [N/−anim]
　　　　　'Have you seen anything? – No, nothing'

　　　　b. *Hefur-ðu   ekki   séð   neitt? –　　Jú, ég sá   eitthvað*
　　　　　have-you NEG seen [A/−anim] – yes I saw [S/−anim]
　　　　　'Haven't you seen anything? – Yes, I have seen something'

(68)　　a. *Sástu   einhvern? – Nei, engan.*
　　　　　saw:you [S/+anim] no   [N/+anim]
　　　　　'Did you see anyone? – No, nobody'

　　　　b. *Sástu   ekki   neinn? –　　Jú, ég sá   einhvern.*
　　　　　saw:you NEG [A/+anim] yes I saw [S/+anim]
　　　　　'Didn't you see anyone? – Yes, I did see someone'

The distributive schema that may be drawn from (67), (68) is reported in (69).

(69)　　　　Icelandic

	Neg.	Pos.
Reply	x	y
Question	NEG z	y

In a fine-grained taxonomy derived from the general typological framework Icelandic would thus be considered a language of a type intermediate between the macro-type (i) with three items (N vs. S vs. A) and the macro-type (ii), sub-type (iia), ⟨N vs. S⟩. Once again, however, we note how the negatively oriented question constitutes the weak point, and the position of Icelandic is revealed better in the diachronic perspective, at least for the two pronouns exemplified, in the passage from a two items system to a single item system, attested, as has already been stated, in the other Nordic languages and Frisian.[39]

By way of conclusion to this section it is also worth mentioning that, within the sub-type ⟨N vs. S⟩, as well as ambiguous cases involving an opposition between positive and negative questions, such as that illustrated by Icelandic, there also exist cases of tension within the opposition between positive replies and questions. There are indications that point in the direction of a functional differentiation of the involved items. These cases seem to be numerically and qualitatively less significant than those discussed above and regard German for both the pronouns *niemand/jemand* and *nichts/etwas*, and Portuguese only for its non−animate pronoun.

The German replies to the entries Q12−15 of the questionnaire are the following:

(70)   a. *Hast du (et)was gesehen? − Nein, gar nichts.*
        'Have you seen anything? − No, nothing at all'
        b. *Hast du nichts gesehen? − Doch, ein bißchen.*
        'Haven't you seen anything? − Yes, a little'

(71)   a. *Hast du jemanden gesehen? − Nein, niemanden.*
        'Did you see anyone? − No, nobody'
        b. *Hast du niemand(en) gesehen? − Doch, ein paar Leute.*
        'Didn't you see anyone? − Yes, a pair of people'

If the replies (70b) and (71b) are not conditioned by the particular context of positively oriented disagreement with respect to the negative question (cf. Bernini 1990: 141−146), the choice of expressions with greater referentiality (cf. also Ramat−Bernini−Molinelli 1986: 251) would be an indication in favour of a potential restricting of *jemand* and *etwas* to the unique value A.[40]

For Portuguese there is instead:

(72)   a. *Viste   alguma coisa? − Não, nada.*
        saw:2SG something   no   nothing
        b. *Não   viste   nada? − Sim, qualquer coisa.*
        NEG saw:2SG nothing yes something

In this case as well we may take note only of the reply to the questionnaire, nevertheless assigning Portuguese, like German as well, to the main type ⟨N vs. S⟩, which is vouched for by the grammars.[41]

6.6. Systems of indefinite and negative pronouns in Europe

As a concrete example of the application of the typology elaborated in the preceding sections, we now take a look at the diffusion amongst the European languages of the various types of the pronouns corresponding to Eng. *nobody/*

somebody and *nothing/something* and of the four basic types (that is, ⟨N vs. A vs. S⟩; ⟨N vs. S⟩; ⟨A vs. S⟩; ⟨S⟩).

(73)   Opposition of quantifiers: macro-types
            nobody/somebody; nothing/something
            Legend:
            Eng: N vs. S vs. A
            IT: N vs. S
            Fin: A vs. S
            Est: S
            CFrs/CFrs: co-presence of different sub-types for 'nobody' and 'nothing'
            shadow: languages with no N items
            *(*):   languages with problematic classification
            −:   boundary of the macro-type ⟨N vs. S⟩
            n.b.:   for the language symbols see the list of abbreviations on p. x.

	Ice*				Lap		Fin	
			NOR		SWD		*Est*	
	Ir	**ScGl**	*CFrs**/CFRS*		*DAN***		LTV	
	WLS	Eng	LFRS				LITH	
	BRE	FR	DUT	GER		POL	BYLR	RUS
	Bas	PRO		RMNS	CZ	SLK	UKR	
POR	SPN	CAT	IT	FRL	SLV	HUN		
		SRD		ALB	SCR	RUM		
			MLT	GRK	MAC	BUL		

The schema reproduced in (73) shows above all the marginality of languages where the pronouns under examination participate in different subtypes. In fact these are limited to colloquial Frisian alone (cf. 6.5.). Danish could also be considered such a case, but the attribution of the two pronouns for 'nobody' and 'nothing' to different subtypes is not straightforward, as discussed in 6.3.2.2. Here it will suffice to point out its position straddling the two types ⟨N vs. S⟩ and ⟨S⟩, indicated in the schema with underlining. From the point of view of geographic distribution, the type ⟨N vs. S⟩ is decidedly predominant. The second most represented type is ⟨A vs. S⟩, which is distributed at the western and northern boundaries of the European territory (Basque; Irish and Scottish Gaelic; Lapp, Finnish). Note that the isogloss of this type crosses the Celtic group, confirming the division of Goidelic and Brythonic, while amongst the Finno-Ugric languages Hungarian shares the dominant European characteristic. The type ⟨N vs. S vs. A⟩ (English) and the type ⟨S⟩ (colloquial Frisian in part; Danish in part; Estonian), decidedly in the minority, are situated on the borders of the areas of diffusion of the two principal types. Recall, however, that Norwegian and Swedish appear to give way in the direction of type ⟨S⟩ and that Icelandic, while distinct from these two and confirming its conservative status, has specialised the pronoun *neinn* to the value A,[42] thus moving closer to the type represented uniquely in Europe by English. From the areal point of view, what seems to emerge from all of these facts is the tendency to extend the type ⟨S⟩ at the expense of the major type and to form a more homogeneous northern area.

The schema (74) reproduces the distribution of the four sub-types of the macro-type ⟨N vs. S⟩.

(74)   Opposition of quantifiers: sub-types <N vs. S>
           nobody/somebody; nothing/something
           Legend:
           Rus: N vs. S$_1$ vs. S$_2$
           IT: N vs. S
           Pro: N vs. SA
           grk: NA vs. S
           CAT/   co-presence of different sub-types for 'nobody' and 'noth-
           cat: ing'
           shadow: languages with no N items
           *(*):   languages with problematic classification
           −:   boundary of the macro-type <N vs. S>

POR					Lap		Fin	
	ICE*							
				Nor	Swd		Est	
	Ir	ScGl	CFrs*		*DAN*****		**Ltv**	
	WLS	Eng	CFrs*/LFRS				*Lith*	
	BRE	FR	DUT	GER		POL	*Bylr*	*Rus*
	Bas	**Pro**		RMNS	CZ	**Slk**	*Ukr*	
POR	SPN	CAT/cat	IT	FRL	*Slv*	HUN		
		SRD		*Alb*/ALB	*Scr*	RUM		
			MLT	grk	MAC	BUL		

As far as the diffusion of the sub-types ⟨N vs. S⟩ is concerned, cases of asymmetry in the behaviour of the pronouns for 'nobody' and 'nothing' are also in a minority: Catalan and Albanian as well as colloquial Frisian, already discussed above. The 'pure' type ⟨N vs. S⟩ is the one most widely represented. Of the other three sub-types, that which is quantitatively most significant is the sub-type ⟨N vs. S$_1$vs. S$_2$⟩, which densely covers the most eastern area (Lithuanian, Belorussian, Russian, Ukrainian), but is also found in Slovenian, Serbian and, partly, in Albanian. The sub-type ⟨N vs. SA⟩ is found in Norwegian, Swedish, and Latvian to the north, partly in colloquial Frisian, and still sporadically in

Slovak and Provençal. Since, from a functional point of view, this sub-type represents an expansion of the S items in the direction of A, it is interesting to find this type in the northern border zone like a hinge between the extreme cases of Danish (and colloquial Frisian) on the one hand and Estonian on the other. Finally, the type ⟨NA vs. S⟩ is the most marginal, being present only in Greek and Catalan, and in the latter only for *res* 'nothing' and not for *ningú* 'nobody'.[43]

6.7. Observations on the S items

As anticipated in 6.3.3., we now turn our attention to an examination of the value S assigned on the basis of the procedure outlined in 6.4. to the indefinites of individual languages, and to studying the behaviour of the counterparts to Eng. *somebody, something* in the context of the following sentence, corresponding to the entry Q18 of the questionnaire.

(75)   *Somebody didn't see something*
         Qualcuno non vide qualcosa.

The literal translation of (75) or the preference accorded to alternative constructions to render the sense of 'There is something that somebody has not seen', will serve as a measure of the existential value of the S item in the various types of oppositions. As we shall see, difficulties do not only emerge in the languages with just one ⟨S⟩ item, and languages of the sub-type ⟨N vs. SA⟩, i. e. those languages with functionally weaker S items (in that they are used indiscriminately for the values N and A as well).

The majority of the languages under examination has two pronouns of type S and standard negation. Aside from languages of the 'pure' type ⟨N vs. S⟩ such as Italian and languages of type <N vs. S vs. A> such as English, languages of type ⟨A vs. S⟩, such as Basque and Finnish also behave in this way, cf.

(76)   Basque
         Norbait-ek   *zerbait*   *ez*   *zuen*   *ikusi*
         somebody-ERG   something(ABS)   NEG   AUX   seen

(77)   Finnish
         Joku   *e-i*   *nähnyt jotain*
         somebody:NOM   NEG-3SG   seen   something:PART

Estonian also knows this strategy: although it is a language with just one item, it makes use of the formative *mitte*, discussed in 6.3.2.3., with which it is possible to indicate an N interpretation in ambiguous contexts. This allows both the pronouns to be used with the value S, as the following example shows.

(78)   *Keegi*   *ei*   *näinud midagi*
         [S/+anim]:NOM NEG seen   [S/−anim]:PART

On the other hand, consider the following examples:

(79)   *Keegi*   *ei*   *näinud mitte midagi*
         [S/+anim]:NOM NEG seen   NEG [S/−anim]:PART
         'Somebody didn't see anything (lit. 'nothing')'

(80)   *Mitte keegi*   *ei*   *näinud midagi*
         NEG [S/+anim]:NOM NEG seen   [S/−anim]:PART
         'Nobody saw anything (lit. 'something')'

    Amongst the languages of the macro-type ⟨N vs. S⟩, the informant for Catalan gives a reply with doubts about its grammaticality:

(81)   ?*Algú no ha vist quelcom.*

As for Greek, some informants reply with S items, cf.

(82)   *Kápoios dén eíde káti.*
         'Somebody has not seen something'

while others do not accept the cooccurence of *kápoios* and negation and give the following reply:

(83)   *Dén eíde káti.*
         'He has not seen something'

Due to the uncertainty of the examples it is better to catalogue Greek as well amongst the dubious cases.[44]
    Furthermore, in Lithuanian, Provençal, and colloquial Frisian the meaning of (75) is not distinguished from that of the entry Q17 (*Somebody didn't see anything/Qualcuno non vide niente*), which should not be surprising given that they are ⟨N vs. SA⟩ languages; the same goes for literary Frisian and Dutch, which belong instead to the 'pure' type ⟨N vs. S⟩.[45]
    Other replies tend to play down the indefiniteness of one or both the quantifiers involved. The languages which have more series of indefinites, such as Russian, Belorussian and Lithuanian, make use of more specific ones.[46] Cf.

(84)   Russian
         koe-kto   *ne*   *uvidel*   koe-čego
         somebody NEG saw:PFV something

(85)   Belorussian
         kual'ki-xto *ne*   *bačyŭ* kual'ki-čago
         somebody NEG saw   something

(86)   Lithuanian
         Kažkas   kažko   *ne-mate·.*
         somebody something NEG-saw

A second strategy consists in translating Eng. *someone* with other existential quantifiers, that however are not intrinsically so in that they appear in the plural, like Italian *alcuni* 'some'.[47] German and Portuguese give replies of this sort. Cf.

(87)   German
         Einige   *haben etwas*   *nicht gesehen.*[48]
         some:PL have   something NEG seen

(88)   Portuguese
         Alguns   *não*   *viram*   *alguma coisa.*
         some:PL NEG   saw:3PL something

It. *qualcosa*, Eng. *something* is rendered with other expressions, albeit general ones, only in Norwegian:[49]

(89)   *Noen*   *så*   *ikke*   *en del*   *ting.*
         somebody saw   NEG   a   part   thing

In Russian and the other languages of this group the choice of more specific indefinites has to do with the possibilities of the system, and is obligatory because the test sentence, although decontextualised, implies a specific reading of the two quantifiers. Amongst the other languages which make use of expedients which may be labeled as being the result of strategies aiming at an increase in referentiality, we find Norwegian, which belongs to type ⟨N vs. SA⟩ and tends, at least in the colloquial varieties, to become a one item language, not to mention German, where we have noted (cf. (71) in 6.5.) a certain 'weakness' in *jemand*. Analogous weaknesses in S items, despite the systems of oppositions to which they belong, may be also noted in Portuguese and Greek.

Two further Nordic languages with weak S items adopt the strategy which reduces the indefiniteness together with a strategy of introducing the topic by means of a presentative construction. These languages are Danish, which has more than once been the object of discussion, and Swedish, which like Norwegian belongs to type ⟨N vs. SA⟩.

(90)   Danish
         Der   *var*   *nogen,*   *der*   *ikke*   *så*   *det*   *hele.*
         There was   somebody REL   NEG   saw DET   all
         'There was somebody who didn't see everything'

(this translation was given as a second alternative next to *Der var nogen, der ikke så noget*, lit. 'There was somebody who did not see something').

The indefinite *nogen* is inserted into the presentative construction *der var X der*, while 'something' is reformulated by means of a universal quantified expression.[50]

In Swedish, instead, the presentative construction contains a referential expression which substitutes the indefinite subject of the original sentence, cf.

(91)   Swedish
        Det fann-s   de   som   inte   såg   någonting
        that find:PRET-PASS DEM:PL REL NEG saw something
        (lit.: 'It was found those who not saw something').

Finally, mention must be made of Irish, which belongs to type ⟨A vs. S⟩ and which has for (75) a presentative construction, although there may be doubts concerning its grammaticality, cf.

(92)   *? Bhí duine   éigin   nach   bhfaca rud   éigin.*
        was person some NEG:REL saw   thing some

The diffusion of the various types of reply and avoided reply throughout the languages of Europe is shown in schema (93), which reproduces the distribution of the sub-types of oppositions ⟨N vs. S⟩ (see (74)). Note that to the West and the North of the ⟨N vs. S⟩ isogloss, Basque, Irish, Gaelic, Lapp and Finnish are of type ⟨A vs. S⟩, Estonian of type ⟨S⟩.

(93)   Replies to Q18
        ( ): languages avoiding reply
        1:   S Neg S
        2:   languages which differentiate Ss
        3:   other expressions for S
        4:   presentative constructions
        ?:   doubts as to grammaticality
        n.b.: for language symbols, see the list of abbreviations on p. x; see
              also the Legend for schema (74)

					Lap2		Fin1	
ICE*1				Nor3	Swd4		Est1	
Ir4?	ScGl	(CFrs*)			*DAN***4		(Ltv)	
WLS1	Eng1	(LFRS*)					Lith2	
BRE1	FR1	(Dut)	GER3			POL1	Bylr2	Rus2
Bas1	(Pro)		RMNS1	CZ1		Slk1	Ukr	
POR2	SPN1	CAT/cat1? IT1	FRL1	*Slv*1		HUN1		
	SRD1		*Alb*/ALB1	*Scr*1		RUM1		
		MLT1	(grk)?	MAC1		BUL1		

Schema (93) brings to light a certain overlapping between the types of quantifier oppositions and the possibilities of translating Q18, as has already been seen in the preceding discussion. From the areal point of view it is interesting to find that the area of greatest 'tension', with the presence of alternative constructions, is straddled across the dense area of the macro-type ⟨N vs. S⟩ and the area ⟨A vs. S⟩, including the languages adjacent to that area (Frisian, Dutch, German).

By way of conclusion we observe also that amongst the values N, S, A, the value S is always present in each of the four basic types and thus occupies a central position in the quantifier systems. In general terms, it may be said that the presence of a quantifier with the value N implies the presence of the corresponding quantifier with the value S. This makes it possible to have languages with N and S quantifiers (for example, Italian), languages with only the quantifier S (for example, Danish in most of its system), languages with neither N nor S quantifiers, a type which Irish seems to come close to (cf. Chapter 7.3.4.), but excludes languages which have only the quantifier N.

In effect the value N may be easily arrived at via an operation typical of the spoken level, that is, by placing the item with the value S clearly within the scope of NEG, as has been seen in Dan. *ikke ... nogen/noget*. Furthermore, that an S item may assume the value of a generic existential quantifier A in interrogatives raises no problems from a logical point of view, in that it has to be assumed that the referent exists in such a way as to be able to be seen (cf. Q12: Eng. *Have you seen anything?*, Dan. *Har du set noget?*). This also brings A into the logical domain of S.

These observations may explain the progressive marginalisation of items with the value N in northern Germanic (greatest in Danish, but absent in Icelandic) and the substitution of lit. Fris. *nimmen* 'nobody' with *net ien* in colloquial Frisian (see 6.5.).

Nevertheless, at the level of usage, the basic nature of items with the value S, as far as it appears from the comparison of the systems made in this chapter, is found to be in a critical position, in that the functional weight of N items is far greater than that of S items. In fact it is important, and is also frequent, especially in the spoken language, to negate absolutely that somebody has done something,[51] while the use of S items in declarative sentences with positive polarity is not as important (and probably not as frequent) in view of their indeterminateness.[52] On the other hand, their very indeterminateness makes them more liable to use in non-factual contexts, such as direct and indirect interrogatives or protases of hypothetical clauses, obviously when there are no items with the value A specifically reserved for such contexts, such as in English.[53] It is, in short, pragmatically more 'natural' to ask *Has someone called?*, or to hypothesise *If someone calls/were to call* [...], rather than to state *Someone has called/calls*.

In these conditions, the operations that allow a grammatical item to take on either the value S or the value N or the value A, illustrated above, compromise its stability. In the case of these operations applying with high frequency, the item with an original S value may become a generic existential (value A) and end up by assuming an intrinsically negative value, as is fully illustrated in 2.3.

In the case of a massive loss of value of the S items and their potentially being drawn to the value of A or even N, the reaction should be in terms of a reestablishing of the S items whether in particular contexts of usage or at the system level.

At the level of usage, proof of this 'reaction' is found in the S items or locutions obtained through strategies of increase in referentiality discussed above (in this section) in particular contexts such as that constituted by the entry Q18 (*Somebody didn't see something* / *Qualcuno non vide qualcosa*) and illustrated, for example, by Norw. *Noen så ikke en del ting* (lit. 'Somebody saw not a part thing').

The exclusion of Ger. *jemand* not only from particular contexts such as Q18 (cf. *Einige haben etwas   nicht gesehen*, lit. 'Some …'), but also from the positive elliptical replies elicited via Q15 (*Didn't you see anyone?* − *Yes, I did see someone*, translated as *Doch, ein paar Leute*, lit. 'Yes, a pair of people'), and its substitution with *einige* 'some' (plural) or with other expressions, illustrates perhaps the start of a process of reconstitution of an S item also at the system level. The same goes for Portuguese, discussed in 6.5. (see example (72)) and in this section (see example (88)).

The extreme case of a reaction by the system to the loss of an S item is represented in languages in which an S item has been reconstructed from an N item. In Europe we have only three examples of this: Maltese, some Gallo-Italic dialects (in particular Bergamasque), some varieties of Rhaeto-Romansh.

In Maltese we have the pronoun *xi ħadd* 'somebody', formed by *xi* 'some' (cf. Aquilina 1965: 98)[54] and from *ħadd* 'nobody', which in turn is derived from class. Ar. *ʔaħad,* where it had the value AS.[55] *Xi ħadd* again might be traced back to the operating of strategies reinforcing the referentiality of *ʔaħad* in order to contrast its development into a negative meaning. The formation of the homologous non−animate *xi ħaġa* 'something', which synchronically is opposed to *xejn* 'nothing', but diachronically connected to the A item *ħāġa* in Egyptian Arabic and other dialects, may be adduced in support of this hypothesis.

The evolution of Maltese is a clear illustration of a case of transition from a stage with only AS items (such as classical and literary Arabic) first to a stage in which the conditions of use discussed above have brought about an intermediate system with only AN items and finally a third stage, that of modern Maltese, in which the S 'slot' was occupied by items re-formed on the basis of the AN items *ħadd* and *ħaġa*, as schematically illustrated in (94).

(94)

	Development of Maltese quantifiers		
	Class. Arabic	interm. stage	Maltese
S		?	xi hadd
	?aḥad		
A			
		ḥadd	
N	NEG?aḥad		ḥadd

The case of the Gallo-Italic dialects and the relevant varieties of Rhaeto-Romansch may be illustrated by Bergamasque,[56] which has the following paradigm:

(95)   *(v)ergü* 'somebody' − *nigü/nisü* 'nobody'
         (v)ergót 'something' − *negót* 'nothing'

Diachronically, the N pronouns show incorporation of the negation *ne(c)-*, the S pronouns the formative *ver(e)-* from Latin *vere*, also found in Tuscan *veruno* (< *ver(e)-unu(m)*) 'anybody, nobody'. In the case of the non−animate pronouns *(v)ergót* and *negót* it is difficult to reconstruct the historical evolution. Within the typological framework outlined here, it is anyway interesting to note that the *-gót* formations (latin *gutta(m)* 'drop') may only have developed from negative polarity items indicating little or insignificant quantities along the lines fully described in 2.3. Later on they entered negative sentences as A items.[57] From the A stage it may be imagined that, once the intrinsically negative form with incorporation of negation *negót* is affirmed, the form **ver(e)gutta(m)* was available, thanks also to the meaning of the prefix *vere-*, to take on the value S when the evolution from Latin to the Gallo-Italic dialects and Rhaeto-Romansch caused a complete restructuring of the system of indefinites and the loss of many Latin S items.[58]

The pair of animate pronouns *(v)ergü* − *nigü* follow essentially the same pattern of development as *(v)ergót* − *negót*. The importance of the N item in constituting the paradigmatic opposition, however, is more evident here, since the S item was analogically rebuilt on the model of the N item *nigü*. In fact, from a probable original **(v)erü* (< *ver(e)-unu(m)*) we have the non-etymological outcome *(v)ergü*. With the other three terms it constitutes a perfect paradigm having four oppositions, based on *-gü* for the animate and *-gót* for the non−animate, and on the formatives *(v)er-* (value S) and *ne-* (value N).

Although somewhat rare, on the basis of the data we have to hand these cases of S items formation based on or derived from N forms in languages with prevalent (see Maltese) or uniquely (see Bergamasque) oral traditions seem to illustrate well how the prominence of N forms in the spoken language renders them more salient than the S forms. At the same time, the semantic importance and basic nature of the latter in the system forces them to be reconstructed whenever they are lost or marginalised due to the conditions governing their use in discourse.

The hypothesis that there exists a 'strong' implicational rule that obliges a linguistic system with N items to also have the corresponding S items, which we have illustrated here and sought to establish on the basis of data drawn only from European languages, is of course to be corroborated by a larger and more representative sample of languages such as that elaborated by Peter Kahrel (in prep.).

7. Morphological typology of negative quantifiers

7.1. Introduction

Chapter 6 dealt in detail with the classification of quantifier systems on the semantic level starting out from the problem of how to unambiguously characterise a negative quantifier in a language. To this end a test was proposed concerning the possibility for the quantifier in question of constructing negative elliptical replies with it (see 6.3.1.). This chapter is instead concerned with seeking the general principles of paradigmatic organisation (i. e. morphological structure) of negative quantifiers, identified in each language by application of the procedure indicated above. The organisational principles and the types of paradigms that derive from them will be characterised according to the grammatical categories of the negative quantifiers and the morphological type to which their formation may be attributed on the synchronic level. The discussion will then move on to consider ways of codifying the main semantic categories in order, finally, to make an attempt at establishing whether more basic items within the inventories of negative quantifiers exist.

In this chapter attention will be concentrated exclusively on intrinsically negative quantifiers, that is, those with N value (: 'nobody', see 6.3.1.). A or S quantifiers will be also taken into consideration, but to a lesser extent.

7.2. The inventories of negative quantifiers: semantics and grammar

The test for negative value in elliptical replies, which has already been used to construct the typology of opposition systems for quantifiers as discussed in 6.3. and 6.4., may also be used to establish the inventory of intrinsically negative quantifiers in each language.

At the the expression level, the inventory will include only those intrinsically negative quantifiers for which autonomous lexemes do exist, to the exclusion of all analytic (often descriptive) expressions which utilise autonomous quantifier forms.[1]

For example, in Italian the inventory may comprise the lexical entries *nessuno* and *niente* (pronouns), *mai* (adverb), *nessuno* (determiner, or adjective, according to the terminology adopted here). The latter is identified on the basis of the following example:

(1)   *Quale automobile preferisci? – Nessuna.*
       'Which car do you prefer? – None (= no (car))'

The inventory of negative quantifiers in Italian will not, however, include adverbial expressions of the type *in nessun luogo/da nessuna parte* (lit. 'in no place') 'nowhere' or *in nessun modo/in nessuna maniera* (lit. 'in no way') 'no way' and suchlike. These prepositional phrases, albeit relatively fixed, are formed from lexical elements, which render the expression 'transparent', when accompanied by *nessuno* in adjectival function, which guarantees intrinsic negativity and the possibility of constructing elliptical negative replies, cf.

(2)   *Dove sei stato? – Da nessuna parte.*
       'Where have you been? – Nowhere'

In German, on the other hand, the question in example (2) has a reply consisting of an autonomous adverbial element, and not an analytic and transparent expression of the type *an keinem Ort*.[2] Cf.

(3)   *Wo bist du gewesen? – Nirgends.*

It is interesting to note that asymmetries in the expression of the different categories of quantification may be also found in the inflectional categories of a pronoun, as is shown by the case of Latin *nihil* 'nothing', used only in the nominative and accusative and substituted in the other cases by analytic expressions (GEN *nullius rei*, DAT *nulli rei*, ABL *nulla re*).

The inventories of negative quantifiers may vary quite considerably in size from language to language. Russian, like other Slavic languages, has an inventory composed of at least 11 elements,[3] cf.

(4)   *nikto* 'nobody' (pronoun), *ničto* 'nothing',
       ničej 'of nobody', *nikakoj* 'no' (adjective),
       nikogda 'never'
       nigde 'nowhere'
       nikuda 'to nowhere'
       niotkuda 'from nowhere'
       nikak 'no way'
       niskol'ko 'in no quantity'[4]
       nipočëm 'for no reason' (only colloquial)[5]

Italian for its part has an inventory which includes only three forms: *nessuno* 'nobody', 'no' (pronoun and adjective), *niente* 'nothing', *mai* 'never'.

In Europe there is no language having the possible minimum of a single negative element. Danish, however, which shows a clear tendency to eschew the use of negative quantifiers (cf. 6.3.2.2.), maintains the adverb *aldrig* 'never' consistent in its negative value, cf.

(5) [Q21] *Hans havde aldrig løbet så hurtigt*
           John had   never run   so fast

Thus, if one may be allowed to project this situation diachronically, the developmental tendencies of Danish may well result in a potential case of an inventory comprising a single negative element, i. e. the adverb *aldrig*.

As can be clearly seen in the inventory of N elements in Russian recorded in (4), the grammatical categories represented are usually substantives (or rather, using more traditional terminology, pronouns, cf. *nikto* 'nobody', *ničto* 'nothing'), determiners (or, according to the more traditional terminology adopted here) adjectives, cf. *nikakoj* 'no', *ničej* 'of nobody', which agree in gender, number and case with the noun to which they refer (cf. *nikakaja*, *ničja* (FEM), *nikakoe*, *nič'ë* (NEUT)), adverbs (*nikogda* 'never', *nigde* 'nowhere' etc.).

Russian's rich inventory of negative quantifiers also allows us list the semantic categories that may be represented by means of autonomous forms in quantifier inventories:

(6)   ANIMATE: *nikto* 'nobody', *ničej* 'of nobody';
          NON-ANIMATE: *ničto* 'nothing';
          TIME: *nikogda* 'never';
          PLACE (with possibly more subtle distinctions as in Russian):
                               nigde (state),
                               nikuda (movement to a place),
                               niotkuda (movement from a place);
          MANNER: *nikak*;
          QUALITY: *nikakoj*;[6]
          QUANTITY: *niskol'ko*;
          CAUSE/PURPOSE: *nipočëm*.

These observations on the inventories from a quantitative point of view and from the point of view of the grammatical and semantic categories represented in them, allow us now to go ahead and deal with their internal structure, in terms of both the paradigmatic organisation of the elements they comprise and of the importance given to each of the semantic categories individuated within them.

7.3. The morphological organisation of the inventories

Of the possible types of morphological organisation of the inventories of negative quantifiers, the most widespread amongst the languages of Europe are derivation by means of negative prefixes and suppletion.

7.3.1. Derivation

The first of the two types, derivation by means of prefixation (more traditionally known as incorporation of negation), is again typically illustrated by Russian, where negative quantifiers are constructed by means of a formative *ni-* prefixed to interrogative pronouns and adverbs. They thus constitute a paradigm whose cohesion is reinforced by the fact that the various S value quantifiers are also formed from interrogative pronouns and adverbs by means of processes of suffixation or prefixation (that is *-nibud', -libo, -to; ne-, koe-*). In Russian, then, there are series of regular formations, as exemplified by the table (7).

(7)		ANIM	NON-ANIM	TIME
	INT	*kto*	*čto*	*kogda*
	N	ni-*kto*	ni-*čto*	ni-*kogda*
	S1	*kto*-nibud'	*čto*-nibud'	*kogda*-nibud'
	S2	*kto*-libo	*čto*-libo	*kogda*-libo
	S3	*kto*-to	*čto*-to	*kogda*-to
	S4	koe-*kto*	koe-*čto*	koe-*kogda*
	S5	ne-*kto*	ne-*čto*	ne-*kogda*

The transparency of the Russian negative quantifiers is enhanced in pronominal and adjectival categories by the common inflectional endings of both the interrogative base and other indefinite formations (for example, the accusative of the animate pronoun: *kogo, nikogo, kogo-nibud', kogo-libo, kogo-to, koe-kogo, nekogo*) and in addition by the fact that in PPs the preposition is placed between the formative *ni-* and the base (for example, *ni s kem* 'with nobody'; *ni u kogo* 'at nobody' etc.).

Negative quantifier paradigms constructed with similar processes to the Russian are found in all the Slavonic languages:[7] Russian, Belorussian, Ukrainian; Polish, Czech, Slovak; Slovenian, Serbo-Croatian, Macedonian, Bulgarian. Apart from the Slavonic languages analogous formations are found mainly in Baltic,[8] in both Lithuanian and Latvian, cf.

(8)   Lithuanian
             niekas 'nobody'/'nothing';
             niekada 'never'; *niekur* 'nowhere'

(9)   Latvian[9]
             neviens (MASC), *neviena* (FEM), 'nobody'; *nekas* 'nothing';
             nekads (MASC), *nekada* (FEM) 'no' (ADJ);
             nekad 'never'; *nekur* 'nowhere'

Latv. *neviens* is not formed from the interrogative (like *nekas*, cf. *kas* 'what?'; *nekur*, cf. *kur* 'where?'), but from *viens* 'one', which is also the base for the indefinites (for example *viens otrs* 'koe-kto' (see Veksler-Jurik 1984: 171)).

The schema of formations is therefore the same as for Russian. It is also the same in Hungarian, where the range of derivation processes by means of prefixation of *sem-* to interrogative elements, although with some disruption due to their morphophonemic nature, is widened by the morphological type of the language, being agglutinating. Cf.:

(10)   *senki* 'nobody', *semmi* 'nothing';
             semelyik 'no' (ADJ), *semmilyen*, *semmiféle* 'of no quality';
             soha 'never';
             sehol 'nowhere'[10]
             sehány, *semennyi* 'in no quantity'
             sehogy 'in no way'
             sehányadik 'no one' (within an ordered set)
             semekkora 'of no size' (Tóth 1964, 143)

Lastly, in Albanian[11] there is a paradigm of negative quantifiers formed with the prefix *as-* and the interrogatives. Cf.

(11)   *askush* 'nobody', *asgjë* 'nothing';
             asnjë 'nobody' (also 'no' ADJ)
             (as)kurrë 'never';
             askind 'nowhere'

The formation of negative quantifiers through regular derivation processes therefore occurs exclusively by means of the prefixation of a negative morph to the paradigm of indefinite-interrogative pronouns. From the quantitative point of view, this type of classification permits inventories of considerable size, in which many adverbial categories are represented, to be obtained. Finally, from the point of view of areal distribution, derivation is spread over a compact zone, namely that of Albanian, Hungarian, the Baltic and Slavonic languages.

7.3.2. Suppletion

Suppletion is not actually a true type of morphological organisation with respect to inventories of negative quantifiers in that it merely comprises a collection of different lexical elements which share certain syntactic behaviours. It may be typically represented by French, cf.

(12)   *personne, nul, aucun* 'nobody', *rien* 'nothing';
         nul, aucun 'no' (ADJ);
         jamais 'never';
         nulle part 'nowhere'

Even *nulle part*, despite the fact that the negative meaning is explicitly codified in the adjective *nul(le)*, has to be considered more an autonomous adverbial form than a descriptive NP beause the regular preposition of place (*en, dans*) is missing and because the lexical item *part* is not interchangeable with other synonymous elements (for example, ****nul lieu*). The members of the French inventory[12] illustrate the diverse nature that the elements of a suppletive collection may have after diachronic processes have turned them into negative quantifiers (see chapter 2). For example, *personne* is also a common noun (*la personne* 'the person'), *rien* too is derived from a noun (Lat. *rem*, ACC. 'a thing'), but synchronically it is an isolated lexical item.

Generally speaking the pronoun-adjective *nul* is particularly interesting: though an outcome of a process of incorporation of the negation, transparent in Latin (*ullus* → *nullus*), synchronically it cannot be interpreted as such, in contrast to the Russian formations in *ni-* discussed above, where the transparent process of incorporation is extended across the entire paradigm. From this it follows that even formations such as the Italian *nessuno* and *niente*, which are the outcome of diachronic processes of incorporation of the negation, must be considered, in our perspective, isolated lexical items without any interrelationship on the morphological level: the inventory to which they belong is of a suppletive type.[13]

Suppletive inventories of N quantifiers are found in western, southern and northern Europe. Cf.:

Welsh (*neb, dim (byd)*),[14] Breton (*nikun, netra, biskoas/ morsè*);[15]

Portuguese (*ninguém, nada, nunca*), Spanish (*ninguno, nada, nunca*), Catalan (*ningú, res, mai, enlloc*), Provençal (*degun, res, jamai*), French (*personne, rien, jamais, nulle part*, but see also (12)), Italian (*nessuno, niente, mai*), Friulian (*nissun, nuie, mai*), Rhaeto-Romansch (*ingün, nüglia, mai, dinglur*), Sardinian (*nissunu, nuḍḍa, mai*);

Icelandic (*enginn / ekkert, aldrei, hvergi*),[16] Norwegian (*ingen, ingenting, aldri*), Swedish (*ingen, ingenting, aldrig, ingenstans*), Danish (*ingen, ingenting, aldrig*);

Greek (*kanénas, típota, poté, pouthená*);

Maltese (*ħadd, xejn, qatt, imkien*).

The remaining European languages not included in the two preceding lists and in the related discussion make up a cross-over zone between the two areas, sharing some of the traits, if somewhat weak, of derivation and some of suppletion. English is typical of this group, in that it forms its series of negative quantifiers with the prefix *no-*, which on its own functions as a negative adjective (cf. *no idea*), but the quantifier bases, which occur regularly in the A paradigm (*any-*) and in the S paradigm (*some-*) are partly lexical items (*body, thing*); one is a relative-interrogative adverb (*where*). Finally the negative quantifier of time constitutes an 'exception', even though a lexical item, *time(s)*, occurs in its positive counterpart. Cf.

(13)   *no, nobody, nothing*, never, *nowhere, no way/nohow*
        any, anybody, anything, ever, *anywhere, anyway/anyhow*
        some, somebody, something, sometime, *somewhere, somehow*[17]

A language which is instead very weakly characterised by a classificational schema of derivational type is Rumanian, where all the quantifiers are indeed formed with *ni-*, but where, at least for 'nobody' and 'nothing', the base form is not at all transparent. No regular paradigmatic correspondances with the inventory of S quantifiers may be found. The latter are instead regularly derived from interrogative pronouns by means of the suffix *-va* (Klein-Ceauşescu 1979: 137 and 50), cf.

(14)   N: *nimeni, nimic, niciodată, nicăieri*
        S: *cineva, ceva, cîndva, undeva*

Between these two extremes German, Dutch and (literary) Frisian show more or less strong traces of regular derivation of negative quantifiers by means of incorporation of a negative element.

In this regard, Dutch exhibits the more regular schema, cf.

(15)   N: *niemand, niets, nooit, nergens*
        S: *iemand, iets, ooit, ergens*

The only exception to the regularity of this paradigm is constituted by the negative adjective *geen*,[18] to which the indefinite article *een* corresponds. Similarly, in Frisian there are alternants of the type *nimmen/immen* and *neat/eat* for the animate and non-animate. In German, instead, the alternants are less regular, here too as a result of diachronic phonetic processes: cf. *niemand* 'nobody' vs. *jemand* 'somebody', *nie* 'never' vs. *je* 'ever', *nirgendwo* 'nowhere' vs. *irgendwo* 'somewhere', but *nichts* 'nothing' vs. *etwas* 'something' and *kein* 'no' vs *(irgend)ein* 'one'. *Kein*, for its part, has a part in the formation of *keinesfalls* 'in no case', *keineswegs* 'in no way', *keinerlei* (ADJ) 'of no type' which constitute a more cohesive sector of the paradigm, albeit marginal; the first two were originally descriptive locutions in the genitive, but they are now fixed, the third results from the application of a word formation rule (cf. Kluge-Seebold 1989, s.v.).

Finally, worth a mention are the inventories of Norwegian (*ingen, ingenting, aldri*), Swedish (*ingen, ingenting, aldrig, ingenstans*), Danish (*ingen, ingenting, aldrig*):[19] characteristics of suppletion (*ingen* vs. *aldri(g)*) overlap here with those of derivation (cf. *ingenting* and Swe. *ingenstans*) of the type already seen in English. They originate from the crystallisation of descriptive NPs with a negative adjective, as the written form of the Norw. locative *ingen steder* 'in no place' still clearly shows (Bjørnskau 1971: 114).

7.3.3. Inflection

Both suppletion and derivation are ways of organising the inventories of forms (in our case of negative quantifiers) which belong more to the domain of the lexicon than to that of the grammar. More precisely, suppletion, as has already been said at the beginning of 7.3.2., clearly belongs to the lexical domain, while derivation, although connected with both the lexicon and the grammar, nevertheless belongs in a not as central sector of the latter as that of lexical morphology.

A type of classification of paradigms of negative quantifiers calling exclusively upon grammatical processes could ideally be realised in a language which possessed a lexical base having the generic meaning of a negative quantifier and a series of morphological processess which modified it, making it take on in turn the meanings of 'nobody', 'nothing', 'never', 'nowhere', etc.

From what has come to light in 7.3.1. and 7.3.2. it is obvious that this type is not found amongst the languages of Europe. Nonethless, the Icelandic negative pronoun/adjective *enginn*, which is inflected for masculine, feminine and neuter genders, seems to come close to it. The masculine and feminine endings, added to the base *eng-*, turn it into the equivalent of the animate negative pronoun/adjective It. *nessuno* (and *nessuna*) and Eng. *nobody* (and *no*); the endings of the neuter turn it into the non animate negative pronoun It. *niente* and Eng. *nothing*. Here is the paradigm of *enginn* (from Kress 1982: 111 with modifications).

(16)

		MAS	FEM	NEUT
SG.	NOM	enginn	engin	*ekkert*
	ACC	engan	enga	*ekkert*
	DAT	engum	engri	engu
	GEN	*einskis*	engrar	*einskis*
PL.	NOM	engir	engar	engin
	ACC	enga	engar	engin
	DAT	engum	engum	engum
	GEN	engra	engra	engra

Schema (16) brings to light the high degree of internal cohesion in the paradigm based on *eng-*; it reproduces in its basic features the paradigm of pronominal inflections used not only for the interrogative pronoun but also for the 'strong' declension of adjectives (cf. Kress 1982, 108 and 84). The irregular singular neuter nominative-accusative form *ekkert* and singular masculine-neuter genitive form *einskis* (in italics in the schema) are not in themselves exceptional in the general frame of the nominal inflectional paradigms of Icelandic.[20] It is also true, however, that the irregularity of *ekkert* seems to recreate a lexical opposition of a suppletive type with respect to *enginn*, being both of them relatively frequent forms.

The possibility of organising the paradigm of negative quantifiers with the purely morphological means described above, implies in fact that a language possesses a sufficient number of 'locative' cases which allow expression of the adverbial categories listed in (6).

Amongst the European (but not Indo-European) languages of this type Hungarian conforms to the derivation type and forms its negative quantifiers with the prefix *se(m)-* (see 7.3.1., ex. (10)).[21] The other European languages with this possibility, Finnish, Lapp and Basque, do not possess negative pronouns and therefore do not even enter into the discussion. Nevertheless, the series of quantifiers with value A in these languages lends itself well, in certain cases, to illustrating concretely the possibility of realising this type, even if not in the pure version hypothesised above.

In Basque, for example, the series of A quantifiers is derived from the base of the interrogative pronouns by means of the prefix *i-/e-* (Saltarelli 1988: 254–255),[22] but part of the adverbial categories listed in (6) is expressed by means of case endings, cf.

(17)[23]   ANIMATE: *i*   -nor

                           [A]   who (ABS)

        NON-ANIMATE: *e-*   *ƶer*

                           [A]   what (ABS)

TIME:	*i-*	no-	*iz*
	[A]	INT	INSTR
PLACE:	*i-*	no-	*n*
	[A]	INT	INESS

Even though in *nor* 'who?' *-r* may not be attributed with the meaning [+ animate], the regularity of formation throughout the categories listed remains evident despite the derivation process and a residue of suppletion (*inor* vs. *ezer*).

An analogous example is supplied by Finnish *missään* 'anywhere', composed from the non-animate pronominal base *mi-*, the inessive suffix *-ssä* and the generalising suffix *-(k)ään* (Whitney 1984: 144 f.), but not by *koskaan* 'ever', in which, however, the usual generalising suffix *-(k)aan* may be identified in the variant required by vowel harmony.

7.3.4. Secondary means of codification

Having examined the manner in which the inventories of negative quantifiers are constituted from a quantitative and a qualitative point of view, we now turn our attention to the strategies used to fill in the gaps in the inventory schemas, in other words how the lack of autonomous codification for certain categories of negative quantification is made up for. We thus come back to the discussion on the asymmetries sometimes found in the inventories of negative quantifiers.[24]

The strategies found in the languages of Europe for expressing those semantic categories not provided with autonomous expressions may be straightforwardly divided into two categories:

  – reconstitution of an expression with N value utilising autonomous N items, in particular the negative adjective;
  – constitution of expressions with non-N value by means of items with the values A or S, or else by means of generalising constructions.

The first strategy is adopted in most of the Romance languages for the negative locative, cf.

(18)   It. *in nessun luogo*, Sp. *en ningún lugar*, Port. *en nenhum lugar*, Frl. *in nissùn puest*

The second strategy is found in the Sardinian *lógu berunu*, lit. 'in place any', a descriptive phrase containing the adjective *berunu* with value A, and also in Welsh *yn unrhyw le* 'in some place',[25] Breton *tu-bennag* (lit. 'place-some'),[26] or Welsh *yn un man, yn unlle* (lit. 'in a place'), which have nuances of constructions with a generalising value; this is best illustrated, in the corpus drawn from our questionnaire, by the Provençal *ounte che siègue* 'wherever it be'.

In Europe, transparent expressions composed with generalising elements are found mainly in Irish, which is close to the extreme case of a language without negative quantifiers and which therefore is faced with the problem of codifying their functions in some alternative way. To this purpose Irish has the widespread, fixed locution *ar bith*, lit. 'on world', postposed to a noun, cf. *duine ar bith* 'anybody' (lit. 'person on world') and *rud ar bith* 'anything' (lit. 'thing on world') already discussed in 6.3.2.4., and also *ar chor ar bith* 'ever' (lit. 'on time on world'), *áit ar bith* 'anywhere' (lit. 'place on world'), *ar dhóigh ar bith* 'anyway' (lit. 'on way on world').[27]

In the framework of the types of organisation of the inventories of negative quantifiers illustrated above, what might be seen in the Irish locutions composed with *ar bith*,[28] leaving aside the fact that they are equivalent to items with the value A and not N, is a strategy which makes use of word formation. In support of this view it may be added that the series of locutions listed above is opposed to an analogous series of locutions formed with the undeclinable element *éigin* 'some' with S value (cf. *duine éigin* 'someone', *rud éigin* 'something', *uair éigin* 'sometimes', *in áit éigin* 'in some place', *ar dhóigh éigin* 'in some way').[29]

In fact, for various reasons, it is preferable to see in the locutions in question a substitute for the autonomous quantifiers. In the first place, as can be evinced from our glosses, the lexical components of the locutions are maximally transparent. These components, for their part, may be substituted by other synonymous elements, cf. *aon duine* 'a person' vs. *duine ar bith* and again *in aon áit* 'in a place', *in aon bhall* 'in a place' vs. *áit ar bith*.[30]

Ar bith is not limited to these locutions, but is a common generalising expression used with indefinite NPs under negation,[31] cf.

(19) *Ní   raibh arán   ar bith   ann*
      NEG was   bread on world there
      'There was no bread' [Q33]

(20) *Níl   tuairim ar bith   agam*
      NEG:is idea   on world by:1SG
      'I have no idea' [Q35]

(21) *Ní   bhíonn   tu-sa   ag tabhairt cúnamh ar bith   dhom*
      NEG is:HAB you-EMPH   by give   help   on world to:1SG
      'You give me no help' (Ó Siadhail 1988: 128)

The various locutions compete with each other without any apparent regularity. In the replies to our questionnaire, for example, *aon duine* is used twice against 7 occurrences of *duine ar bith*, while *rud ar bith* appears 4 times against the 7 of *dada*.[32]

Furthermore, at least in the case of the equivalents of It. *mai*, Eng. *never*, the three alternative expressions in Irish are subcategorised by the tense of the verb; to be precise, *ar chor ar bith* (lit. 'on time on world' and *in aon chor* (lit. 'in a time') occur with the present tense, *go brách* (lit. 'until eternity'?) with the future, *riamh* 'before' with the past. The three expressions seem to establish a relationship of semantic solidarity with the verbal tense, at least from the diachronic if not from the synchronic point of view.[33] A similar situation to that found in Irish is also found in Scottish Gaelic.[34]

To conclude this long excursus into Irish it may be noted that, as proof of the non-quantifier nature of the locutions examined, there is usually no chapter in the grammars of Irish reserved for them and that the relevant information are to be inferred from the dictionaries.

7.4. Types of inventories

Having examined in detail the organisation of the inventories of negative quantifiers and their alternative expressions, we are now in a position to try and make some general observations.

In the first place it appears evident that quantifiers are items of a primarily lexical nature and that even when they form cohesive and diachronically stable inventories, their classification pertains mainly to lexical morphology (see 7.3.1.), and to a decidedly negligible extent to grammatical morphology (see 7.3.3.).

In the European areal perspective, the distribution of the two prominent types of organisation, that is, suppletion and derivation, seem to take the form of a *continuum* along a west-east axis, with suppletion more significantly represented in south-west Europe and derivation in the eastern regions, while central Europe forms the middle ground for the two types which partially overlap. English is an 'exception' and represents a derivative island within suppletion territory. This distribution of derivation and suppletion is also confirmed if the paradigms of N and A items are taken into consideration together, and if the marginal European areas are thus also included (see 6.3.1, 6.3.2). In this perspective the Irish transparent locutions may well represent the extreme case of suppletion, accentuated by the possibility of using various synonyms, while Basque, as English before, constitutes an island of derivation within suppletion territory. The areal distribution of these types, with the gradation from a lesser to an ever greater cohesion of the inventory moving from west to east, recalls the distribution of the structure of noun phrases studied by Bechert (1990). The distribution is summarised in schema (22).

(22)   Derivation and suppletion in the inventories of negative quantifiers
n.b.: The languages where the two types overlap are indicated in
bold type, accompanied by an asterisk for English and Basque
For the language symbols see the list of abbreviations on p. x

Suppletion   Derivation

	Ice				Lap		Fin	
				Nor	**Swd**		Est	
	Ir	ScGl			**Dan**		Ltv	
	Wls	**Eng***	**Frs**				Lith	
	Bre	Fr	**Dut**	**Ger**		Pol	Bylr	Rus
	Bas*	Pro		Rmns	Cz	Slk	Ukr	
Por	Spn	Cat	It	Frl	Slv	Hun		
		Srd		Alb	Scr	**Rum**		
			Mlt	Grk	Mac	Bul		

As far as the relationship between autonomous and secondary expressions of
quantifier categories is concerned, on the basis of the data from the European
languages illustrated in 7.3.2. and 7.3.3. the categories which may be identified
as central are the pronominals [+animate], [−animate] and the adverbial [time].
These categories are shared by all the languages examined with the unique exception of Welsh (which will be discussed shortly). The other adverbial categories listed in (6), that is, those of [place], [manner], [quality], [quantity], [pur-
pose], appear instead to be more marginal, even though the autonomous codification of the category [place] appears to be quite widespread.

Concerning these adverbial categories, the richness of the inventories is clearly
a consequence of the regularity of the formation rule for quantifiers and is more
likely to be found in derivational languages, such as Russian, which served as
our example in 7.3.1. The opposite, however, is not the case: the availability of
a negative quantifier formation rule does not imply quantifier formation for all
the semantic categories listed in (6), as is shown in English which has the items
[+animate], [−animate], [tense], [place], [manner], but not [quality], [quantity],
[purpose] (cf. example 13), or even Rumanian, which is limited to [place] (see
example (14)).

On the basis of these observations concerning the morphological means
available to a language in establishing an inventory of negative quantifiers, we
will now try to check whether the autonomous codification of the various categories in the individual languages of Europe may be reduced to a more general
type of regularity. To this end we start by taking a look at the more marginal
adverbial categories and only afterwards those which we have defined as more
central to the paradigms.

As far as the adverbial categories listed in (6) are concerned and according to the autonomous codifications under examination the following generalisation in implicational terms may be established (albeit conditionally):

(23)   adverbial {mood, quantity, quality} ⊃ adverbial [place] ⊃ adverbial [time]

The presence of intrinsically negative quantifiers of an adverbial category, such as that of mood or quality or quantity (cf. Russian *nikak, nikakoj, niskol'ko*)[35] implies the presence of a negative quantifier of place (cf. Eng. *nowhere*)[36] which in turn implies the presence of a negative quantifier of time (such as Eng. *never*). The implications of (23) may be hierarchically represented as in (24).[37]

(24)   Hierarchy of autonomous codification:

time >	place >	{manner, quality, quantity, etc.}
A	B	C
Breton, Portuguese, Spanish, Provençal, Italian, Friulian, Sardinian	Albanian, Greek, Lithuanian, Latvian, Rumanian, Dutch, Icelandic, (Norwegian), (Swedish), Catalan, French, Rhaeto-Romansh, Maltese	Russian, Belorussian, Ukrainian, Polish, Czech, Slovak, Slovenian, Serbo-Croatian, Macedonian, Bulgarian, Hungarian, English, German

The languages in sector C of the hierarchy (24) have autonomous negative quantifiers for all the relevant categories, those in sector B only for time and place, those in sector A only for time.

In the central sector of autonomous codification of negative quantifiers, which includes the pronominal categories [+animate] and [−animate] and the adverb of time, the data from the European languages under consideration allow the following hierarchy to be hypothesised:

(25)   (+animate & −animate) > time

Indeed, all the languages listed in (24) possess negative pronouns for 'nobody' and 'nothing', while Welsh, not included in the list in (24), possesses only the negative pronouns *neb* 'nobody' and *dim (byd)* 'nothing' and for the adverbial categories makes use of A items, cf. the translations of Q21 (26) and Q22 (27):

(26)   *Ni   redasai   John   erioed   mor   gyflym*[38]
        NEG had.run John [A/time] EQUAT fast
        'John had never run so fast'

(27)   *Nid   oedd gan   John   gyfaill   na   chartref yn   un-man*[39]
       NEG   was   with   John   friend   nor   house   in   a-place
       'John had no friend, no home anywhere'

In support of the hierarchy reported in (25) we may also recall the case of the languages which are substituting S items with N items such as Swedish, where in negative elliptical replies involving the locative adverbial, the usual choice is not for the N item *ingenstans* 'nowhere', but rather for *inte någonstans*, that is, NEG + S adverb[40] — contrary to the elliptical replies with the pronoun for 'nobody', 'nothing' and with the adverb for 'never'. Another indication in support of the hierarchy in (25), although indirectly, is constituted by the case of the Irish A items *aon duine* [+animate] and *dada* [−animate]. In the contexts of Q8 and Q10 these items may constitute negative elliptical replies (cf. 6.3.2.4.) and therefore end up as the first elements of a potential inventory of negative quantifiers in a language which, as has been demonstrated in 7.3.4., has in fact no N quantifiers nor autonomous codifications for items with value A.

To check the general validity of the hierarchy in (25) (as indeed the hierarchy of the negative adverbs proposed in (24)), would obviously require comparison with a more representative range of languages from the typological, genetic and areal point of view.

Even if the vast majority of the European languages that form the focus of our attention conforms to the hierarchy in (25), it is true that in our corpus of data there are cases that render it somewhat problematic, since there exist two languages that have a negative temporal adverb but not the two pronouns for 'nobody' and 'nothing'.

The first of these cases is constituted by the tendency found in Danish and discussed in 7.2. concerning the sizes of the inventories of negative quantifiers. In Danish, in fact, the only negative element still quite stable is the adverb *aldrig* 'never'.

Outside Europe, a similar situation is found in Classical Arabic, where the only element that may appear in elliptical replies with negative value is *abadan* 'never'.[41]

A second problematic point for the hierarchy in (25) is raised by the position of the two negative pronouns for 'nobody' and 'nothing'. As we have seen above, all the relevant European languages possess both pronouns, therefore they do not allow us to conclude if one of the two elements is more 'basic' than the other. Not even the current tendency in Danish concerning the loss of N pronouns helps us to establish a sequence in the loss of the categories codified with N items. As will be recalled (cf. 6.3.2.2. and note 20), the replies to our questionnaire seem to show a greater resistance on the part of *intet*, that is, the

[-animate] pronoun, to the process of loss of N quantifiers, while Jones-Gade (1981: 94) assign greater resistance to *ingen*, that is, to the [+animate] pronoun.

Outside the group of European languages an indication in favour of a greater basicity of 'nobody' may be found in Egyptian Arabic, where *maḥaddiš*, derived from the term *ḥadd* ,with value A, by means of agglutination of the two sentence negation morphemes, that is, *ma-* and *iš* (cf. Bernini 1987b: 47, note 9), may be considered in nature an almost fully N item. In fact it may not constitute an elliptical reply to Q14 and does not therefore satisfy the main test for the identification of N items, cf.

(28)   **La maḥaddiš*[42]
           no nobody

However, it is used to a limited degree in verbal sentences in the function of subject and, like It. *nessuno*, suffices to express negation of the sentence. Cf.

(29)   *maḥaddiš ḍarab-ni*
           nobody wounded-1SG
           'No-one has wounded me' [Q9]

(30)   *maḥaddiš min   il-gunūb   waṣil*
           nobody from ART-soldiers came
           'No soldiers came'

Egyptian Arabic is also an interesting case with regards to the present question because, with the same procedure of incorporation seen for *maḥaddiš*, it has constructed an item with almost full N status even for 'never', on the basis of a generic locution centred on the lexeme *'umr* 'life' accompanied by possessive suffixes, cf.

(31)   *'alašan   ma-'umru-hum-ši   sim'u   n-nas   biyitkallimu*[43]
           because NEG-life-3PL-NEG heard ART-people speak
           'because they have never heard people speak'

Whatever conclusion may be arrived at concerning the predominance of N items with the features [+animate] and [time], i. e. 'nobody' and 'never', with respect to the other semantic categories that we have discussed in this chapter (that is, [-animate] and the other adverbial categories) it will obviously have to follow from a more rigorous survey on the basis of samples from all the world's languages.

Nonetheless, on the basis of the cues given by the data from Danish, Classical Arabic and Egyptian Arabic, it is possible to try and sketch out a functional interpretation of the specific position that the expressions for 'nobody' and 'never' seem to hold in the lexicalisation of intrinsically negative quantifiers.

On the one hand the requirement of an intrinsically negative expression for 'nobody' seems to be linked to the function of negating the referentiality of the subject, usually animate and above all belonging to the presupposed part of the sentence and therefore understood in a referential sense.[44]

On the other hand, the indefiniteness of non-animate items, typically acting as the object of the sentence and therefore included in the asserted part of it, is sufficient to negate their referentiality (cf. Givón 1984: 331–333), as the following example shows:

(32)   A: At CD they know the plans of the supercomputer!
        B: *Nobody/no technician* here has said *a word*.

In (32) B's reply to A's observation denies the implication that 'One of the technicians has passed on information about the supercomputer'. The object *a word*, under negation, being indefinite, is interpreted in a non-referential sense ('There does not exist a word such that ...'). The same does not apply to the subject (??*a technician has not said a word*), whose non-referentiality requires a special marker (*nobody/no technician*) or is predicated by means of a negative existential construction (*there doesn't exist a technician who/no technician has said a word*). The Egyptian Arabic examples recorded in (29) and in note 42 illustrate this situation well. *Maḥaddiš* in fact may only function as the subject of a sentence; in object function the corresponding A item *ḥadd* is found, with, of course, negation on the verb.

Within the diachronic perspective of the origin of negative quantifiers these observations correspond to the possibility of reconstructing for Indo-European only the negative pronoun **nekʷis* 'nobody' and above all to the hierarchy of incorporation of negation, dealt with in detail in 2.1. and in 7.6. respectively.

On the other hand the predominance of 'never' could be linked to the negation of an event for all time/for possible periods of time and not only for the time that the verb tense refers to. Consider the following example:

(33)   A: Charles has dented the wing of the car again.
        B: Well, he never did drive well.

The reply *He didn't drive well* could refer to just the occasion of the collision which damaged the bodywork, while with *never* what is denied is the realisation of 'drive well' in all other possible moments in the past. It is indeed contexts in the past which are crucial for the use of negative quantifiers of time. These quantifiers in Italian, for example, are always expressed even when it is obvious that the negative interpretation is extended to all possible moments; cf.

(34)   *Gianni* era atterrito. Gli fischiavano le orecchie. Non aveva *mai* visto
            né sentito niente di simile.
            [vs. **/?? Non aveva visto né sentito niente di simile]
            'G. was terrified. His ears were buzzing. He had *never* seen nor heard
            anything (lit. 'nothing') like it.'
            [vs. **/?? He had not seen nor heard nothing like it]

A final indication in favour of this hypothesis may be found in the English
based creoles of the Atlantic Ocean and in the Portuguese based creole, so-
called Indo-Portuguese, which in the past tense have a separate negative morpheme derived respectively from *never* and *nunca* as opposed to *no/duon* and *não*
(see Holm 1988: 172, from where the following examples are taken, and 288).[45]

(35)   Miskito Coast English creole[46]
            ai did tayad an neva *kom*
            'I was tired and didn't come'

In the Papia Kristang creole, still Portuguese based, *nunca*, which has given
rise to *ngka*, is instead extended to all tenses. Cf.

(36)   Ngka *ng'-koza*   *n-te*   *mersimentu*
            NEG NEG-thing NEG-have value
            'Nothing has any value'

The frequency of contexts in the past which obligatorily require the use of
an expression for 'never', added to the frequency of contexts in which an expression for 'never' is used to emphatically deny the possibility of realising an event
even outside these contexts (for example, *He will never drive well!*) could greatly
favour the fixing of an intrinsically negative meaning for items originally with
value A or even S, along the lines discussed in detail in 2.3. and again in 7.6.
for the diachronic perspective.[47]

7.5. Negative quantifiers in adjectival function

Regarding the typological regularities illustrated in 7.4. concerning the classification of the inventories of intrinsically negative quantifiers, items with value N
which accompany nominals and which function as noun phrase determiners
merit a separate discussion. Such is the Italian example *nessuno* which, like the
quantifiers *molto, tutto* as well, precedes prenominal adjectives in the noun phrase
and is incompatible with the indefinite and definite articles as well as the demonstrative, cf.

(37)   *(il/ *un/ *questo) nessun altro   povero cristo.*
        the   a   this   no   other poor fellow

The category 'determiner' is particularly evident for the German *kein*, which aside from being in paradigmatic relationship with articles, demonstratives and possessives, all mutually incompatible, has in the singular the same morphological characteristics as the indefinite article and the possessives. Moreover, on the syntagmatic level of agreement within the noun phrase, it agrees with the adjective according to the same rules as them. Cf.

(38)   daß *ein/mein/kein* gutes Deutschland blühe […] (lit. 'that a/my/no good Germany flourishes')
        vs. *das* gute Deutschland […] (lit. 'the good Germany')

Similar observations regarding the syntactic distribution allow items such as Eng. *no*, Dan. *ingen* etc. to be identified as determiners as well.

Still on a strictly morphlogical level, in languages which have agreement for gender, number and possibly case within the noun phrase, the determiner constituted by an intrinsically negative quantifier agrees with the noun to which it refers. See the German example recorded above and, in Italian, *nessun uomo* 'no man', *nessuna donna* 'no woman' (and also in the so-called 'italiano popolare' *nessune idee* 'no(pl) ideas').[48]

Since negative quantifiers functioning as noun phrase determiners are also characterised by these rules of agreement with their respective nouns, and in many languages the agreement rules are the same as for attributive adjectives, one may even speak of quantifiers in adjectival as opposed to substantive function. According to a fairly established traditional terminology, albeit imprecise (for example, pronouns vs. possessive and demonstrative adjectives), in this book we have adopted the term 'adjective' for quantifiers in this function, in the same way we have called 'pronouns' quantifiers in substantive function (such as *nothing*, *niente*, etc.).

Postponing until 8.4. treatment of the interaction between negative determiners/adjectives and standard negation and their obligatoriness with indefinite noun phrases in negative sentences, we will attempt here to describe the morphological types of negative quantifiers in adjectival function which are found in European languages.

Amongst the European languages which have an inventory, albeit minimal (see the hierarchy recorded in (24) and commented on in 7.4.), of N items, there are the following cases:

(A)   languages which use the animate negative pronoun (that is, the one for 'nobody') even in adjectival function;

(B)   languages with a negative adjective which differs from the corre-
            sponding pronoun;
(C)   languages without negative adjectives.

Most Romance languages (Portuguese, Spanish, French, Italian, Friulian,
Rhaeto-Romansch, Sardinian to the exclusion of Catalan, Provençal and Rumanian) belong to the group of languages which utilise the animate negative pronoun as a determiner, that is, in adjectival function; as do the northern Germanic
languages (Icelandic, Norwegian, Swedish, Danish); and also Albanian, Greek
and Lithuanian (cf. *nieku budu* 'no way', where *nieku* is the instrumental of *niekas*
'nobody', see Leskien (1919: 161)).

Amongst the remaining Germanic languages, German is in a position between
the languages of groups (A) and (B) defined above, in that the pronouns *niemand*
and *keiner* are opposed to the adjective *kein*. The remaining Germanic languages
belong instead to the group of languages which use a specific item as negative
adjective: English *no* vs. *nobody*; Dutch *geen* vs. *niemand*; Frisian *gijn* vs. *nimmen*.

Aside from English, Dutch and Frisian, all the Slavonic languages, Latvian
and Hungarian belong to group (B). In some cases the negative adjective is
formed on the basis of the numeral 'one', cf. Polish *żaden*, Czech *žádný*, Slovenian *nobèn/nobêden*. In other cases there are adjectival formations by means of
incorporation of the negation in the interrogative adjective, in turn derived from
the interrogative adverb for 'how?' (see also note 6 to this chapter). Some examples: Russian *nikakoj*, Ukrainain *nijakij*, Slovak *nejaký*, Bulgarian *nikakăv*, Latvian
nekāds, Hungarian *semelyik*.

In many Slavic languages, alongside adjectival forms of this type, to which the
meaning 'of no type' may be attributed (due to the base on which they are formed:
for example, Russian *kakoj?* 'which?'),[49] there is also a possessive adjectival form
('of no'), formed on the corresponding interrogative adjective, cf. Russian *ničej*
(FEM *nič'ja,* NEUT *nič'è*) 'of no' (*čej?* 'of whom?'). Likewise, Hungarian *semelyik* 'no'
(MASC and FEM), is formed on *melyik?* 'which?'. Hungarian also has adjectival
forms with a more specific meaning, cf. *semmilyen, semmiféle* 'of no quality' (see example (10) above). Some languages in this group, in particular Russian, Belorussian, Bulgarian, Macedonian, Serbo-Croatian, Slovenian and Hungarian, seem in
general to avoid the use of these forms, as the translations of the indefinite phrases
in sentence Q22 show (*John had no friend, no home anywhere/Giovanni non aveva amici,
non aveva casa in nessun luogo*), discussed in detail in 8.4. Cf., for example:

(39)   Russian
            U Ivana   ne   byl-o   druz-ej   u   nego nigde
            By John NEG   was-NEUT friends-GEN by   him   nowhere
            ne   byl-o   dom-a
            NEG   was-NEUT house-GEN

(40)   Hungarian

John-nak	*sehól*	*sem*	*volt*	*sem*	*barát-ja*	*sem*
John-DAT	nowhere	NEG	was	nor	friend-3SG	nor

otthon-a
homeland-3SG

In Welsh and Breton negative adjectivals are instead missing, and are substituted with formations with S value (such as Welsh *unrhyw*) or A value (such as Breton *ebed*); they are also missing in Catalan and Provençal, which use the negative 'pronoun' *cap* 'nothing', lit. 'head' (and also in Provençal *ges* lit. 'people', cf. 2.3.) followed by the preposition *de* + NP (partitive construction, as in (39)) in order to insert the indefinite NP into the scope of NEG (for example *s'ausissiá cap de bruch* 'not a sound was heard'; *ai ges d'amic* 'I have no friend' (cf. Wheeler 1988a: 273)). A similar partitive construction which makes use of the pronoun *xejn* 'nothing' is found in Maltese, possibly by way of compensation for the absence of negative quantifiers in adjectival function (cf. a variant of the reply to Q33: *Ma kien-x hemm xejn ħobż* (lit. 'NEG was-NEG there nothing bread') 'There was no bread').

Finally Rumanian, which does not use *nimeni* 'nobody' in adjectival function, unlike its Romance homologues, has recourse to the locution *nici un/o* 'nor one(MASC/FEM)', for example *nici un bilet* 'no(MASC) ticket', *nici o idee* 'no (FEM) idea' (Klein-Ceauşescu 1979: 137).

7.6. No-one, Ulysses and Polyphemus

Still on the subject of negative quantifiers it finally remains to comment on sentences Q8 and Q9. They have been included in the questionnaire for the undoubted interest raised in ascertaining whether the famous metalinguistic riddle of Ulysses at the expense of Polyphemus may or may not be realised in the various languages, a riddle which has sorely tried the ability of many a translator:

Od. IX 366 Οὖτις ἐμοί γ' ὄνομα 'No-one is my name', and 408 ὦ φίλοι, Οὖτίς με κτείνει δόλῳ οὐδὲ [var. ἠὲ] βίηφιν 'my friends, No-one is killing me with trickery, not [or] with might'. The Cyclops' reply disambiguates the term οὖτις and shows how the riddle has succeded: see 410 εἰ μὲν δὴ μή τίς σε βιάζεται οἶον ἐόντα 'if no-one does you violence'.[50] Note that in line 405 onwards the question posed by the Cyclops come running at Polyphemus' call was put in the negative form, characteristic of interrogatives: ἦ μή τίς σευ μῆλα βροτῶν ἀέκοντος ἐλαύνει; ἦ μή τίς σ' αὐτὸν κτείνει δόλῳ ἠὲ βίηφι; 'perhaps one of the mortals is driving away your flocks by force? perhaps someone is killing you by trickery or by might?'

Q8 and Q9 are recorded here as (41) and (42) respectively:

(41) = Q8 *"What's your name?" asked Polyphemus. "No-one" replied Ulysses.*
"Come ti chiami?" chiese Polifemo. "Nessuno" rispose Ulisse.

(42) = Q9 *"No-one has wounded me" cried Polyphemus*
"Nessuno mi ha ferito" gridò Polifemo.[51]

We note straight away that at the spoken level there is no need to make the choices imposed by the conventions of the written form, such as the hyphen in *No-one* or the use of a capital letter for a proper name, as in the title of this section which has intentionally retained the ambiguity by using *No-one*. But even at a spoken level it is not possible to reproduce Ulysses' pun in all languages, whether due to the impossibility of taking up in (42) the morph of (41), or – more often – due to the morphosyntactic constraints imposed on the (negative) sentence (42). Thus Basque has to add the ergative marker *-k* inside Ulysses' 'name' (: *inor-eẓ* 'Anybody-no > No-one' in (41), but *inor-k eẓ* 'anybody-ERG no' in (42) – and not ****inor-eẓ-ek* with the ergative marker at the end, which would have allowed the double meaning intended by Ulysses to be maintained).[52] Thus many languages are obliged – or at any rate prefer – to put the NEG marker in (42), to start with Modern Greek: *(Ho) kanénas (den) me plḗgōse*; cf. in It. *Non mi ha ferito nessuno*: if there were not an alternative with the negative quantifier before the verb (of the type *Nessuno mi ha ferito*), Italian would not be able to translate the pun either. In Hungarian, Lithuanian, Georgian it is also obligatory to have NEG before the verb; cf. also Rum. *nimeni nu văzu nimic* lit. 'No-one saw nothing', with preverbal NEG despite the fact that there is already a negative quantifier before the verb.[53]

Concerning the translation difficulties just now recorded in the note, it is worth noting how the French translation of the Homeric passage in the 'Belles Lettres' cleverly removes the difficulty by avoiding the negative sentence: line 408 which literally reads 'Oh friends! No-one is killing me with trickery, not [*var.* or] with might' is rendered "La ruse, mes amis! La ruse! et non la force! … *et qui me tue? Personne!*' '…and who is killing me? No-one!', while our informant (a classicist!) gives for (42) *'Personne m'a blessé'* (adding: "Je ne vois pas comment rendre exactement le *oûtis* du grec" [I can't see how Greek *oûtis* may be rendered precisely]). Another interesting case presents itself in Estonian where Ulysses' reply in (41) reads *Eikeegi*; but the informant adds: "In the Estonian translation of the Odyssey the answer is 'Ise', the literal meaning of which is ('my-, your- etc.) self'", while for (42) he notes: "in the Estonian translation his [i. e. Polyphemus'] answer is 'Ise tegin', i. e. 'I myself did it'".

As can be seen, a series of ʿNotübersetzungen' – and the exemplification could continue – which in some way tend to save Ulysses' pun which is based on the characteristic of Ancient Greek of not requiring a pre-verbal NEG if there is already a negative quantifier: a clear example of the impossibility of translating 'verbum de verbo' when structural properties of the languages translated from and into come into play at the metalinguistic level (cf. Comrie 1989).

Regarding the Slavic languages, some of our informants have recourse to inversion of the negative quantifier and the verb thus avoiding the need for preverbal NEG: Slovenian (41) …*"Nihče" je odvrnil Odisej* and (42) *"Ranil me je Nihče" je zavpil Polifem*, observing straight away, however, that the normal order should be *Nihče me ni ranil*; Polish (41) … *"Nikt" odpowiedzał Ulisses*, (42) *"Zranił mnie nikt"* … again with the same comment: "The normal translation would contain double negation and a different meaning, i. e. *Nikt mnie nie zranił* meaning 'There wasn't anyone who wounded me'", that is, exactly the sense of what Ulysses wanted Polyphemus to reply to his friends, but certainly not what Polyphemus wanted to mean, since in effect he had indeed been wounded! In other words Polyphemus could not reply in this way and Ulysses' riddle would not work. Even Russian, Belorussian, Macedonian, Bulgarian, Croatian, Czech, Slovak, normally have to mark NEG before the verb (cf. the sentence Q16: 'Nobody saw anything': Russian *Nikto ničego ne videl*, Croatian *Nikto nije ništo vidio*, Bulg. *Nikoi ništo ne vidja*, etc.), hence one has the impression that replies to (42) such as Russian *'Nikto' menja rabil*, Croatian *'Nikto' me je ranio* are if not artificial in order to somehow translate the pun (see the inverted commas added by the informants to the negative quantifiers!),[54] then at least strongly marked.[55]

In conclusion, the Slavic languages and others that, like Hungarian, Rumanian, Lithuanian, have NEG before the verb, are not able to spontaneously reproduce the linguistic trick: Ulysses would not have made out so well if the Cyclops had been native Slavic speakers!

The languages concerned are those which have the greatest diffusion of the negative element in the sentence: Hun. *senki sem látott semmit* lit. 'no-one didn't see nothing', Rum. *nimeni nu văzu nimic*, Lith. *niekas nieko nemate·* compared to languages such as English with a single negated element: *nobody saw anything* (**nobody didn't see nothing* is ungrammatical at least in the standard variety). Compare the well-known examples of dissemination of negation over all the elements of the sentence susceptible to being negated, typical of Russian and of the Slavic languages in general:

(43) *Nikto ni s kem ni o čëm ne govoril*
Nobody NEG with nobody NEG on nothing NEG spoke
'Nobody spoke with anybody about anything'
(Payne 1985: 235)

(44)   *Nikto   nigde   nikogda   ètogo   ne   skazal*
         Nobody nowhere not.ever   that   NEG   said
         'Nobody ever said that anywhere'

(:Tesnière (1966: 236); cf. Moreno Cabrera (1987: 82); For Czech see Mathesius (1937) who aptly notes how this phenomenon, which he calls 'grammatic concord', operates only when there is sentence and not phrasal NEG).

This is the phenomenon which Tesnière (1966: 235–236) called 'négation perméable' as opposed to 'négation imperméable' of the type in (standard, Classical!) Latin

(45)   *nemo   hoc   unquam   dixit* or *numquam   hoc   ullus   dixit*
         nobody that   ever   said   not.ever   that   anybody said
         'Nobody ever said that'

with a single negative element.[56]

Umquam and *ullus* are so-called 'negative polarity' items, that is, items which by dint of always or mostly appearing in negative sentences take on an intrinsically negative value, which they did not originally have (cf. 2.3.; Bosque (1980, 13); cf. also Tesnière (1966, 235) "…mots négatifs non imperméables, qui en principe ne suffiraient pas à eux seuls pour exprimer une négation véritable, mais qui sont faits pour se marier avec les mots négatifs" [non imperméable negative words, which, in principle, would not suffice alone for the expression of a true negation, but which are apt to marry negative words]). Negative Polarity Items (NPI) therefore originate as such inside the scope of NEG; as has been seen in the first part of this book, they are more often than not complements or satellites of the verb, the element in the sentence on which negation is usually focussed: *je ne vois personne* 'I see nobody' (< *persona(m)* 'person'), *no entiendes nada* 'you hear nothing' (< *re(m) nata(m)* 'a born thing'); where *persona(m)* and *(rem) nata(m)* did not originally have negative value. On the basis of the same semantic process the Spanish *en mi vida* 'in my life' assumes the meaning of *nunca* 'never' due to negative polarisation, and in turn *mai* 'never' (Lat. *magis* 'more'!) assumes an adversative-negative value. In Medieval French it is possible to find the type:

(46)   *Pierre n'a pas vu personne*

where the negative quantifier still maintains its original meaning of 'person': 'P. didn't see any person'. In Molière one still finds

(47)   *Ne faites pas semblant de rien*
         'Act as if nothing happened'

where *rien* (< *rem*) has not yet taken on an exclusively negative value which allows (and then imposes, in prescriptive grammars) the elimination of *pas*, and in Québecois French one finds

(48)   *Il connaît pas personne* (Muller 1984: 65).
           'He doesn't know anybody'

This semantic process has made of the many NPIs, such as *mica, pas, brisa, niente, dén* (< *oudén* 'nothing', NEUT) a single negative marker.[57]

The NPIs originate, in SVO languages, to the right of the verb, either as its Object or as satellites, and may subsequently be transposed to the left of the verb in topicalized position or at any rate in a position of strong emphasis:

(49)   *No he estado aquí en mi vida* → *En mi vida he estado aquí*
           'I have never been here → Never have I been here'

(Bosque (1980: 34); note the disappearance of *no* when the satellite *en mi vida* comes to assume full negative value!).[58]

It is, however, important to note that not all NPIs may appear in Subject position:

(50)   a. ***Je ne crois pas qu'un chat*$_{SUBJ}$ *sache cela*
              'I do not believe that a cat know this'

vs.

           b. *Je ne crois pas que Pierre y verra un chat*$_{OBJ}$.
              'I do not believe that Pierre will be able to see a cat'

this confirms that the origin and the function of these NPIs occur in the scope of the verb (von Bremen 1986: 261).

Not all NPIs are grammaticalised as autonomous negative forms: cf. in French:

(51)   *Guy   n'   a   pas   dormi de la   nuit (de la nuit:* NPI)
           Guy NEG   has   NEG   slept of the night
           'Guy hasn't slept the (whole) night'

but not

           b. ***Guy a dormi de la nuit;*

while the following is possible

           c. *Je n'imagine pas que Guy ait dormi de la nuit*
              'I can't figure that Guy has slept the (whole) night'

since the NPI is situated in a clause dependent on another clause which is in itself negative (Prince 1976: 410–411). In an entirely analogous way one finds in Old High German the already recorded (2.2.)

(52)   *ni   was   wiht   gitanes (Tat.* 1,2)
         not was thing done:GEN
         'nothing was done'

with *wiht* 'thing' not yet fused with NEG (which precedes Vb!) to form *nicht(s)* (cf. note 57). A sentence such as *wiht ni was gitanes* would sound highly unlikely, if not downright incorrect (cf. Ramat-Bernini-Molinelli 1986: 241).

The general rule, for negative quantifiers of the type *nessuno, niemand, nobody, nikto* and similar as well, seems therefore to be: in the negative predication an element with a clearly negative character (tends to) precede(s) the verb,[59] that is, Vb must be in the scope of NEG. Those NPIs which have not (yet) reached a full and autonomous negative value (*un chat, de la nuit* and similar) cannot come before the verb if this is not preceded by NEG. When instead the NPI has reached full and autonomous negative value it may be situated before the Vb (whether alone or accompanied by a negative morph, will depend on language specific morphological rules): cf. in Catalan

(53)   a. *No l'hem trobat enlloc*
           'We haven't found him anywhere';
        b. *Enlloc (no) l'hem trobat*

but not

        c. ***L'hem trobat enlloc* (see Wheeler 1988a: 199).

French has *Personne ne m'a blessé* 'No-one has wounded me' and Ger. *Keiner hat mich verletzt* with a single negative morph. The above rule explains the two possibilities in Italian for (41): *Non mi ha ferito nessuno* and *Nessuno mi ha ferito* (but ***Nessuno non mi ha ferito* is ungrammatical!), and in Spanish: *No me ha herido ninguno* and *Ninguno me ha herido* (***Ninguno no me ha herido*).

As has already been mentioned, in Rumanian it is not possible to say ***Nimeni văzu nimic,* but rather *nu* must be placed before Vb: *Nimeni nu văzu nimic,* which causes Ulysses' trick to fail. On the other hand the following is possible:

(54)   *Nu   vine   oricine*
        NEG comes anyone
        (i. e. 'no-one', in a negative context: 'No-one is coming')

which corresponds to the order in Italian and Spanish. (54) is far better than

(54b)   ?*Oricine nu vine*

(see Manoliu Manea 1977: 16): an element with a clearly negative character (such as the universal quantifier *nimeni* 'nobody') tends to precede the verb, while an element less absolutely characterised as negative (*oricine* 'anyone') tends to follow it (but with *nu* before the verb, according to the general rule!).

Languages such as Italian Spanish and Portuguese (which for (42) has *Ninguém me ferio*, for Q16 *Ninguém viu nada* and not ***Ninguém não viu nada*, for Q19 *O João não tinha nada, ele não conhecia ninguém*, still with NEG before the Vb) are situated halfway between 'négation perméable' and 'négation imperméable' and confirm the rule which requires a clearly negative element to be before the Vb.

Let us now also take a look at the origins of the indefinite pronouns/quantifiers with incorporation of NEG: It. *nessuno* < *ne ipse unus*, Old Fr. *neüns* < *ne unus*, Sp. *ni(n)gun(o)* < *neguno* < *nec unus*, Prov. *degun*, Rhaeto-Rom. *ingün*, Rum. *nimeni* < *nemine(m)*, etc. They are essentially constructed like the IE **ne-kʷis*, **ne-kʷos* (Sanskr. *na-kiḥ* etc., Lith. *nie-kas*, Latv. *nekas*), the only negative pronoun which it is possible to reconstruct for the proto-language; and also like Old Slavic *ni-kŭto* (Russian *nikto*, Pol. *nikt* etc.) and the Ger. type *niemand* (< *nie-man(d)*, where *man* 'man' serves the same function as *-unus* in Latin, *-one* in Eng. *none*, *-eís* in Classical Greek *oud-eís* and *mēd-eís*, *-body* in *no-body* etc.). This schema of formations for the negative universal quantifier is therefore widely diffused in its transparency (cf. also Goth. *ni ains-hun* lit. 'not one-and' > 'nobody', OIce. *en-ge* < **ein-gi(n)* lit. 'one-nor', alongside *neinn* < **ne-einn*, etc.).

On the other hand, expressive reinforcements such as (*rem*) *natam*[60] > Sp. *nada*, *nec entem* > It. *neente* > *niente* are typical of the object, representing a negated rheme or comment: see, for example, cases such as *Çid* 475 *todo esto non precia' nada* 'they do not appreciate all this at all (lit. ...all this nothing)'; Giacomo da Lentini, Sonnet IX,6 *né di meve non ho neiente a.ffare* 'and I have nothing to do with me', which behave exactly like those emphatic negative expressions which have not yet been grammaticalised (for example, *Çid* 252 *Non quiero far en el monesterio un dinero de daño* 'I don't want to do a pennysworth of damage in the monastery'; cf. Molinelli (1988: 43−47)). These expressive reinforcements may be moved to the left of the verb following processes of focalisation, as already recorded above; but bear in mind also that not all NPIs may appear in Subject position.

Regarding the negative indefinite 'nobody' it is worth noting that it has instead the possibility of appearing to the left of Vb, that is, in the normal Subject position, as is appropriate to its inherent feature [+animate], without needing to 'copy' the NEG before Vb: *Nessuno venne* 'nobody came' and not ***Nessuno non venne* 'nobody didn't come'. The traditional explanation of the type *Nessuno venne*, *Ninguém viu nada* is that it is a 'raising' of the negation on the universal quantifier, analogous to that which occurs in

(55)   = Q36b *Giovanni non pensa che sia possibile*
          'John does not think that it is possible'

with respect to

(56)   = Q36a *Giovanni pensa che non sia possibile*
            'John thinks that it is not possible'

as if derived from something similar to *Alcuno (non) vide niente* 'Someone has(n't) seen nothing'.[61]

In fact in this case it is likely that the starting point are nominative forms such as *ne ipse unus venit*, without NEG before Vb since the negative element is already in the subject noun phrase, which for its part is regularly found to the left of the verb.

The following models therefore could be drawn up:

a) NEG-Quantifier/Indefinite +Vb (the type *Nessuno venne* 'Nobody came')
b) NEG + Vb + NPI (the type *Non vado passum* 'I don't go a step' > *je ne vais pas* 'I don't go'; *No la he visto en mi vida* 'I didn't see her in my life')
c) NEG +Vb+ (NPI) Quantifier/Indefinite (the type *je ne vois personne* 'I don't see (a person >) nobody'; *âme qui vive* 'living soul')

Note the decidedly more expressive, emphatic character of the Object NPIs or the satellite to the right of the Vb compared to the formations which more frequently form the base of 'nobody': *none* vs. *nothing* (cf. Molinelli-Bernini-Ramat 1987: 176−177).

Once left-transposition of NPIs with negative indefinite value (or negative universal quantifier value) has occurred, some languages such as French, Rumanian and the Slavic languages, have generalised the need for a negative marker before Vb: *Personne ne voyait rien* (=Q16), *Personne n'est venu* (=Q11). But these are grammatical rules which have been extended in a process of mophological uniformity (cf. note 56 and also examples (46) and (47)).

If this is valid we may move on to the following generalisation for European languages: "If an SVO language has the possibility of omitting NEG before Vb when it precedes another negative word, then it will have a negative pronoun 'nobody' with incorporation of NEG; but it will not necessarily have other negative forms (the type *niente, never*) with incorporation".

The capacity for incorporation may be delineated thus:

PRON.[+ANIM] > PRON.[-ANIM] > TIME > LOC.
nessuno   *niente*   *never*   *nigde, nikuda*
> OTHER ADVERBIALS
no way

This hierarchy recalls that of the autonomous expression of negative quantifiers, cf. 7.4., schemata (24) and (25).

Unlike *ne ipse unus* → *nessuno* or even *persona(m)* → *personne*, the negative sense of *alcuno* < *alicunus* < *aliquis unus* is less pronounced; that is, the item is less negatively polarised. And, in fact, it is not possible to say ***Alcuno vide niente* lit. 'Anybody saw nothing' for *Nessuno vide niente* 'Nobody saw anything (lit. nothing)', while *Giovanni non conosceva alcuno* (= Q19 'John didn't know anybody') is possible, although these days of a somewhat affected style.

G. Holtus (1985: 230−231) has briefly dealt with the development of *alcuno*: it may be used as a pronoun and as an adjective, both in positive and negative sense. In the latter case it usually appears accompanied by a negative morpheme; but it is exactly those cases in which the negative morpheme does not appear that are the more interesting for us: for example, *Deliberorno* [...] *che alcuno* (pron.) *per l'avvenire* [...] *deva vendere il grano più di lire dodici lo staro* (pre-1608) 'they stated that no-one should sell wheat for more than twelf liras a [ancient unity of measure]', yet present in modern use (: *In alcun modo si intende agire contro il trattato* 'In no way is it meant to act against the treaty', from TV news, 27.04.88). Note the following, taken from Parini: *colà donde si nega / che ci ritorni alcun*, with obvious echoes of Latin (: *illuc unde negant redire quemquam*, Cat. 3.12 'there, whence it is said that nobody comes back'): of note in the second Italian example is the dependence on a negative verb such as *negare*.[62] This usage is also maintained up to the present day: *Le autorità militari israeliane si sono rifiutate di fare alcun commento sulle circostanze che* ...'The Israeli military authorities have refused to make any comment on the circumstances which ...' (from "Il Manifesto" of 11.02.88). In French, *aucun* has gone further down the line of this development assuming an exclusively negative value (although maintaining the need for another NEG marker before the verb, in accordance with morphological rules specific to French): *aucun n'a cessé d'en témoigner* 'nobody stopped testifying it'; even when it is used as an adjective: *En aucun cas, ils ne sont propres à faire fondre la graisse* 'In no case they are suitable for melting the fat' (examples from Muller (1984: 72−73)).

We have thus seen that a different account of the type *nessuno* with respect to *personne* and their different morphosyntactic conditionings is possible, especially with regards to the need for a NEG marker in preverbal position. The syntactic behaviour of negative quantifiers and their interaction with sentence negation are dealt with in chapter 8.

8. The syntax of negative quantifiers

8.1. Co-occurrence of quantifiers with sentence negation

In general terms, the interaction between sentence negation and quantifiers allows the traditional distinction between languages with simple (or unique) negation and languages with multiple negation, cf. 7.6., to be drawn.

This distinction, however, must first of all take into account the value of the quantifiers involved, whether they are intrinsically negative (that is, with the value N) or not (that is, A or S). The value parameter of the quantifiers involved intersects in turn with the parameter of the possibility of co-occurrence of sentence negation with quantifiers, giving the combinations shown in the following schema, where +NEG indicates the presence of a sentential negation marker and −NEG its absence.

(1)　　Co-occurrence of quantifiers and sentence negation

Quantifier A/S	Quantifier N
+NEG	+NEG −NEG

In the case of non-N languages, that is, those which do not have intrinsically negative quantifiers (such as Basque), or languages which nonetheless have analogous constructions (such as Danish), the quantifier with value A or S must obviously co-occur with the sentence negation morpheme. Cf.

(2)　　Basque <A & +NEG>
　　　　Inor　　　　　　　　*ez*　　*zen*　　　　　　　　*etorr-i*
　　　　[A/+ANIM](ABS)　NEG　AUX:PRET:3SG.ABS　come-PFP

(3)　　Danish <S & +NEG>
　　　　Der　kom　ikke　nogen
　　　　there　came　NEG　[S/+ANIM]
　　　　'Nobody came'

N languages (such as Italian) may have either co-occurrence of sentence negation and a quantifier or a N quantifier incompatible with sentence negation ('−NEG' in the schema). Italian shows both possibilities, depending on whether the quantifier involved is post- or pre-verbal, cf.

(4)   a. *Non venne nessuno* ⟨N & +NEG⟩
        b. *Nessuno venne* ⟨N & −NEG⟩
           'Nobody came'

German, instead, is an example of a language of the type ⟨N & −NEG⟩, negative quantifiers being incompatible with sentence negation, cf.

(5)   a. *Niemand kam*
           nobody came

        b. *? Niemand kam nicht*[1]
           nobody came NEG
           ?'There was nobody who didn't come'/'Everyone came'

Russian, on the other hand, is a typical example of a language allowing only the combination ⟨N & +NEG⟩, as the translation of the examples in (4) shows:

(6)   a. *Nikto   ne   prišël*
           nobody NEG came
        b. **Nikto   prišël*[2]
           nobody came

The fourth case, i. e. S or A and absence of the sentence negation morpheme is not attested for obvious reasons, firstly semantic, regarding the interpretation of the quantifiers − as has been illustrated in 6.3. − but more particularly syntactic, since in such a case the very codification of the sentence as negative would be missing.

The languages of Europe are distributed between the various possible types as follows (cf. 10.7., concerning the parameter of the permeability of NEG):

(i) ⟨A/S & +NEG⟩

CELTIC: Irish, Gaelic
Basque
FINNO-UGRIC: Lapp, Finnish, Estonian

(ii) ⟨N & +NEG⟩

CELTIC: Welsh, Breton
SLAVIC: Polish, Czech, Slovak, Belorussian, Russian, Ukrainian, Slovenian, Serbo-Croatian, Macedonian, Bulgarian
BALTIC: Latvian, Lithuanian
ROMANCE: Rhaeto-Romansh, Rumanian
FINNO-UGRIC: Hungarian
Greek

(iii) ⟨N & −NEG⟩

    ROMANCE: French*, Provençal
    GERMANIC: Icelandic, Frisian, Dutch, German
    SEMITIC: Maltese*

The two languages indicated with an asterisk, that is, French and Maltese, have discontinuous sentence negation. They belong to this type because the quantifiers are incompatible with the postverbal negation morpheme (which, as has been seen, is the main one) even though they require the presence of the preverbal negation morpheme, the one undergoing erosion according to 'Jespersen's cycle' (see 2.) and, at least in French, effectively eliminated in the more colloquial varieties (Ashby 1981). Cf.

(7)   a. French

       Personne n'   *est venu* vs **Personne n'*   *est pas*   *venu*
       nobody NEG1 is come   nobody   NEG1 is NEG2 come
       'Nobody came'

     b. *Jean   ne   mange pas   de   poisson*
       John NEG1 eats NEG2 PART fish
       'John doesn't eat fish'

(8)   *ħadd   ma   ġie*   vs *Ġanni ma   jiekol-x*   *ħut*
       nobody NEG1 came   John NEG1 eats-NEG2 fish
       'Nobody came'   'John doesn't eat fish'

Some European languages allow more than one construction:

(iv) ⟨A/S & +NEG; N & −NEG⟩

    GERMANIC: English, Danish, Norwegian, Swedish

(v) ⟨N & +/−NEG⟩

    ROMANCE: Portuguese, Spanish, Catalan, Italian, Friulian, Sardinian; Albanian

In the Romance languages and Albanian the two constructions are in complementary distribution according to the postverbal or preverbal position of the quantifier, as in the Italian example (4) (cf. again 7.6.).

The geographical distribution of the various types is illustrated in the schema (9), which illustrates the often noted areal marginality of the non-N languages (cf. 6.3.1., 6.4.6. and, for the geographical distribution in general, 4.1.), and shows how the more widely represented types, that is, ⟨N & +NEG⟩, ⟨N & −NEG⟩ and ⟨N & +/−NEG⟩ are uniformly distributed through Europe. It also shows that these types do not, however, fully correspond to the individual linguistic groups, although certain types do predominate in some of them: ⟨N & +NEG⟩ in Slavic, ⟨N & −NEG⟩ in Germanic, ⟨N & +/−NEG⟩ in Romance.

(9)   Co-occurrence of quantifiers and sentence negation: geographical
           distribution of different types
           Legend:
           ScGl: A & +NEG;
           Rus: N & +NEG;
           GER: N & −NEG;
           Eng: A/S & +NEG, N & −NEG;
           IT: N & +/−NEG
           n.b.:   for the language symbols see the list of abbreviations on
                    p. x.

POR	ICE / Ir Wls Bre Bas SPN	ScGl Eng FR PRO CAT SRD	FRS DUT	IT Mlt	Nor	GER Rmns FRL ALB Grk	Lap Swd Dan Cz Slv Scr Mac	Pol Slk Hun Rum Bul	Fin Est Ltv Lith	Bylr Ukr	Rus

	ICE						Lap		Fin		
					Nor		Swd		Est		
	Ir	ScGl					Dan		Ltv		
	Wls	Eng	FRS						Lith		
	Bre	FR	DUT			GER		Pol		Bylr	Rus
	Bas	PRO				Rmns	Cz	Slk		Ukr	
POR	SPN	CAT		IT		FRL	Slv	Hun			
		SRD				ALB	Scr	Rum			
				Mlt		Grk	Mac	Bul			

The isoglosses depicted in schema (9) permit the identification of two main, partially overlapping, subdivisions of the European linguistic territory to be distinguished: on the one hand the type ⟨N & +NEG⟩, represented in the eastern, southern and south-western sectors is opposed to the type ⟨N & −NEG⟩ which is compactly distributed in central and northern Europe, and is thus isomorphic with the distribution of postverbal sentence negation; on the other hand there are the central southern and western areas, where overlapping of the two types (that is, ⟨N & +/−NEG⟩) allows for a further division between a western macro-area, whose common denominator is ⟨N & −NEG⟩ and another eastern area.

Unlike this macro-area, the western area is not tightly-knit and, apart from the overlapping in the southern part of the two types − with or without co-occurence of negative quantifiers and sentence negation − gradates in the northern part towards the marginal area with A and S quantifiers (cf. ⟨N & −NEG; A/S & +NEG⟩ in English, Danish, Norwegian and Swedish).

8.2. Co-occurrence of negative quantifiers

A second aspect of the syntax of negative quantifiers concerns the possibility of more than one negative quantifier occurring in the same sentence, which of course applies only to those languages designated N in 6.3.

Independently of the possibility of co-occurrence of the standard negation morpheme with negative quantifiers illustrated in 8.1. (types $\langle$N & +NEG$\rangle$, $\langle$N & −NEG$\rangle$, $\langle$N & +/−NEG$\rangle$), all the languages examined subdivide into two groups:

− languages which allow a single negative quantifier in the sentence and substitute any others with A or S items which, coming within the scope of NEG, are assigned a negative interpretation;

− languages which allow several quantifiers to co-occur with no restrictions except that of a lexical nature concerning the possibilities offered by the inventory of negative quantifiers itself; in languages with limited inventories but with the possibility of constructing other intrinsically negative locutions (as, for example, the Italian *nessuno* 'nobody', *niente* 'nothing', *mai* 'never' as opposed to the periphrastic expression for 'nowhere' (: *in nessun luogo*, cf. 7.3.2., 7.3.4., 7.4.), the latter may equally co-occur with the more 'basic' quantifiers without restriction.

This aspect of the syntax of quantifiers seems to be correlated with that concerning the potential co-occurrence of sentence negation with negative quantifiers (see 8.1.). However, as will shortly be seen, the latter has a distribution amongst the languages of Europe not entirely isomorphic with that of the types the first gives rise to. To illustrate these regularities we shall take as a typical case the co-occurrence of the two pronouns for 'nobody' and 'nothing', which constitute the lowest common denominator of the inventories of N items present in the languages of Europe (see 7.4., hierarchy (25)), using the replies to sentence Q16 of the questionnaire, cf.

(10)   NESSUNO vide NIENTE / NOBODY saw *anything*.

Italian and English effectively represent the two types defined above: Italian in fact allows the co-occurrence of an unlimited number of expressions containing intrinsically negative quantifiers, while English, at least in the current standard varieties, allows only one negative quantifier (the first in linear order) and uses the corresponding A items for all the others. Cf. again:

(11)   NESSUNO dice MAI NIENTE per NESSUNA ragione
        [N N N N]
        NOBODY *ever* says *anything* for *any* reason
        [N *A A A*]

We will adopt the convention of calling languages like Italian Nx (that is, with x possibilities of co-occurrence of N items) and languages like English N1 (that is, with the possibility of only a single occurrence of an N item).

All languages which allow negative quantifiers to co-occur with sentence negation are Nx languages. They belong to the types $\langle$N & +NEG$\rangle$ (such as the

Slavic languages, the Baltic languages, Rumanian, Hungarian, Greek, Rhaeto-Romansh) and ⟨N & +/−NEG⟩ (such as most of the Romance languages, including Italian). Those languages, such as standard French and Maltese, with discontinuous negation which in the previous section we have classified for convenience as ⟨N & −NEG⟩, are, however, also Nx even though they maintain, at least in some varieties, the preverbal negative element. Cf.

(12)   ⟨N & +NEG⟩
            Russian   *Nikto ničego ne* videl.
            Czech   *Nikdo nic ne*viděl.
            Macedonian   *Nikoj ne* vide *ništo.*
            Lithuanian   *Niekas nieko ne*mate.
            Rumanian   *Nimeni nu* văzu *nimic.*
            Hungarian   *Senki nem* látott *semmit.*
            Greek   *Kanénas den* eíde *típota.*
            Rhaeto-Rom.   *Ingün nun* ha vist *nüglia.*

(13)   ⟨N & +/−NEG⟩
            Portuguese   *Ninguém* viu *nada.*
            Spanish   *Ninguno* vio *nada.*
            Catalan   *Ningú* va veure *res.*
            Friulian   *Nissùn* al a vidût *nuie.*
            Sardinian   *Nissunu* a bbidu *nudḍa.*
            Italian   *Nessuno* vide *niente.*

(14)   ⟨N & −NEG⟩, but with NEG1 V NEG2
            French   *Personne ne* voyait *rien.*
            Maltese   *ħadd ma* ra *xejn.*

Provençal (cf. *Degun* vegué *ren*), which has only the postverbal negative morpheme, may be added to the group. Note, however, that other varieties of Occitan, such as Gascon, still maintain the original preverbal negative element which, moreover, persists in all varieties in certain subordinate constructions (Wheeler 1988b: 273).

Only the Germanic languages, of the type ⟨N & −NEG⟩ but with only postverbal negative elements, are N1 languages.[3] Cf.

(15)   Icelandic   ENGINN sá *neitt.*
            Norwegian   INGEN så *noe.*
            Swedish   INGEN så *någonting.*
            Danish   INGEN så *noget.*

German	NIEMAND hat (*irgendet)was* gesehen.
Dutch	NIEMAND sag *iets.*
Frisian	NIMMEN hat *eat* sjoen.

In brief, the comparison between the possibilities of co-occurrence of several negative quantifiers and the compatibility of negative quantifiers with sentence negation (see 8.1.), seems to underline two facts. First of all, the 'rarity' of languages with uniquely simple negation, that is $\langle$N1 & $-$NEG$\rangle$; in the second place, a certain interdependence between the feature N1 and the presence of postverbal negative morphemes.

In fact, a language having reached the final stage of the so-called 'Jespersen's cycle' seems to be a necessary condition for its being N1 (cf. the Germanic languages vs. French), although not a sufficient one (cf. Provençal and, particularly, the various Gallo-Italic dialects no longer with traces of preverbal negation, all Nx).[4] From all this may be concluded that if a language is N1, then it must also have postverbal negation.

This implication is not falsified by the fact that sub-standard varieties of the same $\langle$N1 & $-$NEG$\rangle$ languages, in particular those of English, German and Dutch, are, as is well known, characterised by the permeability of NEG and are therefore, in our terms, varieties of the type $\langle$Nx & $-$NEG$\rangle$. In fact, as has been seen above, the condition seems to be necessary but not sufficient. In Europe, the only 'illustrious' counter-example comes from Classical Latin, notably $\langle$N1 & $-$NEG$\rangle$ and not a language with postverbal negation.[5]

Yet it is interesting to note that N1 languages, whether Germanic or Classical Latin, are linked by the fact that they possess either a series of quantifiers with value A contrasting with those with value N and those with value S (cf. the type discussed in 6.4.1.), or S items which are 'weak' in the sense illustrated in 6.7. For English and Latin this is illustrated in (16).

(16)　　　English and Latin quantifiers

| | *anybody* | | | *quisquam* | |
| **nobody** | | somebody | **nemo** | | aliquis |

Consider, furthermore, Ice. *neinn* (A) vs. *enginn* (N) vs. *nokkur* (S), and also processes where N elements give way in favour of S elements (yet which also acquire A value) in the other Nordic languages, and finally the 'weakness' of German *jemand, (et)was,* substituted, in ambiguous contexts, by more referential expressions (*einige, ein bißchen,* 6.7.).

We are not able here to determine if it is the process towards N1 that gives rise to A items or, viceversa, whether it is the fixing of A items which favours the feature N1. We put forward this observation as a suggestion for further research concerning the 'rarity' of ⟨N1 & −NEG⟩ languages on the additional basis of a larger comparison with non-European languages.

In effect, the 'rarity' of ⟨N1 & −NEG⟩ seems due to the lack of explicitness of the negative sense in similar structures and hence the need to reinforce it in order to clarify the message.

8.3. The syntax of quantifiers and sentence negation

On the basis of the observations made in the two preceding sections and the types identified there, we turn now to an examination of the combinations of sentence negation, negative quantifiers and the 'basic' order of the constituents which are encountered in the languages of Europe. The combinations are summarised in schema (17).[6]

(17)   The syntax of quantifiers and sentence negation

		Basic order	Position of NEG	Order of the negative constituents
A	1	SVO	NEG Vb	Nx NEG Vb
	2	SVO	NEG Vb	Nx NEG Vb Nx
	3	SVO	NEG Vb	NEG Vb Nx & Nx Vb Nx
B	1	VSO	NEG Vb NEG	(NEG) Vb Nx [?]
	2	SVO	NEG Vb NEG	(N1) NEG Vb Nx
C	1	SVO	Vb NEG	(N1) Vb Nx
	2	SVO/TVX	Vb NEG	N1 Vb & Vb N1

This schema restates above all the tendency to have a NEG marker in preverbal position (it does not matter whether this is by means of a sentential negation morpheme or a negative quantifier) amply illustrated and discussed at various points of this book and in particular in 7.6. With this tendency languages with postverbal position (types C1 and C2 in (17)) and those in particular with the possibility of Vb N1 order (as in English) or Vb Nx order (as in Provençal) are relegated to a statistically marginal position. Note, in particular that in types C1 and C2 it is nonetheless possible to have a negative quantifier before the verb. The only counter-example may be Welsh (the only representative of type B1), which allows the preverbal negation to be deleted. However, the preverbal negation is in fact somehow marked by lenition of the initial plosive consonant or bilabial nasal or even unvoiced liquid of many verbs. Cf. example (18), where *welodd* is the lenited form of *gwelodd*:

(18)   *(Ni)   welodd neb   ddim*
        NEG saw   nobody nothing

On the basis of data drawn from the corpus of the replies to our question-naire, it may be affirmed that, generally speaking, in the linear order of the sentence negative quantifiers occupy the usual position or positions for NPs or adverbs with the same function. See again the Welsh example (18), which re-states the normal VSO order for subject and object nominals, and examples (13) and (14) in the preceding section for SVO order. Concerning the freedom of quantifiers to occupy different positions consider the Italian *Nessuno poteva aiutarli* vs. *Non poteva aiutarli nessuno* 'Nobody could help them'. For adverbials see the following Dutch examples (TVX with the finite form of the verb in second position and the non-finite form in final position):

(19)   *Jan   had   nog   nooit   so   snel   gerend* [Q21]
        John   had   before   never   so   fast   run
        'John had never run so fast'

(20)   *Jan   had   nergens   een thuis* [Q22]
        John   had   nowhere   a   home
        'John had no home anywhere'

Amongst the particular cases of negative quantifier position it is worth men-tioning the case of Fr. *rien*, which is usually placed between the two members of a periphrastic verbal form (cf. *Quelqu'un n'a rien vu* [Q17] 'Somebody didn't see anything').

Also the negative adverb of time is usually, but not obligatorily, placed be-tween the two components of a periphrastic verbal form in Italian (*non era mai corso* 'had never run' [Q21]), French (*n'avait jamais couru*), Provençal (*avié jamai courregu*), Friulian (*nol veve mai curût*), Rhaeto-Romansh (*nu d'eira mai currü*).[7]

The most interesting cases of particular quantifier position are, however, found in languages belonging to types A1 and A2 of schema (17), and especially to type A1, which concentrates all the negative quantifiers before the verb, thus placing the direct object complement in preverbal position and consequently giving rise to a sort of SOV order. The most well-known representative of this type is Russian, cf.

(21)   a. *Nikto   ničego   ne   videl* [Q17]
           Nobody nothing   NEG   saw
        b. *Ivan   nikogda tak bystro ne   begal* [Q21]
           John   never   so   fast   NEG   ran
        c. *U   nego nigde   ne   byl-o   dom-a* [Q22]
           By   him nowhere NEG was-NEUT   house-GEN

This behaviour is shared by the eastern Slavic languages (Russian, Belorussian, krainian) and the Baltic languages, all of which may be included in type A1. 1 he other ⟨Nx & +NEG⟩ languages, that is, those which allow co-occurrence of all the negative quantifiers with the explicit sentence negation marker, are distributed amongst types A1 and A2 according to the quantifiers involved. The distribution is illustrated in schema (22), constructed on the basis of the translations of sentences Q16, Q21 and Q22 of our questionnaire.[8] In this schema, for each of the three quantifiers involved, that is, 'nothing' in object function, 'never' and 'nowhere', the position preceding the NEG Vb complex is indicated by the number *1*, and the position following the NEG Vb complex by the number *2*.

(22)   Position of negative quantifiers

Language	'nothing'	'never'	'nowhere'
Polish	2	1	2
Czech	1	1	2
Slovak	1	1	2
Slovenian	2	1	2
Serbo-Croatian	*2*	*2*	*2*
Macedoanian	2	1	2
Bulgarian	1	1	2
Hungarian	2	1	1
Rumanian	2	1	2
Rhaeto-Romansh	*2*	*2*	*2*
Friulian	*2*	*2*	*2*
Greek	2	1	2
Albanian	2	1	2

Excluding Serbo-Croatian, Friulian, and Rhaeto-Romansh (in italics in the schema), which belong to type A2, the schema appears to highlight a certain propensity for placing the negative quantifier for 'never' in the position preceding the NEG Vb complex (10 cases out of 13) and a clear tendency to put the negative quantifier of place ('nowhere') in the position following the NEG Vb complex (with the single exception of Hungarian). Only three Slavic languages (Czech, Slovak, Bulgarian) have the pronoun 'nothing' preceding the NEG Vb complex.

We have here another manifestation of the asymmetries that charatacterise negative quantifier paradigms. This confirms on the syntactic level the peculiar position of the negative adverb of time already commented on in 7.4.

If languages of type A1, commented on above, are also taken into account,
it is possible to establish the following hierarchy of negative quantifier prepositioning for types A1 and A2:

(23)   Hierarchy of negative quantifier prepositioning
          NEVER > NOTHING > NOWHERE [/ # _____ NEG Vb]

Schema (23) says that in all languages where the negative adverb of place
precedes the NEG Vb complex, the non−animate negative pronoun also does,
and that in languages where the non−animate negative pronoun precedes the
NEG Vb complex the negative adverb of time does too (bar the single exception
of Hungarian).

The regularities and tendencies that have been explained so far would be
better assessed within the framework of a general theory of constituent order
which took into account the pragmatic conditions in which negative sentences
are produced. By definition this is not feasible on the basis of data that have
been collected by sending a questionnaire around.

To conclude this survey of the syntax of quantifiers and sentence negation,
it may be noted that even non-N languages conform to the tendency to assign
to quantifiers with value A the same position as that occupied by noun phrases
or adverbials with the same syntactic function. Cf., for example:

(24)   Irish (VSO)
    a. *Ní   fhéadfadh duine ar bith   cuidiú le-o* [Q20]
       NEG   could   [A/+ANIM] help   with-3PL
       'Nobody could assist them'
    b. *Ní   fhaca mé rud ar bith* [Q12]
       NEG   saw   I [A/−ANIM]
       'I didn't see anything'

(25)   Scottish Gaelic (VSO)
          Cha   chreid   fear-sam-bith   sin (Mackinnon 1971: 253)
          NEG   believes [A/+ANIM]   that
          'Nobody will believe it'

In Basque too, a verb-final language, the pronouns with value A occupy the
same position as the corresponding full nominals in negative sentences, that is,
sentence initial (in the absolute case) with intransitive predicates (cf. example
26a) and, with transitive predicates, sentence initial if in the ergative case (cf.
examples 26b, c) and between the auxiliary and the full verb if in the absolute
case (example 26d).

(26)   Basque

a. *Inor*   *ez*   *zen*   *etorr-i*[9]
   [A/+ANIM](ABS)   NEG   AUX   come-PFP
   'Nobody came'

b. *Inor-k*   *ezin*   *ziezaiekeen laguntza-rik*   *eman*[10]
   [A/+ANIM]-ERG   impossible   AUX   assistance-PART   give
   'Nobody could assist them'

c. *ezer-k*   *ezin*   *ziezaiekeen lagun*
   [A/−ANIM]-ERG   impossible   AUX   assist
   'Nothing could help them'

d. *[Jon-ek]*   *ez*   *zuen*   *inor*   *ezagut-tzen*[11]
   John-ERG   NEG   AUX   [A/+ANIM](ABS)   know-PFP
   '[John] knew nobody'

The order NP$_{ERG}$ NEG AUX NP$_{ABS}$ Vb of example (26d) may be compared
with the following:

(27)   *Jon-ek*   *ez*   *du*   *arrain-ik*   *ja-ten*[12]
        John-ERG   NEG   AUX   fish-PART   eat-APP
        'John doesn't eat fish'

While in Basque the basic SOV order allows a negative interpretation of items
with value A in the preverbal position reserved for focused constituents, in SVO
languages such as Finnish and Lapp the normal SUBJECT-Negative Vb order
(cf. examples (28b) and (29b) below) is inverted. That is, we have Negative Vb-
SUBJECT in the case of quantifiers, which in these languages have value A (cf.
examples (28a) and (29a)), with the consequence that the morpheme which
conveys sentence negation is found at the beginning of the sentence in such a
way as to include the quantifier in its scope and allow a negative reading of it.[13]
Cf. (28) and (29) where a = Q20 and b = Q5:

(28)   Finnish

a. *E-i*   *kukaan*   *voi-nut*   *avustaa hei-tä,*
   NEG-3SG   [A/+ANIM]:NOM   be.able-PPP   assist   3PL-PART
   e-i   *mikään*   *voi-nut*   *auttaa hei-tä*
   NEG-3SG   [A/−ANIM]:NOM   be.able-PPP   help   3PL-PART

b. *Jukka*   *e-i*   *syö*   *kalaa*
   John:NOM   NEG-3SG   eat   fish:PART

(29)   Lapp

a. *I-i*   *oktage*   *sáhttán*   *sin*   *veahkehit,*
   NEG-3SG   [A/+ANIM]   be.able:APP   3PL:GEN   assist
   i-i   *mihkige*   *sáhttán*   *sin*   *veahkehit*
   NEG-3SG   [A/−ANIM]   be.able:APP   3PL:GEN   help

b. *Jovnna i-i*   *bora guoli*
   John   NEG-3SG eat   fish

8.4. The syntax of negative adjectives

8.4.1. Indefinite NPs in negative sentences

A typological comparison with relevance to the syntax of negative quantification concerns the presence or absence of negative adjectives (It. *nessuno,* Eng. *no,* Ger. *kein,* Pol. *żaden,* cf. 7.5.) with indefinite noun phrases having partitive value in negative sentences.

This comparison is illustrated by the Italian and English versions of sentence Q33, which are:

(30)   a. There was *no bread*/There was*n't any bread.*
        b. *Non* c'era pane

In the negative existential sentence (30), Italian expresses the negation on the verb. English on the other hand also expresses it on the indefinite NP: or only on it by means of the negative adjective *no* or, alternatively, also on the indefinite NP by means of the A value adjective *any* if negation is already expressed on the verb.

In each language this type of construction obviously conforms to the regularities discussed in the preceding sections of this chapter concerning the possibilities of co-occurrence of sentence negation with other negative elements. This is demonstrated on the one hand by the two alternatives of the English version of example (30) (English is a language with simple negation) and on the other hand by the Italian sentence *Non c'era nessun pane,* whose meaning is different from (30b) and is equivalent to *There wasn't any kind of bread.*

This last Italian sentence shows another characteristic of the constructions under consideration: languages like English must indicate the non-referentiality of the NP either with an N item or with an A item (cf. ***There wasn't bread*); languages like Italian allow both alternatives, that is, with and without explicit indication of the non-referential NP (but in Italian, as has already been pointed out, the variant with the negative adjective *nessuno* is not synonymous with (30b)). We will return to these observations after having compared the behaviour of European languages with regards to this parameter. The parameter in itself may be summarised as /± obligatoriness of non-referential quantifiers/ for indefinite NPs in the scope of the negation. The discussion will take into account not only Q33 but also the first part of Q22:

(31)   a. *John had no friend* [, *no home anywhere*]
        b. *Giovanni non aveva amici* [, *non aveva casa in nessun luogo*]

This parameter of comparison does not apply to languages which do not have amongst their quantifiers an item for the adjectival category (cf. 7.5.), these being: Basque, Irish, Gaelic, Finnish, Estonian, Hungarian, Maltese.

The Germanic languages behave consistently like English, as is shown by the following examples, in which sentence *a* represents the translation of Q22 and sentence *b* that of Q33.

(32)   Icelandic
        a. *Jón   átti   engan   vin*
           John   had   no:ACC.SG.MASC friend
        b. *það   var   ekkert   brauð*
           that was   no:NOM.SG.NEUT bread
           það   var   ekki   neitt   brauð
           that was   NEG [A]:NOM.SG.NEUT   bread

(33)   Norwegian
        a. *John   hadde   ingen   venn*
           John   had   no:UTR   friend
        b. *Der   var   intet   brød*
           there was   no:NEUT   bread
           Det   var   ikke   noe   brød   der[14]
           that was   NEG [S] bread there

(34)   Swedish
        a. *John   hadde   ing-a   venner*
           John   had   no-PL   friends
        b. *Det   fann-s   int-et   bröd*[15]
           that found:3SG-PASS   no-NEUT   bread

(35)   Danish
        a. *Hans   havde   ingen   ven*
           John   had   no:UTR   friend
        b. *Der   var   ikke   noged   brød*
           there was   NEG [S]:NEUT   bread
           Der   var   intet   brød
           there was   no:NEUT   bread

(36)   Dutch
　　　a. *Jan   had   geen enkele vriend*
　　　　John had no   single friend
　　　b. *Er   was   geen brood*
　　　　there was no   bread

(37)   German
　　　a. *Hans hatte kein-e Freund-e*
　　　　John had no-PL friend-PL
　　　b. *Es gab   kein Brot (mehr)*
　　　　it gave no   bread (more)

Frisian behaves essentially like the other Germanic languages, but the codification of the non-referential NP in Q33 is given as a second alternative to a construction with only negation on the verb; cf.

(38)   Frisian
　　　a. *Jan   hie   net   ien freon*[16]
　　　　John had NEG a   friend
　　　b. *Der   wie   net   brea/ Der   wie   gijn brea*
　　　　there was NEG bread there was no   bread

Apart from in the Germanic languages the same behaviour is found in Lapp, where the NP in question is endowed with an A item, cf.

(39)   Lapp
　　　a. *Jovnnas   i-i   lean   oktage ustit*
　　　　John:LOC NEG-3SG be:PERF [A]   friend
　　　b. *Doppe i-i   lean   oktage láibi*
　　　　there NEG-3SG be:PERF [A]   bread

Almost all the other European languages behave like Italian, that is, they do not obligatorily codify the non-referentiality of the indefinite NP. Some examples:[17]

(40)   Portuguese
　　　a. *O   João não   tinha amigos*
　　　　ART John NEG had   friends
　　　b. *Não   havia pão*
　　　　NEG had   bread

(41)   Provençal
　　　a. *Jan avié pas d'ami*[18]
　　　b. *J'avié pas/pas ges/ges de pan*

(42)　　　Lithuanian

　　a. *Jonas　　　ne-ture·jo　　draugų*
　　　John:NOM NEG-had friend:GEN.PL

　　b. *Ne-buvo　　　duonos*
　　　NEG-was bread:GEN.SG

(43)　　　Russian

　　a. *U Ivan-a　　　ne　　byl-o　　　　druzej*
　　　by John-GEN NEG was-NEUT friend:GEN.PL

　　b. *Ne　　byl-o　　　　xleba*
　　　NEG was-NEUT bread:GEN.SG

(44)　　　Bulgarian

　　a. *Ivan nja-maše　　prijateli*
　　　John NEG-had friends

　　b. *Nja-maše　xljab*
　　　NEG-had bread

Also included in this group was Slovenian, which replied to Q22 but not to Q33 with a marker of non-referentiality, thus diverging decidedly from the behaviour illustrated for the Germanic languages;[19] cf.

(45)　　　Slovenian

　　a. *John　ní　　imel noben-ega　　　　　prijatelia*
　　　John NEG had no-GEN.SG.MASC friend:GEN

　　b. *Ni　　bil-o　　　　kruh-a*
　　　NEG was-NEUT bread-GEN

Finally, in five cases the replies seem to tend towards a certain obligatory presence of the marker of non-referentiality on the NP, yet without fully reproducing the behaviour of the Germanic languages. Such is the case in Breton, Rhaeto-Romansh, Polish and Czech.[20] Breton marks the NP in Q22 and allows both versions, with and without the marker of non-referentiality, in Q33, cf.

(46)　　　Breton

　　a. *ne　　oa　　mignon ebed da Yann*
　　　NEG was friend [A] to John

　　b. *Ne　　oa　　ket　　a　　vara*
　　　NEG was NEG of bread
　　　Ne　　oa　　tamm bara　ebed
　　　NEG was piece bread [A]

The Rhaeto-Romansh informant gives the version of Q22 with a marked NP as more current, cf.

(47)   Rhaeto-Romansh

a. *Jon   nu   veiva (ingü-s) ami-s*
   John not had   no-PL   friend-PL

b. *I   nu   d'eira ingün pan*[21]
   it NEG was   no   bread

Polish and Czech mark the NP in Q22 and in Q33, but in the second sentence the informants place the negative adjective in parentheses, cf.

(48)   Polish

a. *Jan   nie   miał   żadn-ego   przyjaciel-a   żadn-ego   dom-u*
   John NEG had   no-GEN   friend-GEN   no-GEN   house-GEN
   nigdzie
   nowhere

b. *Nie   był-o   (żadn-ego)   chleb-a*
   NEG was-NEUT no-GEN   bread-GEN

(49)   Czech

a. *Ján   ne-měl   nikde   žádn-ého   přítel-e,   žádn-ý*
   John NEG-had nowhere no-GEN   friend-GEN   no-ACC
   domov
   house(ACC)

b. *Ne-byl   (žádný)   chleba*
   NEG-was no   bread

Even in this last group of languages explicit codification of the NP's non-referentiality is, in the final analysis, optional. It therefore seems clear that amongst European languages the Germanic languages (together with Lapp) are distinguished from all the others by their obligatory codification of the non-referentiality of an indefinite NP by means of a negative adjective.[22]

If we exclude Lapp, which has no N items, the languages which obligatorily make the non-referentiality of an indefinite NP under negation explicit are a sub-group of the ⟨N & −NEG⟩ (cf. 8.1.), that is, languages with simple negation according to the traditional definition: as a matter of fact, in all these languages the use of a negative adjective in the NP in question suffices to convey the negative value of the sentence (cf. examples (32)-(37)).

All the languages of type ⟨N & −NEG⟩ discussed above also have negation in postverbal position,[23] but are distinguished by the treatment of the NP in this type of construction: the Germanic languages, as has been seen, negatively mark the NP; the relevant Romance languages, that is, Provençal and French, maintain negation on the verb but place a partitive marker on the NP.[24] For Provençal see example (41) and for French the replies to the questionnaire:

(50)   a. Jean n'avait pas *d'ami.*
        b. Il n'y avait pas *de pain.*[25]

Colloquial varieties of Welsh with a postverbal negative morpheme also exhibit a construction which recalls the partitive construction in Provençal and French, although without explicit markers, cf.

(51)   Welsh[26]
        a. *D-oedd   gan John ddim ffrindiau, dim   cartref yn un-lle*
           NEG-was with John NEG friends   NEG house in a-place
        b. *Nid   oedd dim   bara*
           NEG was NEG bread

In example (51a,b) the indefinite subject is obligatorily placed after the second negative morpheme, while the usual position of definite subjects is between this and the verb, cf.

(52)   *Nid   yw 'r   dyn   ddim yn yr   ardd*
        NEG is ART man NEG in ART garden
        'The man is not in the garden' (Bowen–Rhys Jones 1973: 41)

Partitive constructions are also found in many Slavic languages and in the Baltic languages, which have negative adjectives, and in Finnish, Estonian and Basque which instead do not have negative adjectives. The distribution of obligatory use of negative adjectives and of partitive constructions in the languages of Europe is recorded in schema (53).[27]

(53)   Indefinite NPs in negative sentences
        Legend:
        Ger: obligatory negative adjective
        Rus: partitive construction
        (Ir):   absence of negative adjectives
        n.b.:   for the language symbols see the list of abbreviations on p. x

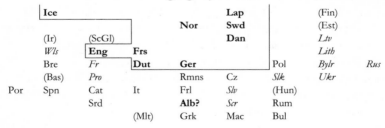

The differences in behaviour on the part of French and Provençal on the one hand and the Germanic languages on the other may be due to the different

conditions that have accompanied the origin and diffusion of postverbal negation in the two language groups (see 3.2., 3.3. and chapter 1. for the Romance
languages in particular).[28]

Synchronically, the behaviour of the Germanic languages illustrated above
reinforces the hypothesis that negation in them is directly linked to the focus
of the sentence, that is to say, to the communicatively most significant element.
It thus obeys mainly pragmatic and not syntactic rules, as is shown by the
'freedom of movement' of *nicht* in German on the one hand and by the fixed
position of the postverbal particle of the Romance languages on the other.

Furthermore, within the Germanic group German and Dutch occupy a particular position in this respect, in that they also obligatorily mark NPs of attributive predicates, unlike English, where the use of a negative adjective is not
obligatory, and the Romance languages, which do not mark the NP, even with
the specific partitive construction seen above. Cf.

(54)   a. Sie sind *keine* Freunde.
        b. They are *no* friends/They aren't friends.
        c. Ils ne sont pas des amis.[29]
        d. Non sono amici.

Suffice it here to mention this regularity, without entering into the details of
the behaviour of the individual languages according to the type of predicate
involved, which would open other problems. In fact, in our questionnaire the
case of indefinite NPs as objects of predicates which describe general qualities,
such as 'to eat fish' in Q5, has already brought to light types of behaviour
slightly different to those in (54), cf. Ger. *Hans ißt keinen Fisch*, Dut. *Jan eet geen
vis*, Fris. *Jan yt net fisk/gijn fisk* and similarly Fr. *Jean ne mange pas de poisson*, but
Eng. *John doesn't eat fish*, and Dan. *Hans spiser ikke fisk*, Ice. *Jón borðar ekki fisk*
etc. like It. *Giovanni non mangia pesce*.

Nor is it possible in the present context to deal in greater depth with the
question of the potential differences of a semantic and/or pragmatic nature
which outside the Germanic languages govern the use of the negative adjective,
which is optional but which is not indifferent to the sentence structure, as is
shown in Italian by the difference between *Giovanni non mangia pesce* 'John doesn't
eat fish' (that is, 'not eating fish is a characteristic of John') and *Giovanni non
mangia nessun pesce* (that is, 'no single (type of) fish'). The question is in turn
linked to that concerning partitives, cf. *Giovanni non ha amici = Giovanni non ha
nessun amico* 'John hasn't any friends' in the case of count nouns, but *Giovanni
non ha acqua ≠ ?/**Giovanni non ha nessuna acqua* 'John has no water' in the case
of mass nouns.[30]

8.4.2. Keine Ahnung!/No idea!

In the Germanic languages obligatory expression of negation by means of a negative adjective on the indefinite NP of the constructions exemplified by Q22 and Q33 has an interesting consequence on the typological level, even if marginal in the general economy of the negation system. It is possible to have negative existential constructions with ellipsis of the predicate.

Consider the following German examples with the corresponding Italian translations:

(55)   a. *Kein Brot!*   *Non c'è pane*   'No bread'
        b. *Keine Ahnung!*   *Non ne ho idea*   'No idea'
        c. *Kein Eingang!*   *Vietato entrare*   'No entry'
        d. *Kein Trinkwasser!*   *Acqua non potabile*   'Not drinking water'
        e. *Keine Rückgabe*   *La macchina non dà resto* 'No change given'

In German only the NP is present, accompanied by the negative adjective. This construction is able to take on generically (non-)referential functions (predicating the non existence of the referent, or its not having); it expresses also prohibitive function (prohibition of doing NP), according to the communicative context in which it is used.

From a formal point of view all five examples (55a-e) may ultimately be considered the result of ellipsis of an existential or locative predicate (for example 'es gibt kein NP' or 'es ist kein NP hier/da') or even a possessive predicate as in *Ich habe keine Ahnung* 'I have no idea'. However, their use in different functions, such as the conative in (55c) and (55d), which corresponds to a descriptive NP with prohibitive function in Italian (whereby (55d) = *Non bere!* 'Do not drink'), makes them autonomous constructions.[31] Consider also, in this regard, the following German-Portuguese comparison taken from the work of Koller (1988: 81), where the essentially conative function of our construction ('Do not give me any money') is rendered in Portuguese with a volitive predicate:

(56)   German   Doch Haendel wehrte ab. "Nein", sagte er leise, "*kein Geld* für dieses Werk"
                    [But Haendel refused it. "No" he said in a low voice, "no money for this work"]

        Portuguese Haendel recusou. "Não, *não quero dinheiro* por esta obra".
                    [Haendel refused it. "No, I do not want (any) money for this work"]

Here it can be seen how, when translating, it is necessary to make the German construction explicit as it corresponds to several functions. Similar observations also apply to Eng. *no* +NP, cf. *No date, No matter!, No idea, No smoking, No study, no supper!, No wonder that* …

The data relating to this parameter of comparison are supplied by the replies to Q35, recorded here as follows:

(57) a. *No idea!*
      b. *Non ne ho idea!*[32]

Amongst the Germanic languages other than English and German, the following supplied the construction with the negated NP:

(58)   Fris.   *Gijn idee.*
       Dut.   *Geen idee.*
       Dan.   *Ingen anelse.*
       Swe.   *Ingen åning.*
       Ice.   *Enga hugmynd.*

The Norwegian reply has the verb in parentheses, *(Jeg har) ingen anelse!* and may therefore be added to the group of replies in (58).[33]

Aside from the Germanic languages, those which reply with a similar construction are French (*Aucune ideé!*), Rhaeto-Romansh (*Ingün'idea*), Albanian (*Asnjë ide!*). The position of these three languages with respect to Germanic is worth a mention, albeit brief.

As has been seen above (cf. example (50) in 8.4.1.), French differs in certain respects from the Germanic languages and replies to Q22 and Q33 with a partitive construction and not with the negative adjective *aucun*. On the other hand, the reply to Q35 with just the NP accompanied by *aucun* links French to the Germanic languages, which share with French the presence of a postverbal negative morpheme incompatible with other N value elements (cf. **aucun NP Vb *pas* : this is the type ⟨N & −NEG⟩, dealt with in 8.1.). These elements, therefore, constitute the main means of conveying sentence negation, which ends up being separated from the verb and placed on the most focal constituent. Regarding the parameter of comparison that we are examining, French is thus assimilated into the Germanic languages with respect to the wider complex of phenomena linked to the postverbal position of negation.[34]

Rhaeto-Romansh may be assimilated to the Germanic languages for its obligatory codification of the non-referentiality of an indefinite NP under negation (: cf. 8.4.1., example (47)), despite the fact that the Lower Engadin variety represented in our questionnaire does not have constructions with discontinuous or postverbal negations. Perhaps in this case it concerns a calque construction from German, the Grisons, as is well-known, being a strong contact area.

Far more problematic instead is the case of Albanian, though not disrupting the typological regularity that we have outlined. It has in common with the Germanic languages the use of the negative adjective in the existential construction Q33 and, in part, in Q22 (cf. note 20), but has the sentence negation in preverbal position. It may be hypothesised that the possibility of having an elliptical construction is nonetheless linked to the requirement of indicating the non-referentiality of an indefinite NP in these contexts. This requirement, however, could in turn be due to factors different from those suggested for Germanic and French. The question deserves further and more thorough examination and above all additional collections of data.

Amongst the other elliptical constructions of the predicate that are found in Europe, worth particular note is that found in the colloquial Welsh variety: an NP is preceded by the postverbal negative morpheme,[35] cf.

(59)   *Dim   sydniad*
          NEG   idea

This construction fits in with the general framework of postverbal negation syntax that we have dealt with above for Germanic and French and has its *raison d'être* also in the lack of N value adjectives in Welsh.[36]

In five cases (Spanish, Catalan, Slovak, Croatian, Latvian) the remaining elliptical replies of the predicate in Q35 have the NP preceded by the same morpheme as that used as a negative co-ordinating conjunction, the only one which may come before an NP in noncontrastive contexts (cf. 5.3.). Cf.

(60)   a. Spanish   *Ni idea*
          b. Catalan   *Ni idea*
          c. Slovak   *Ani nápad*
          d. Croatian   *Ni pojma*[37]
          e. Latvian   *(Man   nav)   ne   jausm-as*[38]
                        1SG:DAT NEG:is   nor   idea-GEN

This construction, which, as can be seen, surfaces in languages relatively distant as far as genetic affiliation and geographic position is concerned, reveals another strategy of focalisation.

The rest of the European languages reply to Q35 with a complete sentence whose predicate, aside from a few isolated cases, is possessive in nature.[39] In addition to Italian *Non ne ho idea*, cf., for example

(61)   Provençal *N'   ai   pas   idéia*
                    NEG   have:1SG NEG   idea
          Rumanian *Habar n-am*
                    idea   NEG-have:1SG

Lithuanian *Ne-turiu*   *supratim-o*
            NEG-have:1SG idea-GEN:PL

   Polish *Nie   mam   pojęci-a*
            NEG have:1SG idea-GEN:SG

 Russian *Ne   imeju   predstavleni-ja*
            NEG have:1SG idea-GEN:SG

Macedonian *Ne-mam   poim*
            NEG-have:1SG idea

   Greek *Dén   ékhō   idéa*
            NEG have:1SG idea

The same also applies to languages which do not have N value adjectives, cf.

(62)   Irish *Níl   tuairim ar bith   ag-am*
              NEG:is idea   on world with-me

     Finnish *E-i   aavistus-ta-kaan*
              NEG-3SG feeling-PART.SG-EMPH

   Estonian *P-ole   mõte-t*
              NEG-be thought-PART

Hungarian *Fogalm-am sincs   ról-a*
              idea-1SG there.is.not on-3SG

   Maltese *M'   għand-i-x   idea*
              NEG by-1SG-NEG idea

9. 'Raising'

We have previously had cause to mention 'negation raising' in dealing with negative quantifiers such as *nobody* (cf. 7.6.) and with sentences Q6, Q7 (cf. 5.4.). In our questionnaire it is represented explicitly with the sentences

Q36a   *John thinks that it is not possible*
        Giovanni pensa che non sia possibile

and

Q36b   *John does not think that it is possible*
        Giovanni non pensa che sia possibile

and also implicitly with the pair

Q23   *John hoped that nothing would happen to him*
        Giovanni sperava che non gli succedesse niente

and

Q25   *John didn't think that anything would happen to him*
        Giovanni non pensava che gli sarebbe successo niente.[1]

This is a phenomenon which linguists have devoted their attention to for a long time: see Jespersen (1917), Wackernagel (1926) etc., and which has become current again in generativists' discussions.[2] This is certainly not the place to go into a detailed critical examination of generative-transformational theory (neither in its extended version: EST, nor in its government and binding version: GB) with its − purely syntactic! − rule of 'Move α'. Even within this theoretical framework there does not seem to be the slightest indication of a 'trace' left by NEG in Q36b (that is *John does not think that* t *is possible, Giovanni non pensa che* t *sia possibile*). But what is more to the point is that within the class of 'verba putandi', that which best characterises NEG-raising, raising is not possible with every verb:

(1)   a. *Mario non temeva che i conti fossero sbagliati*
           'Mario was not afraid that the accounts were wrong'

is quite different to

        b. *Mario temeva che i conti non fossero sbagliati*
           'Mario was afraid that the accounts were not wrong'

even in a context where *non* would be pleonastic, 'expletive'[3] (for example Mario
has received a bill considerably higher that he expected and is afraid that there
is unfortunately no error: an obviously different state of affairs to that in which
Mario is afraid that the accounts are in effect wrong). Similarly we have

(2)   a. *Egli non dubita che il debito gli venga saldato*
          'He doesn't doubt that the debt will be settled'

vs.

       b. *Egli dubita che il debito non gli venga saldato*
          'He doubts that the debt won't be settled'

Even

(3)   a. *Er befürchtet nicht, daß die Genfer Verhandlungen im Sand verlaufen*
          (example from Lerner–Sternefeld (1984: 164))
          'He is not afraid that the Geneva negotiations will come to nothing'

is obviously a quite different thing to the following sentence, with an 'expletive'
NEG in the subordinate clause:

(3)   b. *Er befürchtet, daß die Genfer Verhandlungen nicht im Sand verlaufen*
          'He is afraid that the Geneva negotiations will come to nothing'.

"Es scheint also, daß die Eigenschaft, für die Negation durchlässig zu sein,
mit semantischen Strukturen zusammenhängt" [Then it seems that permeability
as a characteristic of negation is related to semantic structures] (Lerner–
Sternefeld 1984: 165). The realisation of NEG raising seems to be possible only
when the semantic content of the matrix verb is such as to guarantee its subject
(1st actant) a degree of control over the process or state to which it refers: this
applies to 'to think', 'to consider', 'to believe', but not to 'to fear', 'to doubt' (cf.
Ramat (1988b: 660–661) and the bibliography cited in note 2).

In a sentence such as *Non voglio che ti succeda niente* 'I don't want anything to
happen to you' the negative quantifier *niente* is in the scope of the dependent
Vb; but there is no reason for speaking of raising NEG (*non*) before the main
Vb, since in this case – taking a hypothetical *Voglio che ti succeda niente* as the
base form – there should be 0 in the place of *niente*. This is obviously impossible
in Italian syntax: ****Non voglio che 0 ti succeda /...che ti succeda 0*. It should rather
be thought of as reinforcement of NEG by means of repetition (of the type
Non ho visto nessuno) with *niente* more or less equivalent to *alcunché* (quantifier of
type A), *qualche cosa* (quantifier of type S, which, in the scope of NEG, expresses
the same state of affairs as *niente*).

For this reason NEG raising is not a purely syntactic transformation nor a movement rule: it is in any case sensitive to the semantic content of the verbs in question. Furthermore: how is it possible to decide if we have NEG raising in Q36b or lowering in Q36a, given that the truth content is the same? The placing of NEG in the matrix or subordinate clause is not a syntactic strategy but is instead on another level.

There is, in fact, a subtle difference between

(4)   a. *Il ne faut pas que ce mariage se fasse*
          'It is not necessary that this marriage takes place'

and

      b. *Il faut que ce mariage ne se fasse pas*
          'It is necessary that this marriage does not take place'

(examples from Horn (1978: 188), who devotes many pages to what he calls 'NEG transportation', from the subordinate to the main clause). Lerner and Sternefeld (1984: 166) think that (4a) expresses a weaker negation than (4b), while if the following pairs are considered

(5)   a. *Non credo che questo problema possa esser risolto*
          'I don't think that this problem can be resolved'

and

      b. *Credo che questo problema non possa esser risolto*
          'I think that this problem cannot be resolved';

(6)   a. *Hubert doesn't want the secretaries to leave early*

and

      b. *Hubert wants the secretaries not to leave early*
          (example from Sheintuch−Wise (1976: 550)),

it could be said that there is a more drastic affirmation in the (b) examples: in (5b) the problem is declared to be insoluble and the verb *credere* is not in the scope of NEG. 'I have no doubt that the problem cannot be resolved'. In (5a), on the other hand, it is my personal belief that is subject to negation (and I may even be mistaken). In the same way in (6b) Hubert seems to excercise a greater control over the state of affairs than in (6a), where his wish may even be contradicted by the actual facts.

Whatever the case, it is obvious that the position of NEG in this type of sentence is due to pragmatic strategies of topicalisation and focalisation. So-called NEG-raising is not the application of a syntactic rule, rather it is governed by the differing organisation of the cognitive content in function of the speaker's strategies for focalising one or another part of the message (cf. Nuyts' approach, very close to this one (1987)).

How do the languages in our questionnaire behave with regards to this two-fold possibility? Being a problem, as we have said, of a pragmatic nature, it is obvious that any sentence in the questionnaire, out of its situational context, runs the risk of giving too inadequate, or at worst, unreliable information. What-ever the case, the two sentences compared may capture if nothing else the possibility or otherwise of their coexistence within a particular linguistic system.

In fact there exists no language amongst those examined which is not able to distinguish between Q36a and Q36b! The replies to the questionnaire may diverge (slightly) in their morphosyntax between Q36a and b as in the case of French

(7)   a. *Jean pense que ce n'est pas possible*

vs.

        b. *Jean ne pense pas que ce soit possible*[4]

or rely on a lexical opposition as in the case of Lithuanian

(8)   a. *Jonas galvoja, kad tai   yra ne-įmanoma*
           John thinks   that that is   not-possible

vs.

        b. *Jonas ne-galvoja,   kad tai   yra įmanoma*
           John not-thinks   that that is   possible,

but basically the opposition between 'I believe that ... not' and 'I don't believe that' is preserved in every language. We limit ourselves here to reporting three languages belonging to genetically different groups:

(9)   Greek
        a. *Ho Giánnēs pistéuei hóti dén eínai dúnato*

vs.

        b. *Ho Giánnēs dén pistéuei hóti eínai dúnato*

(10)   Bulgarian
        a. *Ivan misli, če tova ne e vǎzmožno*

vs.

        b. *Ivan ne misli, če tova e vǎzmožno*

(11)   Portuguese
     a. *O João pensa che isso não seja possivel*

vs.

     b. *O João não pensa che isso seja possivel.*

It is this very consistency that seems to us to constitute an ultimate proof that so-called NEG-raising is not a movement rule but a real and proper functional opposition, depending on whether or not the main clause Vb is in the scope of NEG. If this is the case, it is understandable then that every language must be able to capture such a functional opposition or, as was said above, the differing functional organisation of the cognitive content. In short, it is not a case such as that seen for Q34 (*In the contest of wits, Ulysses — more often than not — came out the winner*), where we have established the difficulty of many languages in accepting this construction of negative comparison, strongly elliptical and particularly marked (but certainly this does not exlude the possibility of resorting to other types of sentences to express the same state of affairs!). Here the contrast between Q36a and b brings to light deeper aspects than language specific morphosyntactic structures: and these deeper aspects can be expressed in every language.

10. Conclusions

10.1. Parameters of comparison

In concluding this examination of the questionnaire, it is appropriate to introduce a series of binary parameters by which to measure the behaviour of the individual languages. This will also allow us to highlight more clearly the geographical distribution of the phenomena.

For example, the parameter constituted by the behaviour of a Language x with regards to Q1 and Q5 we will call α. Those languages which have the same morph for NEG in Q1 and in Q5, such as, for example, Portuguese, Spanish, Catalan (languages defined as belonging to group (A) in 5.2. – for which the formula 'NO' = 'NEG$_{PRED}$' was actually used) will be $+\alpha$; those instead in which the two morphs are different (as in It. *no* vs. *non* or Ger. *nein* vs. *nicht*: 'NO' $\neq$ 'NEG$_{PRED}$') will be $-\alpha$. Through the succession of + and – values of the individual parameters the various languages thus show their typological profiles which are able to provide a characterisation.

A second parameter β relates Q1 and Q2: languages in which 'NEG$_{HOL}$' formally coincides with 'NO', such as, for example, Portuguese and Spanish, we will call $+\beta$, and languages in which 'NEG$_{HOL}$' does not coincide with 'NO', such as German, we will call $-\beta$.

A third parameter, γ, arises from the comparison between Q2 ('NEG$_{HOL}$') and Q34 ('QUAM NON'), that is, from the potential behaviour of NEG anaphorically related to whatever precedes it in both cases. It has already been seen (5.2. at the end) that such use is relatively rare in Q34. The impression given is one of a construction which, because of its extremely elliptical nature (... *than not, che no*), is strongly marked. We should therefore expect a high number of $-\gamma$ cases.

The fourth parameter δ concerns the coincidence or otherwise of the morph in Q3b and Q5, that is, 'NEC$_F$' and 'NEG$_{PRED}$' (cf. 5.3.). Languages with coincidence of the morph in Q3b and Q5, such as Russian (*i ne* ... in Q3b and *ne* in Q5), are $+\delta$. Languages such as Italian, with *né* vs. *non*, are $-\delta$.

The fifth parameter, ε, refers to the difference between NEG in declarative and in imperative sentences (see 5.6.). Languages where 'NEG$_{PRED}$' and 'NEG-PROHIB' coincide (for example, Italian: *Giovanni non mangia* and *non attraversate!*) are $+\varepsilon$. Languages such as Greek (*dén* vs. *mḗ*) are $-\varepsilon$.

The final parameter, ϑ, concerns the permeability of NEG (see 7.6. and 8.1.-3.): languages with permeability (for example, Russian) are $+\vartheta$, languages without permeability (for example, English) are $-\vartheta$.

(1)   Parameters of comparison of negative structures in Europe

Legend:
+α: Q1=Q5 ('NO'='NEG$_{PRED}$'); +β: Q1=Q2 ('NO'='NEG$_{HOL}$'); +γ: Q2=Q34 ('NEG$_{HOL}$'='QUAM NON'); +δ: Q3b=Q5 ('NEC$_F$'='NEG$_{PRED}$'): +ε: Q37a=Q5 ('NEG$_{PROHIB}$'='NEG$_{PRED}$'); +ϑ: 'permeability'; languages which have no N value items (cf. chapter 6) are designated Ø with respect to ϑ

Language	α	β	γ	δ	ε	ϑ
Ir	+	+	−	−(*)	−	Ø
ScGl	+	+	−	−	−	Ø
Wls	+/−	−	−	−(*)	−	+
Bre	(+)/−	−	−	−(*)	−	+
Bas	+	+	−	+	+	Ø
Prt	+	+	+	−	+	+/−
Spn	+	+	+	−	+	+/−
Cat	+	−	−	−	+	−
Pro	−	−	−	−	+	−
Fr	−	+/−	−	+/−	+	+
It	−	+	+	−	+	+/−
Frl	+	+	+	+	+	+/−
Rmns	−	+	−	+	+	+
Srd	−	+	−	+	+	+/−
Rum	+	+	−	−(*)	+	+
Ice	−	−	+	−	+	−
Nor	−	−	−	−	+	−
Swd	−	−	−	−	+	−
Dan	−	−	−	−	+	−
Eng	+/−	−	+	−	+	−
Frs	−	−	−	+(**)	+	−
Dut	−	−	+	−	+	−
Ger	−	−	−	+	+	−
Pol	+	+	−	−(*)	+	+
Cz	+	+	−	−(*)	+	+
Slk	−	+/−	−	−(*)	+	+
Slv	+	+	−	−(*)	+	+
Scr	+	+	−	−(#)	+	+
Mac	+	−	−	−	+	+
Bul	+	+	−	−	+/−	+
Ukr	+	+	?	−(*)	+	+(%)
Bylr	+	+	+	+	+	+
Rus	−	+	−	+	+	+
Ltv	+	+	−	+/−	+	+
Lith	+	+	+	−	+	+

Language	α	β	γ	δ	ε	ϑ
Lap	+	+	−	−(*,**)	+	∅
Fin	+	+	−	−(*,**)	+	∅
Est	+	+	−	−	−	∅
Hun	+	+	+	−(*)	−	+
Grk	−	+	−	−	−	+
Alb	−	+	+	+	−	+/−
Mlt	−	+	+	−	+/−(&)	+
Trk	−	−	?	−	+	+
Arm	+	+	−	−	−	+/−
Grg	−	−	−	−	−	+

(*)   NEG reinforced in Q3b, of the Rumanian type...*nici nu*; +/−δ; see 5.3.
(**)   See further on in 10.5.
(#)   Croatian varieties are instead −δ(*)
(%)   For Ukrainian the parameters have been deduced from information reported in Rudnýckyj's grammar (1964)
(&)   'NEG$_{PRED}$' and 'NEG$_{PROHIB}$' in Maltese have in common the postverbal morpheme -*x*, but not the preverbal (*ma* vs. *la*).

It is clear that many other parameters still could be added to those listed here. However, we consider that, given the centrality of the sentences involved in the NEG system, these are the most salient.[1]

The typological profiles of the languages of Europe for the parameters under consideration are reported below in schema (1). Profiles of Turkish, Armenian and Georgian have been added to the bottom of this list by way of illustration. In the present work these three languages, very marginal with respect to Europe, have been only fleetingly taken into consideration.

10.2. Parameter α: Q1 ('NO') and Q5 ('NEG$_{PRED}$')

As far as the first parameter of comparison is concerned, that is, 'α', the table echoes what was set out analytically in 5.2. In particular, identity of the two constructions is found on the Atlantic side of Europe (Scottish Gaelic, Irish, Welsh, English (only in part), Breton (only in part), Basque, Portuguese, Spanish, also Catalan) and in the whole of (central- and north-) eastern Europe including most of the Balkan area (: Friulian, Lapp, Finnish, Estonian, Latvian, Lithuanian,

Polish, Czech, Belorussian, Hungarian, Rumanian, Slovenian, Croatian, Serbian, Macedonian, Bulgarian). The two areas are tightly-knit, if the exceptions of Slovak and Russian are excluded. The central-western zone, the northern and the mediterranean side are instead $-\alpha$, as schema (2) shows.

(2)   Parameter $\pm\alpha$: 'NO' and 'NEG$_{\text{PRED}}$'
    Legend:
    Ir: $+\alpha$
    It: $-\alpha$
    Eng/Eng: $+ \& -\alpha$
    n.b.: for the language symbols see the list of abbreviations on p. x.

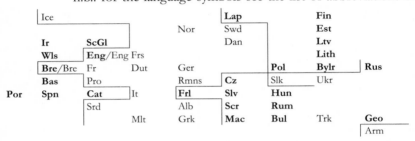

Languages without prosentences, which make use of ellipses (Scottish Gaelic, Irish, Welsh, Breton (in part), English (in part), Lapp, Finnish, Estonian) and those which use the same negative morpheme for Q1 and for Q5 are both included amongst the $+\alpha$ languages. On the other hand, as can clearly be seen, the former constitute an exception in the European context where the overwhelming majority of languages have at least the negative prosentence.

From the point of view of the means of expressing negation in Q1 and Q5 and the corresponding $+/-\alpha$ parameter, the following groups may be distinguished amongst the $+\alpha$ and $-\alpha$ languages:

i. $[+\alpha]$: echo replies for Q1 with the same means used for Q5;
ii. $[+\alpha]$: the same negative morpheme, but stressed in Q1 and unstressed proclitic in Q5;
iii. $[-\alpha]$: different negative morphemes for Q1 and Q5, but with the same etymon; differentiation has arisen after crystallisation of different phonetic forms for the stressed and unstressed positions in Q1 and Q5 respectively;
iv. $[-\alpha]$: different negative morphemes following diachronic development of a new negative morpheme in Q5 (usually postverbal as in the Germanic languages (cf. chapter 2), but also preverbal, as in Modern Greek);
v. $[-\alpha]$: different negative morphemes resulting from different diachronic formations.

From the areal and diachronic point of view, the overwhelming majority of the languages of Europe are $+\alpha$ (either type i. or ii.). The $-\alpha$ languages, concentrated in the central zone from the extreme north (Icelandic), to the extreme south (Maltese), are in their turn mostly of type iv. (and in this case the negative morpheme for Q1 represents the original etymon); there are few languages belonging to type iii. (Italian, Sardinian, Rhaeto-Romansh, Slovak) and even fewer belonging to type v. (Russian, Albanian and Welsh only as far as *naddo* is concerned).

10.3. Parameter β: Q1 ('NO') and Q2 ('NEG_HOL')

From a quantitative point of view cases of +β are almost twice as frequent as those of −β (28 vs. 15). In two cases the replies to the questionnaire were +/−β (: Fr. Q1 *Non* and Q2 …*ses amis non* alongside *ses compagnons n'en mangent pas*; Slovak Q1 *Nie* and Q2 …*ale jeho priatelia nie* alongside *jeho priatelia nejedia*).

One can no doubt imagine that there are other languages amongst those in our questionnaire giving −β, which allow formal correspondence between 'NEG_HOL' and 'NO' in yes/no questions, especially at an informal level: *no* without the verb and therefore in holophrastic function, represents a rapid and economic solution. This occurs in cases where the presence of a Vb to complete the sentence is not morphologically obligatory: cf. also (Q1) in Welsh: *A wyt ti wedi gweld John?* (lit. 'Are you after see John?') − *Naddo* 'No', or *Nag ydwyf* (lit. 'Not I am'), with repetition of the verb of the question − as in (Q2) …*ond nid yw ei gyfellion ddim* (lit. 'but NEG is of him companions NEG', i. e. '…but his companions do not').

In any case the quantitative data which emerge from the inquiry conducted on the questionnaire are as reported above. Consequently −β presents a reduced distribution which practically coincides with the Germanic languages, to which from amongst the Slavic languages is added only Macedonian (with repetition of the Vb in the second part of Q2). The geographical distribution of parameter β is illustrated in schema (3).

10.4. Parameter γ: Q2 ('NEG_HOL') and Q34 ('QUAM NON')

It has already been said that given the strongly marked elliptical construction of Q34, a high number of −γ cases is a priori to be expected. It is interesting to note that amongst the +γ cases (in all only 12 in our sample of languages) as many as 9 accompany +β, that is, those cases in which the negative morph of Q2 (= that of Q1) appears effectively with the function of 'NEG_HOL' (… *i suoi compagni no* 'his companions no'). This is indication of a certain tendency in the

(3)   Parameter $\pm\beta$: 'NO' and 'NEG$_{HOL}$'
           Legend:
           Ir: $+\beta$; Ice: $-\beta$; **Fr**/Fr: $+\&$ $-\beta$
           n.b.: for the language symbols see the list of abbreviations on p. x.

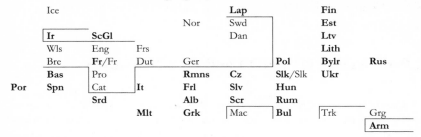

languages in question to make use of elliptical constructions, even though strongly marked like Q34. On the other hand there are only 3 cases where $+\gamma$ corresponds with $-\beta$ (Icelandic, English, Dutch), as shwon in schema (4).

Having observed how in this case there are no languages with $+/-\gamma$, note also that the geographical distribution of the parameter does not seem to assume the form of any specific area: $+\gamma$ appears to be randomly distributed within a Europe essentially averse to the strongly marked construction of Q34.

(4)   Parameter $\pm\gamma$: 'NEG$_{HOL}$' and 'QUAM NON'
           Legend:
           It: $+\gamma$; Ir: $-\gamma$
           n.b.: for the language symbols see the list of abbreviations on p. x.

Ice				Lap			Fin	
			Nor	Swd			Est	
Ir	ScGl			Dan			Ltv	
Wls	**Eng**	Frs				Pol	**Lith**	
Bre	Fr	**Dut**	Ger			Pol	**Bylr**	Rus
Bas	Pro		Rmns	Cz		Slk	Ukr	
Por Spn	Cat	**It**	**Frl**	Slv		Hun		
	Srd		**Alb**	Scr		Rum		
		Mlt	Grk	Mac		Bul	Trk	Grg
								Arm

10.5. Parameter δ: Q3b ('NEC$_F$') and Q5 ('NEG$_{PRED}$')

The data relative to parameter δ have already been extensively discussed in 5.3. Here it remains only to add a couple of observations concerning the classification $+\delta$ and $-\delta$. In Frisian, for Q3 there is *Jan seit (neat) en docht neat*, for Q5 there is *Jan yt net fisk*: *neat* 'nothing, nichts' represents an emphatic expression of negation compared to the usual negative particle *net*. Frisian is therefore essentially $+\delta$. In Lapp, Q3b *üge* is composed of the negative verb (*ü*, 3SQ) and the suffix *-ge*, which is used to coordinate two negative sentences. Lapp is therefore a $-\delta$ language, with NEG also expressed in the second member of the coordination. The same applies to Finnish *eikä*.

From a quantitative point of view, there is a very clear majority of $-\delta$ languages: only 9 cases of $+\delta$ (and 2 of $+/-\delta$). With respect to the geographical distribution shown in schema (5) this means that, like in the previous case, occurrences of $+\delta$ are distributed over the territory and do not form tightly-knit areas of any significance.

(5)   Parameter $\pm\delta$: 'NEC_F' and 'NEG_{PRED}'
      Legend:
      Bas: $+\delta$; It: $-\delta$; **Fr/Fr**: $+\& -\delta$
      n.b.: for the language symbols see the list of abbreviations on p. x.

	Ice							
				Nor	Lap		Fin	
	Ir	ScGl			Swd		Est	
	Wls	Eng	**Frs**		Dan		**Ltv**	
	Bre	**Fr/Fr**	Dut	**Ger**		Pol	Lith	
	Bas	Pro		**Rmns**	Cz	Slk	**Bylr**	**Rus**
Por	Spn	Cat	It	**Frl**	Slv	Hun	Ukr	
		Srd		**Alb**	Scr	Rum		
			Mlt	Grk	Mac	Bul	Trk	Grg
								Arm

10.6. Parameter ε: Q37a ('NEG_{PROHIB}') and Q5 ('NEG-PRED')

The fifth parameter is concerned with whether the morphs for 'NEG_{PROHIB}' and 'NEG_{PRED}' (see 5.6.) coincide ($+\varepsilon$) or differ ($-\varepsilon$). The geographical distribution, represented in schema (6), highlights how the feature $+\varepsilon$ characterises most European languages, forming a large tightly-knit area, with the unique exception of Hungarian and, in part, Bulgarian which is a $+$ and $-\varepsilon$ language. The $-\varepsilon$ languages are situated at the margins of this area; included amongst these are languages which, as far as negative structures are concerned, do not in general share the more common characteristics of the languages of Europe (see, for example, 5.1.; 6.1.-3.).

(6)   Parameter ± ε: 'NEG$_{PROHIB}$' and 'NEG$_{PRED}$'
            Legend:
            It: + ε; **Ir**: − ε; **Bul**/Bul: + & − ε
            n.b: for the language symbols see the list of abbreviations on p. x.

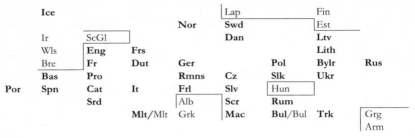

10.7. Parameter ϑ: 'permeability' of NEG

A new parameter emerges from the comparison of sentences Q9 and Q8 regarding Ulysses and Polyphemos, a parameter, which by convention will be designated ϑ, regarding the 'permeability' of NEG, that is, whether or not there must be a negative morph preceding the Vb, even in the presence of a negative quantifier such as 'nobody', 'nothing' (see 7.6. and in addition 8.1.-3.). Languages where this is obligatory will be designated + ϑ, those where it is not − ϑ and those, such as Italian, where the presence of the negative morph depends on the order of the elements in the sentence, + / − ϑ. Languages which do not have negative quantifiers (see 6.3.), for which the symbol Ø was used in schema (1), are of course indifferent to this parameter.

Ulysses' riddle will not work in + ϑ languages. Note that this parameter, unlike the others which may be applied to the sentences of the questionnaire and which are based on a principle of coincidence or non coincidence of morphs,[2] allows a third possibility, relating to the order of the elements in the sentence: it is then a 'positional' parameter.

From the point of view of linguistic families it is worth noting how the Germanic group is consistently − ϑ and the Slavic group just as consistently + ϑ, while the Romance languages are divided between the three possibilities, although they are mostly + / − ϑ: the typology does not coincide with genetic relationship. Concerning the diffusion of the third group (+ / − ϑ), it would appear from the geographical distribution depicted in schema (7) that a Mediterranean Latin area may be distinguished − with Albanian added to the Romance languages (but excluding Provençal). On the other hand Hungarian and Rumanian, both $+\vartheta$ languages, do not behave like most of the other languages of the respective families to which they belong, but like the Slavic languages with which they are in close contact.

(7)   Parameter $\pm\vartheta$: 'N' and 'NEG$_{\text{PRED}}$' (Permeability of NEG)
        Legend:
        Bre: $+\vartheta$; ICE: $-\vartheta$; *It*: $+\&-\vartheta$; Ir: $\emptyset$
        n.b: for the language symbols see the list of abbreviations on p. x.

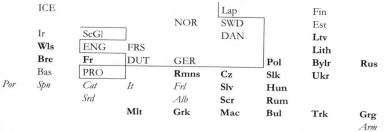

10.8. Concluding remarks

If now, after the analytical and detailed observations of the preceding chapters, we wish to conclude with some comments of a more general nature, it appears that on the typological level the various geographical distributions schematised in (2) – (7) confirm the existence of a central Romance – Germanic 'core area', already well known in historical linguistics. This is particularly evident in schema (6), which at the same time shows the marginality of the Celtic, Finno-Ugric and Mediterranean (Maltese, Albanian, Greek) languages; see also (3).

Also of interest is the distribution according to three macro-areas which emerges from (2), with languages such as English, Welsh and Breton ($+/-\alpha$) crossing over the boundaries. Such a distribution closely resembles the division of the European linguistic continuum from west to east as identified by Bechert (1976).

With reference to Greenbergian typology based on the order of basic elements Bechert distinguishes two basic types: one western and one eastern, with transition areas and two separate linguistic islands (Basque and Hungarian). It is clear that all the elements examined in this sort of typology taken together allow a greater articulation of the possible types: not only 'S', 'V' and 'O' which already allow six different types, but also – as is well known – all the accompanying elements (genitive/adjective and noun, pre- and postpositions, relative clauses, noun and its gender, etc. (cf. Bechert 1990)). In our case, the parameters, in themselves, allow only two alternatives (or at most three, counting the $+/-$ possibility). It is, then, highly significant that in spite of such a restricted number of possible alternatives a geographical distribution takes shape, coinciding in large part with that which emerges for Europe from more 'powerful' parameters of analysis. Nor should schemata such as (4), with random distribution and which do not show any particular 'Sprachbund', be considered a counterexample to what has just been said: the strongly marked nature of the elliptical construction of Q36 ('QUAM NON') is in itself sufficient explanation of its sporadic appearance in only a limited number of the languages of Europe.

We are fully aware of the fact that the analysis we have presented in this book is far from representing a full account of the NEG behaviour in all its details, even less a fully coherent typological explanation. Nevertheless it is not without importance to conclude that our observations clearly show how the phenomenology of negation, as far as Europe is concerned, is also part of a systematic framework in which factors related to historical developments as well as typological evolution have had a decisive role. This is in keeping, as we noticed above, with many other researches which in recent times (above all in the frame of the 'EUROTYP' project)[3] have shown that Europe does really represent a particular linguistic area with a core group of languages constituting the so-called 'Standard Average European'.

Notes

Introduction

1. "La négation exprime fondamentalement un sens ou une valeur actionnelle de rejet, de refus, de confrontation de jugements ou d'actes" [Basically negation expresses an actional sense or value of rejection, of refusal, of comparison of judgements or acts] (Callebaut, 1992: 6). This is also applicable to cases of litotes (an affirmation expressed in the form of a negative contrary; a device which diminishes the perception or fact): *This wine is not bad* ≅ [[it is not the case that] this wine is bad] to express the fact that the wine in question is really rather good. A negative sentence, then, denies only that which is affirmed (or presupposed) in the corresponding positive sentence. It is an evaluation of a proposition. Negation "affirme quelque chose d'une affirmation qui, elle, affirme quelque chose d'un objet" [states something about a statement which states itself something about an object], (Bergson 1957: 287 (cf. Muller 1991: 22, 34)).
2. Amongst the languages where the affirmative declarative sentence is the marked form, Palmer (1986: 79) mentions Huichol (Uto-Aztecan); the unmarked form is in fact the interrogative sentence:

   (i)   *mázá tikuucúu*
            deer asleep
            'Is the deer asleep?'
            vs
   (ii)   *pée-tía*
            ABS:DIRECTION-go
            'He left'

   Tamil may also be mentioned, where following phonetic erosion the NEG marker in vowel form may disappear, which does not happen with other consonantal markers (for example, those marking future, past: cf. Ramat 1994).
3. The 'Consiglio Nazionale delle Ricerche' financed, for a two years period, the research (CNR, CT86.01493.08 and CT87.01034.08) which also received funding from the 'Ministero della Pubblica Istruzione' ("fondi 60%") in 1987 and 1988. Each part of the book has been discussed by both authors. However, Paolo Ramat is responsible for the drafts of 1.; 2.; 3.; 4.1., 4.2.; 5.3 – 5.; 7.6.; 9.; and Giuliano Bernini for 4.3.; 5.1., 5.2.; 6.; 7.1 – 5.; 8. The Introduction, the Foreword of Part two, and the Conclusions were written jointly. We would like, above all, to thank our colleagues who acted as informants for their respective mother-tongues and also those who were willing to discuss various sections of the book with us; particular thanks are due to Armin Schwegler, Peter Kahrel and Gianguido Manzelli.

Chapter 2

1. It is difficult to make any pronouncement on the clitic status or otherwise of preverbal NEG: we have seen how in initial position NEG may be strongly emphatic (cf. already Meillet (1929 >) 1977: 255). Regarding Celtic Pokorny (1959: 757) speaks of a "proklitisches **ne*" [proclitic **ne*] which would have given **na* "im Vorton in der Verbindung air. *na[ch]*, mcymr. *nac* (usw) 'nicht'" < **ne-kʷe* [in pretonic position in the combination OI *na[ch]*, MWelsh *nac* (etc.) 'not']. The creation

of forms such as Lat. *nolo* 'I do not want' and OE *nellan* 'not to want', *not* < *ne wot 'he doesn't know', etc., hardly seems to demonstrate autonomy, even as regards stress, of *ne, even in preverbal position. This is in fact the situation also in Baltic and Slavonic (cf. for example Lith. *nesti* '(there) is not', Serbo-Croat *nêĉê* 'he doesn't want', etc.: see Joly (1981: 115). However, in Latin we have *néscío* 'I do not know' and not *niscío. Neckel (1913: 2) asserts that *ni*, *ne* was proclitic in Gothic, Old English, Old Saxon. But when we find in Gothic *ni rodida im* (Mc. 4.34) 'he didn't speak to them' or in OSax. *thu ni maht bidernien leng willeon thînan* (*Hel.* 4618 ff.) 'you cannot hide your will for long', it doesn't seem as though there is any indication of NEG being in an unstressed, proclitic position. Aside from the preverbal position, we find in Middle Eng. *naught* < OE. *na-wiht* (and not **n[a-w]íht*); in Middle Frankish *nûwet*, *niewet*, in Latin *nihil* < *né-hilum (not *nil). Forms such as *ne-kʷe, *ne-kʷos cited in 2.2. would appear to counter the hypothesis of an original proclitic NEG; in these forms the unstressed element may perfectly well be representated by *-kʷe*, *-kʷos*: cf. the stress in the Sanskrit forms *ná-kis* 'no-one', *ná-kim* 'nothing at all'; Gr. *oú-tis*, *mê-tis*. In conclusion, concerning the reconstruction of the IE phase, it seems that Meillet has again been proved right ((1929 >) 1977: 255): "Le mot *né, qui indiquait le caractère négatif de la phrase, était autonome" [The word *né, which indicated the negative character of the sentence, was autonomous].

2. Note, in this context, the use of the partitive genitive – typical of negative constructions: cf. Fr. *je n'ai pas d'argent* 'I don't have any money', Russian *on ne prinës podarka* (GEN) 'he has not brought a/the present' – in the example from Lucretius, as also in the previously quoted example from *Tat.* 1.2 (: *ni was wiht gitanes*): a clear indication that *hilum* (like *wiht*) maintains a trace of its lexical meaning (cf. again Goth. *jah in jainamma daga mik ni fraihniþ waihtais* (Genitive!), *Joh.* 16, 23, 'and on that day you asked me nothing', not to mention *und hita ni beduþ ni waihtais*, *Joh.* 16, 24, 'and up to now you have not asked anything' with a significant repetition of NEG before the genitive: in itself such a repetition would not be semantically necessary, but it indicates that the fixed negative phrase is now taking shape (*ni waiht(ais)*; cf., for example, *du ni waihtai* (DAT), 2 *Tim.* 2.14, 'not at all'). In the Anglo-Saxon riddles the semantic ambiguity between the term *wiht* 'thing, creature' and the second NEG element is intentionally exploited:

Wætan ne swelgeþ,   ne wiht iteþ
foþres ne gitsað: fereð oft swa þeah
lagoflod on lyfte   (Exet. Book, N. 58, 10–12),

translated as follows by Ann Harleman Stewart (1985: 70): 'She does not swallow wet, nor eat anything / nor does the creature eat not crave fodder; [she] travels often even so the sea-flood in the air' (≅ the well bucket), cf. also riddle No. 4.

3. See the following exemples from Berthold von Regensburg (13th century; examples from Valentin 1993):
   i. *ich enweiz für baz* 'I do not know more' with just the old NEG particle;
   ii. *und enkünnent sie der kunst niht* 'and they do not know anything of the art', with double NEG;
   iii. *und hât sie leider niht geholfen* 'and she has unfortunately not helped' with postposed NEG.
   The same development is also found in Northern Germanic: cf. *né át vættr* 'you don't have a thing' (where *vættr* = Goth. *waihts*) > *át vættr* at the beginning of the sentence (: Neckel (1913: 4), contrasts *veit-at* 'I do (not) know at all', at the beginning of the sentence, with *ne veit(-at)* internal to the sentence). Note also that Dutch *en* (*< *ne*) became homophonous with *en* < *ende* 'and', thus creating a dangerous semantic ambiguity: cf. van der Horst–van der Wal (1979: 18); Burridge (1983).

4. Significantly, also found in creoles; for example, in Louisiana creole: *Mo lese pa rjẽ* lit. 'I leave no nothing' > 'I have left nothing' (see Posner 1985: 181).

5. Cf. already in Plautus, *Pseud.* 397: *...quoi neque paratast gutta certi consili* '...who has not even a drop of a clear purpose'. In the 'Parody of the Lex Salica' (8th. c.) we find an excellent example of this lexeme not having yet reached full desemanticization: *in cuppa non mittant nec gutta* 'they shan't put even a drop in the cup' (note *ne(c) gutta* > *negóta, negót, nagót* and the like!). French also still preserves *goutte* as an emphatic reinforcement of NEG (= NPI): *je n'y vois goutte* 'I can't see at all' (see Molinelli 1988: 66).

6. Cf. in OSp. *non los preçiemos dos nuozes* 'We don't consider them worth two nuts', OFr. *je ne le pris une nois*. As in the case of *gutta*, *Tropfen* 'drop', one often finds the same terms of comparison.

Chapter 3

1. It should be also noted that for this same reason the negative construction is generally more complex than the corresponding affirmative.

2. A sequence that is consistently found in Middle English and Middle German resulting from the discontinuous construction *ne*+Vb+NEG: *þat þei scholde not drede to don it* 'that they should not (> shouldn't) fear to do it'; *it is not longes gon* 'it is not (isn't) long ago'; *Ir sult nicht weinen um den willen mîn* (*Nibel.* 69.3) 'ihr sollt nicht um meinetwillen weinen / you should not weep because of me'; cf. also Fr. *Vous (ne) devez pas pleurer à cause de moi*, vs. It. *Voi non dovete piangere a causa mia*, with NEG before the modal verb, since Italian has not had the discontinuous construction (Vennemann 1989: 29).

3. Thanks to our friend Gianguido Manzelli for his accurate clarification of the Hungarian situation.

4. The genesis and grammaticalisation of such a pattern in Afrikaans as a case study is dealt with in detail in 4.3.

5. Cf. Dahl (1979: 95): "Danish, Norwegian and Swedish can be said to have made a half-way reintroduction of preverbal Neg". Observe the difference between the main clause with Vb+NEG and the subordinate clause with NEG+Vb: Norw. *Jeg vet ikke hvorfor jeg ar så trist* 'I don't know why I'm so sad' vs. *han beklaget at han ikke hadde kjøpt billett til henne* 'he regretted that he didn't buy the ticket for her'. "In addition, preverbal Neg placement occurs frequently in Swedish child language" (Dahl, ibidem). Notice what has been observed regarding the 'naturalness' of preverbal NEG!

6. Peripheral to the present argument, but nonetheless important in itself, is the fact that verbal categories such as tense, mood, diathesis are, in the negative constructions of the Uralic languages (including the Finno-Ugric), distributed between negative AUX and lexical Vb according to the following hierarchical scale: Imperative > tense/person/number > mood > aspect > diathesis: the imperative is the verbal category wherein the characteristic negative verb prefers to appear. Finnish has lost the category of tense in its negative AUX (cf. Finn. *sano-i-mme* 'we said' and *e-mme sano-neet* 'we didn't say', with past tense marker *-neet* on the lexical verb and not on the negative verb: see Comrie (1981a: 350–351)).

7. "*ain't* is completely idiosyncratic and unrelated to any positive form", as opposed to, for example, *doesn't, oughtn't* and even *haven't*: Zwicky–Pullum (1983: 508), who conclude that *n't* represents an inflected affix rather than a clitic.

Chapter 4

1. Cases of borrowing of negative morphs between languages are indeed very rare; and these have no influence on the NEG system in the host language.

2. For this reason Afrikaans may be considered a fully-fledged West Germanic language, unlike, for example, Tok Pisin, which does not belong unambiguously to any genetic affiliation despite its English lexical base.

3. The sentences in example (13), apart from highlighting their common and divergent features with respect to negation, also exemplify the huge discrepancies between Afrikaans and Dutch with regards to verbal morphology. The verbal paradigm in Afrikaans has a base form, *eet* 'to eat' in the case of the present example, without person distinction, which contrasts with the past participle *geëet*; the Dutch counterpart *eet*, as third person present indicative form, contrasts with the first and third person plural *eten* on the one hand and on the other the past tense *at*, the past participle *gegeten* and the infinitive *eten*.

4. In the morphemic interlinear translations of this and of the following Afrikaans examples the past auxiliary *het* is glossed 'have' because it is the uninflected base form, although it is derived from the 3rd person singular form *heeft* of the Dutch verb *hebben* 'to have'.

5. In fact, a fourth cause may be added, being the influence of the French negative construction *ne...pas*, noted by Hesseling ((1897 >) 1979: 5). This hypothesis seems, however, not to have received much support, probably because the French particles are linked to the verb and not to the sentence final position. The French influence might have come from the presence of Huguenots at the Cape after the repeal of the Edict of Nantes in 1685.

6. In this research tradition, the reluctance to recognise non-European influences and a probable partial creolisation in the history of Afrikaans is not unconnected to the ideology of white supremacy. See the cautious but scientifically well-founded critique of it by Valkhoff (1966: x-xi) and again (5–6), where, recalling Saussure, he coins the expression "diachronic purists" in referring to the exponents of this tradition. See also den Besten (1986: 191).

7. Quoted by Valkhoff (1966: 15, note 25) and also by Raidt (1983: 190, note 49).

8. Cf. Nienaber (1955), quoted in den Besten (1986: 211 *passim*) and also by Valkhoff (1966: 17, note 28).

9. Den Besten's hypothesis is supported by observations of a formal type, by means of which the deep structure of the Nama sentence is analysed, and takes into account restrictions imposed by Universal Grammar (1986: 219–221).

10. See the discussion in Valkhoff (1966: 25–40), who contests Hesseling's hypothesis, according to which the slaves spoke a Malayo-Portuguese creole at the Cape.

11. The argumentation is den Besten's (1986: 211). In 1677, 190 slaves of Asiatic origin were disembarked at the Cape (Holm 1989: 340), while in successive decades the numbers reached their thousands (Raidt 1983: 15). The Asiatic varieties of Portuguese creole have only preverbal negative morphemes, derived from Portuguese *nunca* 'never' (for example *ngka* in Malacca, *nungka* in Java). With modals, existential 'be' and the copula only, they use derivations from Old Portuguese *non* (cf. *nontem* 'there is not', *nonpodi* 'to not be able to' in Ceylon), cf. Teyssier (1986: 594, 595).

12. There are only two sentences, which den Besten records from a well-known work by Franken of 1953, that is: *Na misti dali pro mi* 'Don't hit me!' (literally 'NEG it is necessary [< *mister* 'business, need', cf. *ser mister* 'to be necessary'] to hit for me'), going back to 1765, and *Nonti platoe* 'I have no money' (literally 'Not-there-is money').

13. For the inventory of negative morphemes in Afrikaans and the main rules of syntax which characterise them see also Burgers (1971: 88–90, 102, 132, 133, 137–138, 159–160, 163–164).

14. The use of the grave accent in *nòg* 'nor' is an expedient to distinguish this conjunction from *nog* 'still, yet'. In Dutch *nog* 'still, yet', although homophonous with *noch* 'nor' as in Afrikaans, is distinguished in the written form by the use of ⟨g⟩ vs. ⟨ch⟩.

15. We leave aside other more detailed aspects of constituent order rules, such as that concerning the positioning of non-finite forms in both main and subordinate clauses, as they are not relevant to the position of negation.

16. In the colloquial language both morphemes may become enclitics and be reduced to *-ie*, cf. den Besten (1986: 203).

17. This notation refers to the relevant items of the Questionnaire on negation illustrated in the Foreword to Part two of this volume.

18. The lexical alternatives in (31a) and (31b) are of no relevance here and derive from the different meanings of *leave* in Afrikaans. Sentence (32) has created various difficulties in translation and one of the two informants preferred the insertion of a negative conjunction in the subordinate clause. The absence or presence of final *nie* is agreed upon by the two informants (cf. (31a, 32a) vs. (31b, 32b)). Finally, it is interesting that a single negative conjunction for both conjuncts is possible (cf. (32b)).

19. This is and instance of *nie* having comment status with respect to the whole sentence, cf. 3.2.

20. Note that the construction under comparison is that of standard negation. In the presence of negative quantifiers , which in these languages obligatorily occupy the preverbal position, negation may, of course, be indicated on the quantifier and in sentence final position, as happens in Nama, cf. *khoi-xareï ge //nati miï tama hā* 'Nobody says so', literally 'man-no DECL thus to.speak NEG ASPECT' (den Besten 1986: 212).

21. The two examples are taken from the novel *Gabriela, Cravo e Canela* by Jorge Amado, Rio de Janeiro, Record, 1987, pp. 62, 86 respectively.

22. No mention is made of this, for example, in Gärtner (1989), who discusses a lengthy series of features which characterise Angolan or Mozambique Portuguese with respect to the Lusitanian standard. Since this researcher's data are drawn from written texts, it may be concluded that our construction is probably limited to colloquial registers as in Brazil, but with the difference that there it is considered very sub-standard.

23. This creole is spoken by a small community in the Cartagena hinterland in Colombia. For a characterisation of it in the context of Spanish-based creoles, see Lipski – Schwegler (1993: 415 – 419). Schwegler (1991b) deals in detail with negation in Palenquero.

24. Angolar is a creole spoken on the island of São Tomé by approximately 9,000 people, descendents of a community of runaway slaves from the sixteenth century (cf. Holm 1989: 280). Observations made 'in the field' concerning Angolar negation are recorded in Schwegler (1992), who discusses the evidence in favour of the possibility of a construction with only the sentence final particle also occurring in this creole.

25. In this example Valkhoff also gives a version with the first particle *na* in parentheses, implying optionality. In Ferraz – Valkhoff (1975: 24), however, it is stated that "P[rincipense] has only kept final *fa*". Still in Principense, Boretzky (1983: 102) states that "In einigen wenigen Fällen hat sich eine ältere, umklammernde Form der Negation erhalten, wie sie auf der Nachbarinsel S. Tomé noch üblich ist" [In some few cases an older, embracing form of negation was preserved, similar to the one still in use on the island of S. Tomé].

26. See the discussion in Holm (1988: 173 – 174). The possibility that *fa* is the result of a Portuguese relexification of particles of African languages is put forward, although with considerable caution, by Boretzky (1983: 102), who links the Portuguese etymon *foge* 'it flees' proposed by Schuchardt for *fa* in 1888, with the possibility in Yoruba of having "Negationsverstärker" [negation reinforcers] (*ibidem*) homophones of the verbs *mó* and *rá* with the meaning 'to vanish'. The connection is suggestive, even if a direct contact between Yoruba and the Portuguese of the fifteenth and sixteenth centuries cannot be demonstrated. Furthermore, as is clear from the

numerous examples recorded in Rowlands (1969: *passim*, but in particular 13), *mɔ́* 'anymore' and *rárá* 'at all' are lexical items which are not undergoing grammaticalisation.

27. According to Kouwenberg (1992: 264) in 1992 there were only five speakers left. The system of negation in this creole is fully described in Kouwenberg (1994).

28. The conditions under which this creole was formed, reconstructed by Smith – Robertson – Williamson (1987), are unlike those identified for other Caribbean creoles. These researchers explain the massive presence of Ijo lexicon with the phonological characteristics of creolised Dutch as the result of a process of relexification of a Dutch creole by well-knit groups of non-Ijo slaves as part of the processes of forming a new ethnic identity. As far as the syntax is concerned, however, Kouwenberg (1992) highlights the role of adaptive strategies "aimed at the creation of a linguistic system which optimally exploits perceived similarities" (296).

29. This example taken from Boretzky is in turn taken from Westermann's grammar. Boretzky's original gloss, in German, is: 'ich-neg-sein, dann/als er-kommen neg'.

30. The remaining 3 cases are Austronesian languages, of no relevance here.

31. The particle *báá* may be optionally inserted in sentence initial position (Brown 1994: 165).

32. This traditional etymology is challenged by Kihm (1994: 46 – 47), who stresses the role which West African negative items might have played in the genesis of *ka*.

33. The Atlantic creoles under discussion here represent the exception with respect to the type of negation found most frequently amongst creoles. Those researchers most concerned with sub-stratum phenomena place a great deal of emphasis on the evidence that they provide in that it refutes the supposition that preverbal NEG is a creole 'universal'; cf., for example, Boretzky (1983: 104). See Schwegler (1991b: 50 – 51) for an interpretation of this characteristic in terms of a simplification of grammatical material and/or its being phonetically weak in the lexifying languages.

34. The brief historical references noted here are taken from Holm (1989: 259 – 268 for the Portuguese expansion; 322 – 325 for Dutch colonisation).

35. Cf. again 3.2. and the discussion of similar developments in some northern Italian dialects.

36. In the Asiatic creoles there are actually cases where the older unstressed particle is maintained, on which see note 11.

37. Note that in Berbice creole there is also *nɛnɛ* 'no', evidently from Dutch *nee(,) nee* 'no(,) no' (cf. Kouwenberg 1992: 284).

38. The source of the example is line 644 of the play *Floresta d'enganos* by Gil Vincente, 1536, in which an old judge makes fun of himself by dressing as a black woman and speaking in the 'reconnaissance language' (Naro 1978: 321). For a critical evaluation of Naro's literary sources and their dating cf. Goodman (1987), who contests the European origin of the initial processes of pidginisation.

39. See also what is said by Schwegler (1992: § 4.3.), who records, however, only information drawn from Lusitanian informants in the United States.

40. Schuchardt says only "Häufig wird auch *não* wiederholt" [Often *não* is also repeated] (1888: 252), but does not mention the question. The absence of a comma before the second negative element is not a certain indication that recategorisation has taken place, as the examples were collected and transcribed by officials of the 'Nieuwe Afrikaansche Handels-Venootschap' [New African Commercial Society] of Rotterdam (1888: 250). As far as attempts to find indications in favour of the change hypothesised in (48) are concerned, it is curious to note that Schuchardt, in the same article, says that he linked this type of negation to the "kapholländisch" type, but that his informants proved him wrong, in that the reply by a black to the question *fizestes que te mandei?* [sic] 'have you (PL in the original) done what I ordered?' is in all probability ("wird sein" in the original) *não, senhor, não fez* 'no, sir, I haven't done (it)'. Schuchardt confines himself

to noting: "Es besteht ein Widerspruch zwischen den beiden Angaben" [The two reports are contradictory] (1888: 252).

41. Cf. also Holm (1989: 264) and the different sociolinguistic conditions which were characteristic of the Portuguese commercial expansion routes as compared to those typical of the plantations, which gave rise to the genuine creoles.

42. The reader is again referred to Schwegler's accurate observations (1992).

43. Schuchardt notes that while on the west African coast Portuguese creoles were formed on the islands of Cape Verde as well as on the facing mainland (in Guinea Bissau), in the Gulf of Guinea, in a similar geographical situation, the 'Inselkreolisch' has no corresponding 'Festland-kreolisch'.

44. Instead of the construction with *moenie*, the construction used here is that with the imperative form of the verb, which is still possible today, even though it is not the most frequently used. Cf. Burgers (1971: 137).

45. Note, in this example, *e* for *i* in the ending of the verb *ir* 'to go' and, as before in (68), the third person singular verb used with a subject (here not expressed) in the first person.

46. Perhaps these unfavourable conditions are also reflected by the optionality of final *nie* when preceded by a negative indefinite.

47. The point is discussed in detail by den Besten (1986: 203−210) in order to refute the idea that the Afrikaans construction derives from Dutch dialects. Cf. also 4.3.1.

48. There is greater unanimity of opinion concerning knowledge of Portuguese at the Cape during the subsequent centuries, partly because court records indicate that 20% of the trials in which slaves were involved required the hearing to be translated into Portuguese (or into Malay) (Holm 1989: 341).

49. Cf. again Valkhoff (1972: 95). According to Valkhoff (1966: 33, 161) the same Jan van Riebeeck must have known literary Portuguese as well as the creole.

50. The Asiatic varieties of Portuguese creole extended as far as the island of St. Helena in the Atlantic. Furthermore, the Cape of Good Hope seems to have depended more on the Asiatic colonies than on the mother country for its supplies (cf. Valkhoff 1966: 61−62).

Foreword

1. The sentences in the questionnaire, recorded in detail in the appendix, will be indicated with a Q. The functional value of NEG which appears in each one will be given between ' '. The label by which the individual replies have been classified on the computer will be given in italic capitals. The sentence Q3 (*John neither speaks nor moves; Giovanni non parla né si muove*) which is aimed at exemplifying the behaviour of disjunctive sentential negation will therefore be 'NEC...NEC$_S$' and Italian will have *NOT1* for the first NEG and *NEC1* for the second (while the somewhat stylistically elevated variant *Giovanni né parla né si muove* would have both the negations labelled *NEC1...NEC1*). Hence the symbol appearing between ' ' has no crosslinguistic variation, while sequences of *NEC*s and *NOT*s, etc., of course constitute the *typological profile* characteristic of each individual language.

Chapter 5

1. On the basis of this interpretation in terms of conversational maxims (Grice 1975), we may perhaps speak of short answers as being a universal pertaining to the pragmatic organisation of discourse.

2. The literature on ellipsis is very extensive and goes beyond the relevant limits and aims of this study, suffice it here to make reference to Halliday and Hasan (1976: 142 – 225) and, for some questions regarding Italian, Marello (1984).

3. Cornish also made exclusive use of ellipsis, cf.

a-gerough-why   an   pow-ma? –   Caraf/   Na-garaf
INT-like-you:PL ART country-this? like:1SG/ NEG-like:1SG
'Do you like this country? – Yes / No' (Smith – Hooper 1972: 27).

4. In Estonian *ei* is the negative particle crystallised from the 3SG of the Uralic negative verb (cf. 3.4. and the replies to Q5).

5. Cf. the Finnish reply to Q13:

E-t-k ö   ole näh-nyt   mitään? – Ole-n   (kyllä)   näh-nyt
NEG-2SG-INT be see-APP anything? be-1SG certainly see-APP
jo-ta-in
some-PART-NON.ANIM
'Haven't you seen anything? – Yes, I have seen something'

6. Breton could also be assigned to the intermediate type of which more below, in that affirmative replies always allow ellipsis of all elements but the most focal one.

Mat   eo e   Lannion? –   Nann/ Ya.
good is in Lannion   no   yes
'Is it nice in Lannion? – No/Yes'
Yaounank eo da   c'hoar? – Yaounak (eo)
young   is your sister   young   is
'Is your sister young? – Yes'
(Press 1986: 109 – 110)

7. Example (7b) is taken from Parkinson (1987: 273), according to whom the echo-type replies are the only ones found in Portuguese (but note postposed *sim* in his own example). See also 4.3.4.1., examples (66), (67).

8. *Dydy* is a form resulting from apheresis of the negation *nid* and from contraction of the full form of the auxiliary *ydyw.*

9. The inversion of the two parts of the construction is much more problematic: **/? *I suoi compagni no, ma Giovanni mangia pesce*; for this reason one may speak of anaphoricity of negation.

10. Because it does not seem to be relevant, as far as current knowledge goes, we do not take into consideration the possibility or the obligatoriness of an adversative conjunction, like the Hungarian *de* in this contrastive context. It is found here and there in various languages as well as in Hungarian.

11. Q5 is in German *Hans ißt keinen Fisch*, given that the object is indefinite. The same goes for Dutch.

12. Our informant notes: "In Dutch, the particle *wel* [OppNeg] is usually added to mark the opposite of negation. This literal translation is grammatically correct, but highly marked: strong accent (intonation) must be put on *Jan* and *wel* in order to make the sentence interpretable".

13. The connection between the expressive means used by the languages of type (C) and those used by the languages of types (D) and (E) is much more complex if one thinks of short answers as containing indications of modality, corresponding to Italian *forse no*, English *perhaps not* and German *vielleicht nicht*, which show the same behaviour. A complete typology of all the constructions of this type would require an adequate collection of data including also the corresponding positive expressions, which do not behave like the negatives (cf. It. *forse sì* , Eng. *maybe yes*, Ger. *vielleicht schon*).

14. In Finnish the main verb may also be repeated after the negative verb, giving *hänen ystävänsä eivät syö*. From this point of view it behaves like the last type on our *continuum*, that is, with repetition also of the main verb in the second part of the conjunction. The same happens in Lapp.

15. In fact the informant who provided us with the Swedish data gave first the following translation: [...] *men inte hans kamrater*, that is, literally, 'but not his companions', which is essentially negative focalization of the NP and corresponds to a strategy of constituent negation (cf. also 3.1.). The same strategy is found in the reply supplied by the Estonian informant: [...] *aga mitte* (NEG) *tema kaaslased*.

16. This datum is in partial contrast to Sadock and Zwicky's assertion (1985: 191) concerning the obligatoriness of the reduction in certain languages and notably Icelandic. According to the two authors, reductions of the type seen for the negative reply are barely acceptable in Icelandic, cf. *Ertu amerikumaður? – ?Já, það er ég* 'Are you American? – Yes, I am'.

17. This distribution seems linked, at least partly, to the Germanic type of negation which, although postverbal in German, Dutch and Frisian, is placed in rhematic position and sometimes constitutes the only focal element, cf. *Ich sehe den Zusammenhang(TOP) nicht(FOC)* 'I don't see the connection' (but see the discussion in 3.2.).

18. In these three suggested translations, given in this order by our informant, we have first of all negative focalisation (that is, constituent negation), then maximally explicit rendition, and finally rendition by means of a prosentence.

19. This is the reply given by a native speaker. The alternative, given by a bilingual with Provençal as the second language is thus: *Jan manja de peis, mai pas seis companhs*.

20. The first of the two alternatives uses a prosentence, *nie*, differing from the unstressed sentence negation morpheme *ne* which appears on the verb *jedia* in the second alternative.

21. If this were proved, it would constitute another characteristic that the Germanic and the Gallo-Romance languages (including Catalan) have in common (cf. 4.2.).

22. The second variant (reply from a university teacher) has, however, for Q3 *pas ... pas*, with the same morph as Q5. In fact, the possibility is not to be excluded that in various languages, alongside *NOT1 ... NEC1*, for Q3, *NEC1 ... NEC1(/2)* coexists, as in an elevated variety of Italian (cf. Foreword to Part II, note 1). This is the case in Greek, for which, alongside a Q3 *dén .. oúte* [that is, *NOT1 ... NEC1*] in the replies of three university students, we also have *oúte ... oúte* [that is, *NEC1 ... NEC1*] in the reply of a teacher colleague. *NOT1*, a marking evidently drawn from English, makes reference to the sentence negation morpheme. The index 1 distinguishes, if somewhat marginally, this morpheme from that which in certain languages (for example French, Estonian) is reserved for phrasal negation (: *NOT2*), cf. 5.4.

23. In negative sentences the verb is obligatorily preceded by the clitic *ne-*.

24. **John neither speaks and doesn't move* is obviously impossible, as is also **Giovanni né parla e non si muove*: there may be 'telescoping' of *NEC1* over *NEC2* but not vice versa.

25. The reply from our German informant is of this type: *Hans spricht nicht und rührt sich nicht*, thus introducing a clear differentiation with Q4 (: *Weder Hans noch seine Freunde wollten gehen*, of the type *neither ... nor*). French also follows this line, although with reinforcement of NEG in Q3b: *Jean ne parle pas et ne bouge pas non plus* (next to the elevated form ... *ne parle pas ni ne bouge* [without *pas*!]).

26. The cases of identity or non-identity constitute individual parameters of comparison, for which see chapter 10.

27. In Q3a Maltese allows *ma* (as in Q5) as well as *la*: *Ġanni ma jitkellimx* (or *la jitkellem*) *u lanqas jiċċaqlaq*.

28. In our corpus the languages that use different adversative conjunctions in Q6 and Q7 are: Basque (*baina* vs. *baizik*), Catalan (... *però sí que menja carn* vs. ... *sinò a una festa*), Icelandic (... *en hann borðar kjöt* vs. *heldur í partíi*), Polish (... *ale za to je mięso* vs. ... *lecz na party*), Croatian (... *ali jede meso* vs. ... *već na zabavi* [but the Serbian reply is: ... *već meso* and ...*već na zabavi!*]), Bulgarian (...*no jade meso* vs. ... *a na edin prazdnik* [but the Macedonian reply is: ...*no jade meso* and *no na zabava!*]), Finnish (... *mutta lihaa hän syö* [Vb.3SG] vs. ... *vaan juhlassa*), Estonian (... *küll aga liha* vs. *vaid pidul* [but ... *aga ühel pidul* is also possible!]. These are stylistic options, not morphologically obligatory oppositions, like the Italian *ma* vs. the literary *bensì*.

29. As in the preceding note, it is as well to restrict ourselves with such wording: we in no way exclude the possibility that 'raising' also exists in those languages for which our informant has instead limited her or himself to providing only the literal translation of the sentence.

30. Finnish and Lapp in fact have different morphemes for NEG~PRED~ and NEG~PROHIB~ (for example Finn. *e-* vs. *älä-*). Nonetheless they are catalogued with the languages whose morphs coincide for the two types of negation in that the two forms used are part of the same paradigm of the negative Vb. Compare, in this respect, the different situation for Estonian illustrated in note 31.

31. In Estonian the negative Vb has crystallised in the single uninflected form *ei*, but in the imperative the negative Vb has maintained an inflection, thus:
Q37a *ära*   *mine*   *üle*,   *John!*
         NEG:IMPER:2SG   go:IMPER:2SG   there John
Q38a *ärge*   *minge*   *üle*   *mu lapsed!*
         NEG:IMPER:2PL   go:IMPER:2PL   there my children
Thus the 'NEG~PRED~' morph is different to that of 'NEG~PROHIB~'.

32. The impersonal prohibitive is quite normal in Italian when not addressed to a particular interlocutor: e.g. *Vietato attraversare* 'Forbidden to cross'; but obviously ***Giovanni, vietato attraversare!*, with direct allocution, would not be possible.

Chapter 6

1. Universal quantifiers will not be examined here. For a general picture of the problems presented by the use of quantifiers in negative sentences see, among many others, Jespersen (1917: 84–90); Horn (1978: 138–148 and 1989: 204–267); Payne (1985: 233–239). For a treatment of quantifiers, both negative and existential, in broader typological terms reference should be made to Haspelmath (1993).

2. Within the theoretical and formal framework of S. Dik's (1978 and 1989) 'Functional Grammar' Kahrel's is the only attempt at a typology based on a sample which, while not large (38 languages), seeks to reflect the typological, genetic and areal variety of the world's languages. In the formal terms of 'Functional Grammar' his types are defined thus: a. neg plus indefinite (cf. (i)); b. neg plus zero quantification (cf. (iii)); c. neg plus special indefinite (cf. (ii)); d. zero quantification (cf. (iv)). Kahrel's typology actually includes five types, the last of which, not found in Europe, consists in a negative existential construction, cf. Fula *walaa ko ɓe-ngindʼi* (lit. be=NEG REL 3PL-want) 'There is nothing they want' (Kahrel, in prep., p. 9).

3. Dahl's observations are modestly presented in the margins of his well-known and much quoted work on the typology of sentence negation, the distribution of the types across languages being given as an "impressionistic generalization" (ibid.).

4. Regarding this set of problems, a brief mention of the syntactic function of negative quantifiers is made by Payne (1985: 238): "It also appears that inherently negative quantifiers themselves

in at least one language [Tiwi, in Australia] are restricted to subject position". Payne deals with the problem with reference to possibilities in the distribution of negated quantifiers of the type 'not many/many not'.

5. For Latin see the detailed analysis of non-negative pronouns in Orlandini (1981). The system of quantification in Italian is now thoroughly described, though in terms which go beyond our field of interest, in Longobardi (1988).

6. The bibliography on English quantifiers is extremely abundant, suffice it here to note by way of illustration the early work of Lakoff (1969), the more recent work of Hirtle (1988) and above all Tesch's empirical research (1989) on the use of *some* and *any* and the quantifiers formed with them in spoken and written British, with the aim of checking and correcting where required the presentation of the relevant rules in the teaching of English.

7. Reference to the English paradigms A and N, central to all treatments of negative quantifiers, is also used with the aim of making comparisons in Giuseppe Longobardi's and Raffaella Zanuttini's works on negation in the Romance languages and in particular the Italian dialects, within a generative framework (cf. Zanuttini (1987 and 1989), Benincà (1989: 15–16)).

8. This is also the more current usage in the grammars of European languages, which often deal with these items in the chapter on indefinite pronouns (and adverbs) (cf. also Ger. *unbestimmte Fürwörter/Umstandswörter*, but Russian *neopredelennye mestoimenija* 'indefinite pronouns' vs *otricatel'nye mestoimenija* 'negative pronouns').

9. Kahrel makes the same observation, and even considers inherently negative quantifiers to be almost exclusively restricted to the European territory.

10. Notably *nada* is derived from the Lat. *(rem) natam* and not from incorporation of the negative morpheme as, for example, Eng. *never*.

11. In our questionnaire contexts of this sort are provided by entries Q14 and Q12. In the discussion which follows the assignment of the value N or S or A to other quantifiers in the various languages has been carried out on the basis of information from grammars and dictionaries, accordingly acknowledged.

12. In glossing the quantifiers a features notation in [ ] is adopted in order to avoid giving misleading translations. Note that A is the value of the generic existential quantifier as opposed to N and S, and that 'anim' stands for animate.

13. As will be seen further on, these are quantifiers with the value A, which are in opposition to the corresponding S quantifiers *norbait*, *zerbait*.

14. *Ketään* and *mitään* are formed from interrogative pronominal bases, respectively *ke-* 'who?' and *mi-* 'what?', followed by the partitive suffix *-tä* and the generalising particle *-än*.

15. It goes without saying that in non-N languages the Ulysses riddle (see Q8, Q9 in the questionnaire) cannot work. Cf. 7.6.

16. The inclusion of English in this group will be discussed a little further on.

17. Colloquial Frisian has *neat* 'nothing', but *net ien* 'nobody'. The different quantifier inventories of the two varieties of Frisian will be discussed further on in section 6.5.

18. The Ulysses riddle does of course work in Danish, but on this see 7.6.

19. In Jones and Gade's (1981: 94–96) excellent grammar the example sentences with indefinite pronouns in the replies are never elliptical. We take note of them, even if this may only be due to the well-known habit of grammars of reporting complete sentences.

20. The internal structure of the quantifier paradigm is discussed further on (see Chapter 7). As for Danish, note that according to Jones–Gade (1981: 94) *ingen* and *ikke nogen* are "at least as common", while "there is a tendency to negate *noget* by means of *ikke noget* rather than *intet*" (p. 96). The latter is considered by the authors to be rather a negation of *alt* 'all', in expressions of the type *alt eller intet* 'all or nothing'. In adjectival use we have only *nogen*, which is also used

in the plural in the affirmative (that is, with the value S), but never in the negative (that is, to render the value N) and also, potentially, in interrogative and conditional sentences, or in non-factual contexts where it takes on the value A (p. 95).

21. Cf., for example, Collinder (1969: 150), who glosses these with 'somebody' and 'something' respectively.

22. *Mitte* is used in the function of constituent negation, cf. *mitte esirinnas* 'not in the foreground', *mitte arvestama* 'to overlook' (lit. 'to not consider'), *mitte avada* 'not to be opened'. In combination with *ei* and also with the imperative form of the negative verb *ära* (pl. *ärge*) it serves as a 'double' emphatic negation, cf. *ära tee seda mitte!* 'don't do it!', lit. 'NEG:IMPER:2SG do this:PART NEG' (Saagpakk 1982: 500−501). Lavotha (1973: 93) also reports cases of prefixation of *mitte* as in *mittesöödavaid* 'not edible'.

23. Our informant, a lecturer at the University of Uppsala, expressly indicated in the replies to the questionnaire the optionality of *ei* ("*Ei* can be omitted"), which is therefore understood in the same way as the negative prosentences seen in English and Italian and for which see 5.1.

24. These are A items, as opposed to the S items *duine éigin* 'man some' and *rud éigin* 'thing some'. Cf. 6.3.3.

25. Some languages, such as English, do not give elliptical replies in the context of a reply of positive disagreement exemplified here (see Bernini 1990: 141−146). This fact, however, has no bearing on the interpretation of the quantifiers that appear here, the sentence anyway expressing reference to a real, factual state of affairs.

26. The sentence serves the purposes of the survey but is obviously unlikely in a discourse of non-linguists. It is, however, plausible, although improbable, in contexts such as the following: after a hurried robbery of an employee in a crowded post office a police officer briefly questioned those present. All were aware of what was happening and noticed the robbers' appearances, others didn't have time to take note of all the useful details. Upon arrival of the inspector in charge of the investigation the officer reported the results of his brief enquiry to him saying "Almost everyone saw everything perfectly; somebody didn't see something".

27. The order in which the relevant contexts are arranged reflects their relative importance for the purposes of comparison. The sequence of question and reply in the entries in the questionnaire, apart from that relating to their polarity, is, of course, inverted (cf. example 26 above).

28. In the corpus elaborated by Tesch (1989: 338) *some* and its formatives are in the overwhelming majority (90% (p. 238)) in declarative affirmative contexts. Yet roughly half the occurrences of *any* and its formatives are, however, found in affirmative declarative contexts (for example *I thought any fool would know*, where the existence of the referent is merely assumed, but not taken for granted). The other half of the occurrences of *any* and its formatives are distributed amongst negative declarative sentences (approx. 30−40%, for example *I shan't get any scripts from the assistants before then*) and positive questions (approx. 10%, for example *but is there any truth in there?*). It is extremely rare to find them in negative questions.

29. For example, in Vlasto (1988: 130), *kto-to* is translated as 'a certain person, someone', *kto-nibud'* 'someone, anyone'. Dahl (1970: 37) had already observed that indefinites in *-nibud'* favour a similar distribution to the Eng. *any,* occurring in negative (sic!), interrogative and conditional sentences. Cf. also the following opposition (ibid., 38), where a different distribution of presuppositions is called into play: *Kto-to pozvonil?/Did someone ring?* vs *Zvonil kto-nibud'?/Has anyone called?*.

30. The reason for this is evident in the distribution of the three items in Russian with respect to English (cf. 6.4.1.) and in their behaviour in negative declarative sentences, cf. *Nikto ničego ne videl* 'Nobody saw anything', and not ***Nikto čego-nibud' ne videl.* For a rigorous analysis in terms of generative semantics of the meaning and distribution of the Russian indefinites in *-to* and

-nibud' see again Dahl (1970), who criticises the use of the feature [+/− specific] and traces the opposition between the two quantifiers back to the different positions assumed by them at deep structure. The indefinites in *-to* require a predicate of existence in the highest node in the base structure, in turn dominated by a declarative performative predicate (ibid., 35).

31. For Ukrainian cf. Rudnyćkyj (1964: 64): *xtos'* 'jemand' ('somebody') vs. *xtobud'* 'irgendeiner' ('anybody'); *ščos'* 'etwas' ('something') vs. *ščonebud'* 'irgend etwas' ('anything').

32. Cf. also Joseph—Philippaki Warburton (1987: 68): "The distribution of these two types of forms [i. e. in our terms those with the value N and S] is not entirely complementary". Of the four examples recorded by Joseph and Philippaki Warburton, three are direct questions, while the fourth is a declarative sentence with deontic modality: *prépei kaneís ná prosékhē hótan miláei* (lit. must [NA/+anim]:NOM CONJ pay.attention when speaks). The two researchers translate it as 'Someone must pay attention when he talks', but, on the basis of the meaning that may be inferrable from the example as a generally valid order, the following translation seems better 'One must pay attention when one speaks', with an impersonal construction. Thus the assignment of the value NA to *kaneís* is confirmed, in opposition to value S assigned to *kápoios*.

33. The morphemic gloss of the two auxiliaries (AUX) is the following: *duzu*: PRES:3SG.ABS:2SG.ERG; *dut*: PRES:3SG.ABS:1SG.ERG.

34. Cf. Braune-Ebbinghaus (1981: 104), who always quote the forms in question accompanied by *ni*. Apart from *hwashun* there is also *manna*, with the same meaning, and the adverb of time *hwanhun* 'ever'. The examples are taken from the Wulfila Bible edited by Wilhelm Streitberg, cf. Streitberg (1971 (< 1909)).

35. *Ainnohun* corresponds here to the Gr. *tina állon* 'someone/anyone else'.

36. 'Syntatic type' refers schematically to the types illustrated in 6.1., reproduced here for convenience:

   a: N, cf. Ger. *Hans hat [N]niemanden gesehen*;
   b: NEG N, cf. It. *Giovanni [NEG]non vide [N]nessuno*;
   c: NEG A, cf. Eng. *John did [NEG]not see [A]anybody*;
   d: NEG S, cf. Hindi [S]*koī [NEG]nahī̃ āyā thā*.

37. Mention may be made only fleetingly of the delicate sociolinguistic problem concerning the interweaving of language varieties shared by the same social groups and of the problems of the diffusion of features from top to bottom and vice versa. This, perhaps, is the case regarding the presence of *net wat* in the literary language variety.

38. Cf., for example, *Hann segir aldrei neitt*, lit. 'he says never nothing', Kress (1982: 109).

39. In addition to Frisian and Danish, discussed in 6.3.2.2, the two types are distributed amongst the more or less colloquial varieties of Norwegian as well ("[...] the expression: *ikke noen*, [...] often replaces *ingen*, especially in colloquial speech", Marm—Sommerfelt (1981: 131)). Different types of oppositions according to the language variety taken as the norm are also found in Welsh. For one of our three informants *rhywun* 'someone', *rhywbeth* 'something' may also appear in negative questions, giving a system ⟨N vs. SA⟩, whereas for the other two informants they form a system ⟨N vs S⟩ as they oppose to *neb* 'nobody' and *dim* 'nothing'. Cf.
   Oni   welaist ti   rywun/rywbeth? -   (Do,) gwelais   rywun/rywbeth
   NEG   saw   you   someone/something   yes   saw:1SG   someone/something
   'Didn't you see anyone/anything − Yes, I did see someone/something'
   The indefinite pronoun forms that appear in the examples have undergone the usual lenition when used in the function of direct object of the verb in finite form.

40. Note that our informant does not give the reply *Doch, etwas*, even after the third form selected as translation of the question Q13, i. e. *Hast du nicht was gesehen?* A reply such as *Doch, jemanden*, in Q15 would indeed be hard to accept.

41. For Portuguese, prescriptive grammars do not specifically mention *qualquer coisa* except in the lists of indefinites (cf. Vázquez Cuesta – Mendes da Luz 1980: 402); its value seems to be rather that of 'whatever' (ibid. 514).

42. In the diachronic perspective, it is interesting to note how, of the two inherited pronouns in Icelandic, the one with incorporation of negation (*neinn* < *ne+einn* 'not one') has taken on the value A, while the one that probably originally had the value A, that is, *enginn* (< *ein-gi(n)*, with *-gi(n)* = Goth. *-hun*, generalising suffix comparable to Lat. *-cum* of *quicumque*; cf. Ramat (1988a: 136)), has become fixed with the value N.

43. This is what emerges from our questionnaire. The grammars instead do not register asymmetries of this type in the whole paradigm, cf. *ha vingút ningú aquesta tarda?* '¿ha venido alguién esta tarde?'/'has anybody come this evening?', *hi ha res de nou?* '¿hay alguna novedad?'/'are there any news?', *l'heu trobat enlloc?* '¿lo habéis encontrado en alguna parte?'/'did you meet him anywhere?', *l'has vist mai per aquí?* '¿lo has visto alguna vez por ahí?'/'have you ever seen him here?', *teniu gens de pa?* '¿tenéis algo de pan?'/'have you got any bread?' (Badía Margaritt 1975: 41 of vol. 2).

44. The informants who gave the reply (83) observed that in negative sentences there is a tendency to omit *kápoios*; they consider the sentence *Kápoios dén eíde típota* (lit. 'sombody NEG saw nothing') ungrammatical in reply to Q17 (*Somebody didn't see anything*). This is instead grammatical for the informants who replied with (82) to Q18. However, the latters allow as an alternative *Merikoí dén eídan típota*, lit. 'Some didn't see nothing'.

45. It is as well to note that the reply of our Serb informant allows the translation of (75) [= Q18]) (cf. *Neko nije nešto video* vs. *Neko nije ništa video* 'Somebody didn't see nothing'), while the Croatian informant gives the same translation for Q17 and Q18, that is, *Netko nije ništa vidio* 'Somebody didn't see anything /**something'. It is of course possible that faced with a sentence of this sort, particularly 'marked' and not particularly clear outside of an appropriate context, speakers react in different ways.

46. Ukrainian, which has various series of indefinites comparable to those in Russian and Belorussian (cf. Rudnyćkyj 1964: 64), can probably be added to this list, although we do not have replies to the questionnaire for this language.

47. For discussion of these various types of quantifiers in Italian see Longobardi (1988: 651 – 652).

48. Another variant suggested by our informant is *Einige sahen einiges nicht*, where *einiges* in the singular is again intrinsically existential. The disheartened final comment to this entry in the questionnaire is: "unklarer Satz" [unclear sentence].

49. If the interpretation is correct, the same goes for Lapp which, however, on the basis of the replies to the questionnaire, does not seem to have a term for 'something'. Cf.

    Muhton   i-i   oaidnán moadde diŋgga
    [S/+anim]   NEG-3SG   seen   [A?]   thing?

    The varieties of Lapp in greatest contact with Russian have instead developed series of indefinites, both negative and positive, according to the type ⟨N vs. S_1 vs. S_2⟩. The negatives are formed with the particle *ni*, obviously a Russian loan (Kuruč 1985: 548 – 549).

50. The impression of 'weakness' that these two items give in Danish is indirectly confirmed by the reply to Q15 (*Så du ikke nogen? – Jo, jeg så en* 'Didn't you see someone? – Yes, I saw one'), where the use of the pronoun *en* 'one' is part of the increasing referentiality strategy in this particular context showing a positive reply to a negative question.

51. Discussion of the functional importance of N items is taken up again in more detail in 7.4.

52. In Gricean terms, S items, designating only existence (of animate and non-animate referents, but also referring to time and place of an event), do not violate only in a few contexts the maxim of quantity ("give as much information as is required") and perhaps also that of manner ("avoid ambiguity") (see Grice 1975).

53. The use of S items is probably more frequent in contexts of this sort, but we do not have statistical data regarding this.

54. *Xi* in the final analysis is derived from *šay*ʔ 'thing' like the postverbal negative morpheme and takes part in the formation of indefinite interrogative pronouns in almost all the Arabic dialects (cf. Fischer–Jastrow 1980: 85).

55. Cf. Wright (1933: 236 of vol. II):

    ʔaḥadu   *n-nas-i*
    [A/+anim] ART-people-GEN:DEF
    'one of the people'
    mā   *jāʔib-i*   *aḥadun*
    NEG came-1SG [a/+anim]
    'nobody came to me'

56. The relevant data may be found in Rohlfs (1968: §§ 497, 498, 499).

57. See, still in 2.3., the Romance, Germanic and Celtic documentation of words for 'drop' used as negative polarity items.

58. It may also be hypothesised that *(v)ergót* was re-formed on the basis of *negót* with a strategy of increase in referentiality, that is, by trying to reproduce a positive meaning of the type 'really a drop'. However, the presence of *veruno* in Tuscan, with a value fluctuating between A and N, makes this course of development less plausible. Obviously the two hypotheses ought to be evaluated on the basis of philological documentation.

Chapter 7

1. In the languages in which they appear, autonomous forms, which are found as independent entries in the dictionaries, may of course be substituted by descriptive expressions, cf. Rus. *nipočëm* vs. *ni v kakom slučae* 'in no case' (Ožegov 1968, s.v. *nipočëm*].

2. For similar contrastive comments cf. also Schwarze (1988: 313).

3. Obviously, only the base forms of a paradigm, being also entries in the dictionary, and not all the possible inflected forms for the different syntactic relations, are included in the calculation (for example ACC/GEN *nikogo* '(of) nobody'; DAT *nikomu* 'to nobody'; INSTR *ničem* 'with/by nothing', etc.; or also *ničej* (NOM.MASC), *ničja* (NOM.FEM), *ničʔe* (NOM.NEUT), *ničʔi* (PL), *ničʔego* (GEN.SG.MASC/NEUT), *ničʔej* (GEN.SG.FEM), etc.).

4. This is a category which is in fact not present in English. In the following example it must be translated by means of a periphrasis: *Skol'ko knig ty prinës? – Niskol'ko* 'How many books have you brought? – I haven't brought any, I have brought no books' (cf. also Ghere–Skvorzova 1952: 333).

5. Cf. Ožegov (1968, s.v.). Alongside these autonomous forms there are, of course, transparent forms, cf. the already recorded *ni v kakom slučae* 'in no case' (note 1) and again *nikoim obrazom* (INSTR) 'in no way'.

6. This is the semantic category (*kačestvo*) proposed for negative adjectives (It. *nessuno*, Eng. *no*, Russian *nikakoj*, Bel. *nijaki*) by Krivickij *et al.* (1978: 163) in their Belorussian grammar. Adverbial categories are listed by Krivickij *et al.* (1978: 166–169) for Belorussian and by Maslov (1981: 317) for Bulgarian: *narečija mesta* 'adverbs of place', for example Bulg. *nikăde, otnikăde*, respectively for place/movement to and from a place; *narečija vremeni* 'adverbs of time', Bulg. *nikoga*; *narečija obraza dejstvija* 'adverbs of manner of action', Bulg. *nikak*; *narečija pričiny i celi* 'adverbs of cause and purpose', Bulg. *za niščo*, which is, however, a secondary locution. Regarding adjectives of the

Russian type *ničej*, Bel. *ničyj*, Bulg. *ničij*, Krivickij *et al.* (1978: 163) suggest the category *primadležnost'* 'belonging', which may well be considered as implying the category animate.

7. As well as from grammars and dictionaries, the data discussed here are drawn from the entries Q21 (*John had never run so fast and he couldn't go on any longer*) and Q22 (*John had no friend, no home anywhere*) of the questionnaire.

8. The pronouns *niains* (NOM.SG.MASC), *niainâ*, or also *ni ainâ* (NOM.SG.FEM) 'nobody' and the negative adjective *niainonts* (NOM.SG.) are also attested in Old Prussian (Schmalstieg 1974: 106-107 and 83 respectively). The attestation of a non-animate negative pronoun is doubtful. According to Schmalstieg (107) the assignment of neutral gender to *neaineassa* (GEN.SG., *hápax legómenon*, cf. *beggi mes asmai stêison* NEAINEASSA *wertei kan mes madlimai* [denn wir sind der KEINES werdt das wir bitten] 'because we are not worthy of anything of that which we pray for') by previous researchers is in fact debatable, in that it is based uniquely on the corresponding German *keines* of the original version of the Old Prussian catechisms.

9. Cf. Veksler—Jurik (1984: 10 and 172). In sentence Q22 the negative adverb does not appear in the Latvian translation, instead there is an S item accompanied by the negative coordinating conjunction *nedz*, cf.

Džonam   ne-bija   nedz draugu   nedz kaut kur   mājas.
John:DAT NEG-was nor friends:GEN:PL nor some where house:GEN (= LOCATIVE)
'John had no friend, no home anywhere'

10. Amongst the negative quantifiers of place there are still: *sehova* (movement to a place) *sehonnan* (movement from a place) and, with deictic adverbs, *semerre* (movement to a place), *semerröl* (movement from a place), which may be formed by making use of locative suffixes. Note also *semennyiért* 'of no value' (*sem-ennyi-ért*, lit. NEG-so much-value).

11. The formation possibilities in Albanian for the same categories are numerous, as may be inferred from Buchholz—Fiedler's (1987: 311—331 and 370—371) grammar. Cf., for example, *moskush* (NEG-who), *kurrkush* (never-who), *askurrkush* (NEG-never-who); *asnjeri* (NEG-someone), *mosnjeri* (NEG-someone). The possibilities are multiplied by the use of the prefix *hiç-*, a Turkish loan (but originally Persian), cf. *hiçgjë*, *hiçasgjë*, *hiçmosgjë* etc. 'nothing' (Buchholz—Fiedler 1987: 312).

12. *Nul* is relatively marginal in the system, in fact "[il] reste presque uniquement confiné à la langue écrite" [it is almost exclusively restricted to the written language] and furthermore it may only fill the function of subject in the sentence (Gaatone 1971: 181). Even *aucun* is relatively marginal (Gaatone 1971: 172—177).

13. Suppletion may even penetrate inflection, as the case of the Lat. pronoun *nemo* 'nobody' shows:
NOM *nemo;* ACC *neminem;* DAT *nemini;* GEN — ;   ABL —
                                    nulli   nullius   nullo.

14. In this list we give, in order, the equivalents of Eng. *nobody* and *no, nothing, never, nowhere.*

15. *Morse* is recorded by Hemon (1984: 66), who gives as example: *n'o charas morse* 'il ne les aima jamais' [he never loved them]. The fully negative value of *morse* and of its rival *gwech ebed* (lit. 'time in the world') is taken indirectly from Marvennou (1978: 74). For *gwech* 'time' see Hemon (1975: 171). Our informant replies to Q21 with *biskoas*, cf.

biskoas n'   e-noa redet Yann ken buan
never NEG was run John so fast
'John had never run so fast'

According to Thurneysen (1970 (< 1913): 231), *biskoas* (cf. M.Bret. *bez-goaz, bezcoaz, biscoaz* 'ever (never)', Wel. *byth* 'ever, forever', Corn. *byth, by, bythqueth* 'ever (never)') is a Goidelic loan, for which cf. Ir. *bith, ro-bith* 'long period', "[...] a rare word [...] probably not to be separated from *bith* 'world' ". For the latter word see also the discussion in 7.3.4.

16. In Icelandic suppletion is evident in the case of *enginn* vs. *aldrei*. Despite their forms, *enginn* and *ekkert* belong to the same inflectional paradigm and thus depict an organisation differing from both derivation and suppletion, as will be argued in 7.3.3.

17. This is an open organisational schema, which also includes comparative expressions (cf. *no more/longer*, *any more/longer*, *some more/longer*); theoretically, new elements may always be joined to the bases *no*, *any* and *some*, giving rise to phrases rather than to new lexemes (see *some people* vs. *somebody*).

18. From M.Dut. *negheen*, cf. MHG *nichein* 'nec unus' > Ger. *kein*. Historically, therefore, it is a different derivation process. Synchronically the negative morph (which is *n-*) is no longer recognisable in *g-*, *k-*.

19. Bear in mind, however, the position of Danish and, in part, of Norwegian and Swedish, discussed above with regard to the oppositions between N and S items.

20. *Einskis* is a case of double inflection, historically justifiable for the base *einn* 'one' from which *enginn* is derived, and extended from this to the generalising suffix *-gi* as well (with devoicing due to regressive assimilation). The other forms are the outcome of phonetic processes and the reanalysis of the composite **einn+gi* (> OIce. *engi*), which has caused the loss of the inflection on the suffix (Ramat 1988a: 236). Cf. OIce. *ekki* 'nothing' < **ei(n)t-gi*, *einum-gi*, *einungi* (DAT.SG.MASC) next to *engum* (Ranke−Hofmann 1967: 35 and 54).

21. The marginal forms of negative adverbs formed by preposing *sem-* to deictic adverbs extended with the suffixes of locative cases, such as *semerre* (movement to a place), *semerről* (movement from a place), do not fall within our type not only due to the formant *sem-* but also because of the already locative meaning of the base.

22. The language variety to which reference is made here is the so-called unified Basque or *euskara batua*, based on the varieties spoken in the region of Vizcaya and Guipúzcoa (Saltarelli 1988, 'Introduction'). In the Navarro-Laburdin variety, on the French side of the Pyrenees, quantifiers with value A are formed with the prefix *ne-* (for example, *nehor* 'anyone') and, alongside *ezer* 'anything', *deus* is also used (Allières 1979: 98).

23. The usual gloss INT indicates here the base of the interrogative pronouns. Obviously *inor* (as also *ezer*) receives case suffixes which encode its syntactic function (cf. *inor-ek*, ERG; *inor-i*, DAT; *inor-en*, GEN and so on, cf. Saltarelli (1988: 55)).

24. Cf. 6.3. concerning the asymmetries in value between members of a paradigm and 7.4. regarding more specifically the asymmetries in the inventories of negative quantifiers.

25. These are the replies given by the three informants for our questionnaire. Lewis's pocket dictionary (1988, s.v. *nowhere*) gives *dim yn unlle* 'nowhere' that is, 'not in a place'.

26. *Bennag*, or even *pennac*, *bennak* (cf. Hemon 1975: 142−144) has the value both of 'any, some' (cf. *en ul lech bennac* 'in some place') and of '(so)ever' (cf. *piu pennac* 'whosoever', *e pe leac'h-bennag ez eot* 'wherever you will go').

27. Data taken from De Bhaldraithe (1987), s.v. *nobody, nothing, never, nowhere, nowise*.

28. This type of locution is Pan-Celtic and is also found in Brythonic. Cf. Wel. *dym byd* and in particular Bret. *ebed* (also *en bet*, *ebet*, *erbet* (Hemon 1975: 155)), formed with the preposition *e(n)* 'in'. Cf. also the reply to Q11:

    ne   teuas   den   ebed
    NEG came man in.world
    'Nobody came'

29. Cf. De Bhaldraithe (1987), s.v. *somebody, something, somewhere, somehow* respectively. For *uair éigin* cf. instead Ó Dónaill (1977, s.v. *uair*).

30. Note also the presence of the preposition *in*. Cf. again De Bhaldraithe (1987) s.v. *nowhere*.

31. And also in interrogatives, in accordance with the uses of items with A value , cf.
    ach an   mbeidh pai   ar bith   ag Pádraig […]?
    but INT will.be reward on world by Patrick
    'but will Patrick have a reward […]?' (Ó Siadhail 1988: 75)

32. We limit ourselves to note the variation which stands out in contexts that are very similar, cf.
    Q10 *Céard a fheiceann tú? − Dada, a dúirt Seán.*
        'What did you see ? − Nothing, said John'
    Q12 *An bhfaca tú rud ar bith? − […] Ní fhaca mé rud ar bith.*
        'Have you seen anything? − I haven't seen anything'
    The variation seems quite different to that obtaining in Italian between *niente* and *nulla* (cf.
    Brunet 1981: 145 and 149), which in a neutral context such as that of the sentences in the
    questionnaire may not in fact alternate.

33. For the glosses cf. De Bhaldraithe (1987, s.v. *never*) and Ó Dónaill (1977, under the respective
    entries).

34. Cf. *fear sam bith* 'man in the world', *gin* ('kind' if derived from *gin* 'beget', cf. MacBain (1982:
    194)); *càil* 'condition', *dad* 'thing', *rud sam bith* 'thing in the world' as locutions with the value A.
    Cf. *feareigin* 'man some' (animate masculine S item), *té-eigin* 'one some' (animate feminine S item);
    cuideigin 'place some', *rudeigin* 'thing some' as locutions with the value S (Mackinnon 1971, 87 f.).
    Cf., for example,
    Chan eil càil   ceàrr   air Calum
    NEG is [A/-anim] mistaken on Calum
    'There is nothing wrong with Calum'
    A   bheil rud sam bith anns a'   bhocsa?
    INT is   [A/-anim] in+ART box
    'Is there anything in the box?' (Mackinnon 1971: 88)

35. Manner is perhaps the more salient of the more marginal categories, cf. Eng. *no way*, and could
    constitute a further stage in the series of implications of (23).

36. The presence of negative quantifiers for the categories of movement to a place and movement
    from a place, as already exemplified for the Slavonic languages and Hungarian, seems to depend
    on the relevance of these distinctions in the language in question.

37. In (24) Norwegian and Swedish are bracketed because they have adverbial negative quantifiers
    of place, although relegated to the fringes of the system.

38. One of three informants gave a slightly different translation:
    Ni   redodd John erioed   cyn gyflym-ed
    NEG ran   John [A/time] so fast-EQUAT

39. While in (26) there is an autonomous form of the adverb of time, in (27) there is a secondary
    rendering by means of a prepositional phrase, which allows for various lexical choices, as the
    translations of the other two informants show:
    Nid   oedd gan John na ffrind na chartref yn unrhyw le
    NEG was with John nor friend nor house in [S/ADJ] place
    D-oedd   gan John ddim ffrindiau, dim   cartref yn un-lle
    NEG-was with John NEG friends NEG house in a-place

40. One of our informants feels *ingenstans* to be a rather 'brusque' reply, more typical of child
    language.

41. Cf. Wehr-Cowan (1976, s.v. ⟨'bd⟩): "always, forever; ever, (with neg.) never (in the future), not
    at all, on no account; (*alone, without negation*) *never! not at all! by no means!*" (our emphasis). Doniach
    (1982, s.v. *never*) records instead *lā abadan*, lit. 'not ever'. Otherwise, Classical Arabic, with rigid
    VSO order, has only A items, which in sentences are always preceded by negation, placed before

the verb. In the dictionaries these items are always accompanied by the negation morpheme when it is necessary to indicate its negative value, cf. *lā ʔaḥada* 'nobody' (lit. 'not somebody'), and thus *lā šayʔan* 'nothing' (lit. 'not thing'), *lā fī ʔayyin makānin* 'nowhere' (lit. 'not in some place') (Doniach 1982, s.v. *nobody, nothing, nowhere* respectively). In fact, Classical Arabic seems to often make use of negative existential constructions (the fifth type individuated by Kahrel (in prep), cf. chapter 6, note 2):

fī bilādi-nā laysa   ḍayfan
in city-1PL not.exists visitor

which is the translation of the slogan 'In our city nobody is a stranger'.

42. The only possible reply is non-elliptical, cf.
Ma-šuft-iš   ḥadd
NEG-saw:1SG-NEG   any
'I haven't seen anyone'

43. Cf. Bernini (1987b: 48). The Egyptian Arabic locution corresponds to the Spanish *en mi vida* 'in my life' with the value 'never'; cf. Molinelli – Bernini – Ramat (1987: 182) and here in 7.6.

44. The perspective presented here follows Givón's (1984: 326 – 328). Note that in the corpus of narrative English discussed there, the negative sentences containing a non-referential subject comprised only 10% of the total and of these only two (out of seven) contained the pronoun *nobody.*

45. The fact that the use of *neva* in the Atlantic creoles may be the result of relexification of a hypothetical Portuguese (proto-)pidgin is irrelevant to our discussion, even if an independent development of the two uses were to carry greater weight.

46. In the contexts of this example both Italian and English exclude the use of *mai/never*, in that the action of coming refers to a single point in time given in the context of the conversation.

47. In effect, on the basis of the dictionary of frequency drawn up by Bortolini – Tagliavini – Zampolli (1971) using a corpus of literary written Italian, *mai* is considerably more frequent than *niente* and *nessuno.* The respective values of usage, taking into account both the absolute number of occurrences and the coefficients of distribution between the types of texts under examination are: 551.76, 324.34, 309.92. Furthermore, *mai* turns out to be equally distributed between the types of text under consideration (coefficient of distribution : 80.31) the same as *nessuno* (coefficient of distribution 80.29), but unlike *niente* (coefficient of distribution: 55.16), whose occurrences are concentrated in cinema and theatre texts and, to a lesser extent, in novels.

48. Furthermore, in Italian *nessuno* may be reinforced with the superlative suffix, cf. *per nessunissima ragione* 'for no reason at all', which brings it closer to the category adjective.

49. Cf. also Germ. *keinerlei*, indeclinable, which is however a secondary formation.

50. Comrie (1989: 53) quite rightly observes that 'nobody' in Greek was *oútis*, with acute accent, since the indefinite *tis* is placed as enclitic to the NEG morph *oú*, while *Oûtis* with a circumflex is only possible if *tis* is taken as the final syllable of a single word. In fact, the accusative *oútin* (and not **Oútina*) is attested in Homer: the already quoted *Od.* IX 366 – 367 reads in fact in its entirety: οὖτις ἐμοὶ γ᾽ ὄνομα· Οὖτιν δέ με κικλήσκουσι / μήτηρ ἠδὲ πατὴρ ἠδ᾽ ἄλλοι πάντες ἑταῖροι. 'No-one is my name. My mother and my father and all my other companions call me No-one'; and in his reply to Ulysses Polyphemus takes up the same accusative form: see line 369 (cf. also Eurip. *Cycl.* 549). But this difference doesn't affect the success of Ulysses' riddle: "Perhaps the Cyclops were not only one-eyed, but also tone-deaf; at any rate, they seem not to have reacted to this difference", Comrie (1989). On Ulysses' riddle see also Seiler (1995).

51. That splendid mine of metalinguistic observation *Through the Looking-Glass* also takes the cue from Homer: *"I see nobody on the road", said Alice. – "I only wish I had such eyes", the King remarked in a fretful tone. "To be able to see Nobody! And at that distance too!…?".*

52. Our Basque informant artfully suggests for (42) a way of salvaging Ulysses' pun: *Inor ez da ni zauritu nauena*, lit. 'No one is the one who wounded me', keeping *inor* in the absolute case (= zero inflection); it is nonetheless a ruse.

53. In view of the impossibilty of adequately translating Ulysses' riddle, our informant has translated 'No-one' in (41) as *naiba* 'demon, devil' which may have an indeterminate-negative value and which, unlike *nimeni*, does not obligatorily require NEG in front of the Vb.

54. For Serbian the informant states that *Niko me je ranjo*, if pronounced with [iː] is possible due to homophony with *Niko*, diminutive of *Nikola*; the same does not seem to apply to Croatian, where there is *nitko*, no longer homophonous with 'Nicky'. For his part the Croatian informant also uses inverted commas for (42): '*Nitko' me ranio*, adding that *Nitko me nije ranio* would be the normal construction. In any case, in Serbian the normal form of (42) is *Niko me nije udario* (cf. the reply to Q16: *Niko nije ništa video* 'Nobody saw anything').

55. This seems to also apply to those cases such as Macedonian, Bulgarian and Slovak in which our replies apparently carry no awkwardness (*Nikoj me rani*, or *Nikto ma poranil*) on the basis, still, of comparison with Q16 and analogous sentences (: Mac. *Nikoj ne vide ništo*, Bulg. *Nikoi ništo ne vidja*, Slovak *Nikto nič nevidel*; Czech *Nikdo nikoho neviděl* 'Nobody saw anybody').

56. At this point a diachronically interesting discussion arises, concerning the oscillation between two extreme poles of a typology of NEG, from greatest impermeability (= a single negative element in the sentence) to greatest permeability (= *n* negative elements in the sentence): cf. chapter 2 above and Ramat (1988b). It is unfortunately not possible to follow this line here; suffice it to observe that, for example, in Old English and still in Middle English multiple NEG, permeable, was quite possible and that today it appears in sub-standard varieties and, most predominantly, in 'Black English' (Ramat− Bernini−Molinelli 1986). For the reverse development, from impermeable NEG in Old Czech (: *každý nevie* 'everybody not-knows' or *nikto vie* 'nobody knows') to permeable NEG in Modern Czech (: *nikto nevie* 'nobody not-knows') see Mathesius (1937). On the other hand, in Old Russian *Nikto prišël* 'Nobody came' was possible (: impermeable NEG) rather than the modern *Nikto ne prišël* (Payne 1985: 237): within the same linguistic tradition there is therefore oscillation between mono- and multiple NEG; cf. Plaut. *Miles* 1411: *iura te non nociturum esse homini … nemini* (rather than *ulli*) 'swear that you won't harm any (lit. no) people', with the obvious aim of reinforcing expressively the negative meaning of the sentence (Molinelli 1988: 34) − that is with the intervention of pragmatic factors in grammatical processes.

57. See also the substandard Italian forms such as *Abbiamo raggiunto niente* 'we have reached nothing' studied by P. Molinelli (1988: 63−81). For analogous typological developments outside the European framework see G. Bernini (1987b) (for Arabic) and Brugnatelli (1987) (for Berber and Maghreb Arabic). Differing in part is the case of German *nicht* (< *ni eo wiht* lit. 'not ever thing') Eng. *not* (< *na wiht* lit. 'not thing') which already have the old negative morpheme *ni* incorporated.

58. The historical origin of NPIs and so-called 'forclusifs' of the type *jamais, pas, personne* (a term introduced by Damourette and Pichon in 1928 to indicate a concept of which the speaker excludes the reality) on the one hand, and the variety of grammatical categories to which 'forclusifs' belong (adverbs, pronouns, determiners) on the other, make this term somewhat unfelicitous. On the one hand *âme qui vive* 'living soul' is indeed established and behaves exactly like *personne* ('forclusif'), on the other hand *personne* obviously has a completely different syntactic behaviour to *jamais*!

59. On the general tendency to have NEG to the left of Vb see Bybee (1985: 176−178, basing on Dahl's data: Dahl 1979). Bear in mind that postverbal negation of the type *Hans spiser ikke fisk*

[=Q5, Danish] 'John doesn't eat fish' turns out in effect to be less widely diffused in absolute terms, even in second language acquisition, than the preverbal type (see 3.1.).

60. Already present in Plautus: *Ita rem natam intellego* (*Cas.* 343; cf. also *Bacch.* 218; *Truc.* 962).

61. This is the 'reading' of the facts that is usually given, even in the generative framework: cf. Rizzi (1982: 121 ff.) (although with the reservations expressed by von Bremen (1986: 229 ff.) concerning the reliability of the data); Bosque (1980: 34 ff.). See also chapter 9.

62. Concerning these 'negative implicative verbs' Givón (1973: 917) very appropriately mentions that they may ultimately become real and proper NEG markers. Such is the case in Bemba (a Bantu language) for *kaanaa* 'to fail, decline': *uku-bomba* 'to work', *uku-kaanaa-bomba* 'to not work'. Cf. Eng. *Delegates failed to attend the convention* which is more or less equivalent to *Delegates didn't attend the convention.*

Chapter 8

1. The 'positive' reading of this sentence in fact requires a 'marked' intonation.

2. In older phases, however, Russian allowed the construction of the type *Nikto prišel*, as has already been noted in 7.6., note 56. For the alternating of these constructions in the history of Russian, including the possibility of saying *Ne prišel nikto*, see Savel'eva (1989).

3. The same also goes for those Nordic languages which have preverbal negation in subordinate clauses. The morph used (*inte, ikke*) is that which originally arose in postverbal position but which was later found in preverbal position following restructurings in the order of nominal and verbal constituents only in subordinate clauses.

4. Consider, for example, negation of verbal infinitives: French *ne pas aller* (NEG1 NEG2 Vb) vs. Bergamasque *andá mía* (Vb NEG) 'not to go'.

5. The sub-standard varieties of Latin were, however, of the type Nx, as amply illustrated in chapter 3. Recall also that the varieties gradually adopted as the standard literary varieties in the course of the history of the three Germanic languages in question were indeed Nx (cf. again chapters 2., 3.).

6. In the column headed 'basic order' the verb is indicated with V, according to the Greenbergian tradition, rather than with Vb, as is the custom in this book.

7. The expressions corresponding to 'never' instead follow the verb in Sardinian (*no aia kkurtu mai*), Spanish (*no habia corrido nunca*) and Catalan (*no havia corregut mai*). In Portuguese 'never' precedes the verb (*nunca tinha corrido*) and in Rumanian it is placed in sentence initial position (*Niciodată Ion nu alergase*).

8. Q16: *Nobody saw anything./ Nessuno vide niente.*
   Q21: *John had never run so fast./ Giovanni non era mai corso così velocemente.*
   Q22: *John had [...] no home anywhere./ Giovanni [...] non aveva casa in nessun luogo.*

9. The auxiliary *zen* has to be glossed: PRET:3SG.ABS.

10. In (b) and (c) the negation is incorporated in *ezin* (cf. *ez* in example (a)). The morpheme by morpheme gloss of the auxiliary *ziezaiekeen* is: POTENTIAL:PRET:3SG.ABS:3PL.DAT: 3SG.ERG.

11. The auxiliary *zuen* is glossed thus: PRET:3SG.ABS:3SG.ERG.

12. *Du* is glossed thus: PRES:3SG.ABS:3SG.ERG. In the corpus of the replies to our questionnaire the following example is in fact also found (=Q19a):

Jon-ek   ezer   ez   zuen
John-ERG [A/-ANIM](ABS) NEG have:PRET:3SG.ABS:3SG.ERG
'John had nothing'

with the order NP$_{ERG}$A$_{ABS}$NEG Vb, which depends, however, on the fact that the auxiliary has here the function of a lexical verb, as the following example shows (=Q16):

Inor-k   *ez*   *zuen*   *ezer*   *ikusi*
[A/+ANIM]-ERG NEG AUX [A/-ANIM](ABS) seen
'Nobody saw anything'

13. Similarly, in Danish the S items used in place of the N items must fall within the scope of NEG, with the consequence of anomalous constituent orders, as in the following case:

    Der   *kom* *ikke*   *nogen*
    there came NEG [S/+ANIM]
    'Nobody came'

    where the subject follows the negative morpheme *ikke* (vs. *Det ved Hans ikke*, lit. 'that knows Hans NEG').

14. For the first of these two versions it is also possible to have the following variant: *Der var ikke noe brød*, lit. 'there was NEG S bread'.

15. There is also the construction without the negative adjective (*Det fanns inte bröd*), but according to our informant it is not the prefered one.

16. Recall (cf. 6.5.) that in colloquial Frisian *net ien* has taken the place of *nimmen* 'no' (ADJ).

17. In the cases in which Q22 cannot be used for comparison because it has been translated with a negative co-ordinate construction, only Q33 has been used, cf.: Rumanian: a. *Jon nu avea nici patria nici casă nicăieri* 'John had neither homeland, nor house anywhere', b. *Nu era pîine* 'There was no bread'; Greek a. *Ho Giánnēs dén eíkhe oúte phílo, oúte spíti pouthená* 'John had neither friend, nor house anywhere', b. *Dén eíkhame psōmí* 'We didn't have any bread'. The same goes for Latvian: b. *Tur ne-bija maize-s*, lit. 'there NEG-was bread-GEN.SG' (for sentence (a) see note 9 in chapter 7.). Ukrainian may also be added to this group, cf. *Vi ne maete dimk-a na lito* 'You don't have a dacha' (lit. 'You NEG have little house-GEN for summer'), *V doma ne-mae molok-a* 'At home there is no milk' (lit. 'In+house NEG-has milk-GEN') (Rudnyćkyj 1964: 17).

18. These are the replies of a native speaker. Those of a speaker of Provençal as a second language show variations which are irrelevant to the constructions under consideration, cf. *Jan aviá pas d'ami*.

19. If we equate the Irish *ar bith*, which is in fact a marker of non-referentiality (cf. 7.3.4.), with the use of negative adjectives, we have a situation which mirrors that of Slovenian, cf.

    a. *Ní*   *raibh cara*   [*ná baile*]   *ag Seán*
       NEG was friend [nor house] by John

    b. *Ní*   *raibh arán*   *ar bith*   *ann*
       NEG was bread on world there

20. Albanian also shows this peculiarity, in that it marks the NP of Q33 but, unlike the other languages under consideration, only the second NP of Q22, cf.

    a. *Gjoni s'*   *ka* *shokë* *asnjë shtëpi* *në asnjë vend*
       John NEG had friend no   house in no   place

    b. *S'*   *kishtë asnjë bukë*
       NEG was   no   bread

    The use of *asnjë* in *asnjë shtëpi* in (a) is probably conditioned by the caesura between the two parts and the ellipsis of the verb which somehow makes the repetition of the negation necessary (compare the Italian and English versions in (31)). Other languages which show the same behaviour, such as Slovak, give the non-referential NP marker as optional in Q33 as well, cf.

    a. *Ján*   *ne-má*   *priateľ-a,*   *nijak-ého dom-u*   *nikde*
       John NEG-had friend-GEN no-GEN house-GEN nowhere

b. *Ne-bol   tu   (nijakỳ)   chlieb/ Ne-bol-o   tu   chlieb-a*
NEG-was there no:NOM bread NEG-was-NEUT there bread-GEN

21. Another translation supplied by our informant contains an indication of place, but not the negative adjective:

I nu   d'eira pan (+ indication of place)
it NEG was   bread

22. The position of Lapp is somewhat anomalous. Note, however, that the various varieties of Lapp are in contact with Norwegian and Swedish, as well as Finnish and Russian (Comrie 1981b: 102).

23. Recall, however, that the reverse does not apply: not all languages with postverbal negation are automatically ⟨N & −NEG⟩, cf. Welsh, Breton, Maltese.

24. Outside the range of ⟨N & −NEG⟩ languages, a partitive construction is found, still competing with a non-partitive one, in Breton (cf. example (46b)), which, as is well known, is exposed to French influence.

25. A more detailed discussion of the rules regarding the usage and interpretation of *de* in these contexts may be found in Gaatone (1971: 101−124). Gaatone considers the locution *(ne) … pas de* "comme un quantitatif ordinaire [qui] représenterait la quantité nulle dans une série de quantitatifs comprenant *peu, beaucoup, assez, trop, combien*" [as an ordinary quantifier which represents zero quantity in a series of quantifiers comprising 'a few', 'much', enough', 'too much', 'how much'] (121−122). From this perspective *pas de* would be entirely equivalent to a negative adjective from a functional point of view.

26. More elevated varieties, which do not use the postverbal negative morpheme, conform to the majority of European languages, cf.

a. *Nid   oedd gan   John gyfaill*
NEG was with John friend

b. *Nid   oedd yna   fara*
NEG was there bread

For sentence (a) a second informant gave instead a translation with negative co-ordination of both indefinite NPs, that is, *Nid oedd gan John na ffrind na chartref yn unrhyw le* (lit. 'NEG was with John nor friend nor house anywhere'). Sentence (b) is that which has the greatest number of variants, which are often a cross with the more or less colloquial varieties. The second of our informants has given, for example, *Nid oedd unrhyw fara* ('NEG was any bread') with the A value adjective *unrhyw*, while the informant who gave categoric postverbal negation also gave, as a variant, the same sentence recorded above in this note. Observe that the word for 'bread' appears in the forms *bara/fara* (['vara]) according to rules of lenition.

27. For the Slavic and Baltic partitive constructions see the examples in this section. For the others cf.

Basque: a. *Jon-ek   ez   zuen   adiskide-rik*
John-ERG NEG had:3SG.ABS:3SG.ERG friend-PART

b. *Ez   zegoen   ogi-rik*
NEG was:3SG.ABS bread-PART

Finnish a. *Juka-lla   e-i   ol-lut   yhtään ystävä-ä*
John-ALL NEG-3SG be:APP at.all friend-PART

b. *E-i   ol-lut   leipä-ä*
NEG-3SG be-APP bread-PART

28. The same consideration also goes for Maltese (and the Arabic dialects of northern Africa, cf. again 3.2.). The replies to the questionnaire for Maltese are:

a. *Ġanni   ma   kell-u-x*   *hbieb*
   John   NEG was:to-3SG-NEG friends
b. *Ma   kien-x   hemm hobż*
   NEG   was-NEG   there bread

As can be seen, Maltese, although it does not have negative adjectives, does not make use of partitive constructions. Note, however, an alternative version of (b): *Ma kien hemm xejn hobż*, lit. 'NEG was there nothing bread'.

29. *Des* is the regular partitive article in positive sentences, cf. *Ils sont des amis* 'They are friends'.

30. Some interesting ideas concerning a comparative analysis of Italian and German in this regard are found in Schwarze (1988: 672−673). For comparisons between Ger. *kein* on the one hand and Port. *não/nenhum* on the other see Koller (1988: 81−83; 102−103).

31. From a structural point of view the autonomy may in fact be contested, in that constructions of this sort, the result of ellipsis of a possessive predicate, maintain the accusative ending in the masculine singular, as shown, for example, by *Keinen Schimmer!* 'No idea' (lit. 'No glimmer (ACC)') for *Ich habe keinen Schimmer*, one of the replies to Q35 given by our informant.

32. These colloquial expressions seem to us better able to bring out the construction under consideration, despite the risk of getting full replies (for example *I have no idea*) in languages, such as English, which allow the construction with only the NP negated; and, on the other hand, of getting elliptical replies (for example *Nessuna idea!*) which are appropriate and actually used in reply to the question *Ne hai idea?/Hai idea se X?* 'Have you any idea?/Have you any idea if X?' On the contrary these are not used in reply to questions of general information such as *Giovanni è tornato?* 'Has John come back?'. Stereotyped expressions of the type *No smoking/Vietato fumare* would instead not have supplied replies sufficiently comparable due to diverse stereotypes and the different lexical choices available, as is shown by the case of German *Rauchen verboten* (vs. *?Kein Rauchen*).

33. Interesting, amongst the Germanic languages, the Icelandic alternative to the construction recorded above (i. e. *Ekki hugmynd*, lit. 'NEG idea') confirms the pragmatic valencies of Germanic negation discussed at the end of the previous section.

34. For these features the reader is refered back to chapter 1 and to 3.3.

35. The correspondance of this morpheme with the negative pronoun for 'nothing' makes the partitive interpretation of this construction plausible (see also example (51) above), at least taking the diachronic perspective into account. Recall also, with respect to this, the It. negative existential construction *Niente pane*, lit. 'nothing bread' (but *??Niente idee*, lit. 'nothing ideas'), a usage limited to the colloquial spoken language and subject to pragmatic restrictions (cf. Badan 1985: 29−31).

36. Recall also, however, the alternative *ekki hugmynd* of Icelandic, quoted in note 33.

37. Lit. 'nor of idea'. The Serb informant instead gives *Ne-mam pojm-a*, lit. 'NEG-I.have idea-GEN'.

38. As before with Norwegian, we also consider the parentheses around the verbal predicate in Latvian a reliable indication in favour of the elliptical construction.

39. Four languages reply using the verb 'to know', cf. Port. *Não sei* 'I don't know'; Friulian *No sai* 'I don't know'; Sardinian *Non d isko* 'I don't know it'; Czech *Vůbec nic nevím* 'In general nothing not-I.know'; Belorussian *A adkul' mne vedac'?*, lit. 'But from where to me know?'; Lapp *I-n dieđe*, lit. 'NEG-1SG know'. A non-possessive predicate is found in Portuguese *Não faço (nenhuma) ideia*, lit. 'I don't make (any) idea'.

Chapter 9

1. As will be seen immediately below, 'to hope' and 'to think' behave differently, so that these two sentences are not the most appropriate for confirming NEG-raising. The same obviously also

applies to Q24 (*John didn't think that nothing would happen to him; Giovanni non pensava che non gli sarebbe successo niente*) and Q26 (*John didn't think that something would happen to him; Giovanni non pensava che gli sarebbe successo qualcosa*); raising, though, is related to the behaviour of negative quantifiers.

2. The bibliography is immense. We mention here only a few references: Sheintuch—Wise (1976); Horn (1978: 157 and 161–162) with Russian examples; Forest (1983) with reference to the previous bibliography; Orlandini (1985), etc. See also in the generativist framework the contributions to the special issue of *Rivista di Linguistica* 1993/5 (which totally ignore non-generativist previous work).

3. On the so-called expletive NEG see Vendryes (1950), who calls it 'abusive'; Muller (1983); Queffélec (1988); Forest (1993: 109–121).

4. Cf. also the first of the two variants given for Q36 in Provençal: *Jan penso qu'acò es pas poussible* vs. *Jan penso pas qu'acò fugue poussible.*

Chapter 10

1. In any case, listing the replies to the questionnaire together facilitates cross-reference of the data not only according to the binary schema adopted here, but also in a multiplicity of ways, checking, for example, the frequency with which a $+\alpha$ reply accompanies $-\beta$, $+\gamma$ reply etc.

2. For example the coincidence or non coincidence of 'NO' in the replies to yes/no questions (Q1) with 'NEG$_{HOL}$' (Q2), see parameter β, discussed in 10.3.

3. The project, sponsored by the European Science Foundation, will produce nine volumes (published by Mouton de Gruyter), referring to topical aspects of the languages of Europe, as e.g. 'Pragmatic Organisation of Discourse', 'Subordination and Complementation', 'Adverbial Relations', etc. The areal/typological dimension is present in most of the volumes.

References

Allières, Jacques
1979   *Manuel pratique de basque*, Paris: Picard.
Andersen, Roger (ed.)
1983   *Pidginization and creolization as language acquisition*, Rowley (Mass.)/London/Tokyo: Newbury House.
Antinucci, Francesco
1981   "Tipi di frase", in: Annarita Puglielli (a cura di), *Sintassi della lingua somala*, Studi somali 2, Roma, 219 – 302.
Antinucci, Francesco – Virginia Volterra
1975   "Lo sviluppo della negazione nel linguaggio infantile: uno studio pragmatico", *Lingua e stile* 10: 231 – 260 (also in Domenico Parisi (a cura di), *Studi per un modello del linguaggio*, Roma, CNR, 1975, 135 – 172).
Aquilina, Joseph
1965   *Teach Yourself Maltese*, London: The English Universities Press.
Ashby, William J.
1981   "The loss of the negative particle ne in French: A syntactic change in progress", *Language* 57: 674 – 687.
Attal, Pierre
1984   "Deux niveaux de négation", *Langue française* 62: 4 – 11.
Badan, Marco
1985   "Alcuni aspetti del sistema della negazione", in: Christoph Schwarze (Hrsg.), *Bausteine für eine italienische Grammatik*, Bd. 2, Narr: Tübingen, 11 – 67.
Badía Margarit, A. M.
1975   *Gramática catalana*, 2 vols. (2nd edition), Madrid: Gredos.
Banfi, Emanuele
1985   *Linguistica balcanica*, Bologna: Zanichelli.
Bechert, Johannes
1976   "Bemerkungen zu Greenberg's 'Basic Order Typology'", *Papiere zur Linguistik* 10: 49 – 66.
1990   "The structure of the noun in European languages", in: Johannes Bechert – Giuliano Bernini – Claude Buridant (eds.), 115 – 140.
Bechert, Johannes – Giuliano Bernini – Claude Buridant (eds.)
1990   *Toward a Typology of European Languages*, Berlin: Mouton de Gruyter.
Benincà, Paola
1989   "Note introduttive a un atlante dialettale sintattico", in: Giuseppe Borgato – Alberto Zamboni (a cura di), *Dialettologia e varia linguistica. Per Manlio Cortelazzo*, ["Quad. Patavini di Linguistica", Monografie 6, Padova: Dipartimento di Linguistica dell'Università e Centro per gli studi di fonetica del CNR], 11 – 17.
Bergson, Henry
1975   *Oeuvres*, Paris: Presses Universitaires de France.
Berneker, Erich – Max Vasmer
1971   *Russische Grammatik*, 7e Auflage, Berlin: de Gruyter ('Sammlung Göschen' 4066).

Bernini, Giuliano
1987a   "Attempting the reconstruction of negation patterns in PIE", in: Anna Giacalone Ramat – Onofrio Carruba – Giuliano Bernini (eds.), *Papers from the 7th International Conference on Historical Linguistics*, Amsterdam: Benjamins, 57 – 69.
1987b   "Le negazioni in arabo dialettale", in: Giuliano Bernini – Vermondo Brugnatelli (a cura di), 41 – 52.
1990   "Per una tipologia delle repliche brevi", in: Maria-Elisabeth Conte – Anna Giacalone – Paolo Ramat (a cura di), *Dimensioni della linguistica*, (Materiali linguistici 1) Milano: Angeli, 119 – 149.
1992   "Forme concorrenti di negazione in italiano", in: Bruno Moretti – Dario Petrini – Sandro Bianconi (a cura di), *Linee di tendenza dell'italiano contemporaneo*, Roma: Bulzoni, 191 – 215.
Bernini, Giuliano – Vermondo Brugnatelli (a cura di)
1987   *Atti della 4a giornata di Studi Camito-semitici e Indeuropei*, Milano: Unicopli.
Berruto, Gaetano
1990   "Note tipologiche di un non tipologo", in: Gaetano Berruto – Alberto S. Sobrero (a cura di), *Studi di sociolinguistica e dialettologia italiana offerti a Corrado Grassi*, Galatina: Congedo, 5 – 24.
(den) Besten, Hans
1986   "Double Negation and the Genesis of Afrikaans", in: Pieter Muysken – Norval Smith (eds.), *Substrata versus Universals in Creole Languages*, Amsterdam: Benjamins, 185 – 230.
Bhatia, Tej Kr.
1978   *A syntactic and semantic description of negation in South Asian languages*, Diss., University of Illinois at Urbana-Champaigne.
Bianconi, Sandro
1980   *Lingua matrigna*, Bologna: Il Mulino.
Bîtea, Ioan N.
1984   "Towards a Theory of Simple-Statement Negation, I, The Scope of Simple-Statement Negation", *Revue Roumaine de Linguistique* 29: 499 – 512.
Bjørnskau, Kjell
1971   *Praktisches Lehrbuch Norwegisch*, Berlin: Langenscheidt.
Bloch, Jules
1946   *Structure grammaticale des langues dravidiennes*, Paris: Maisonneuve.
Boretzky, Norbert
1983   *Kreolsprachen, Substrate und Sprachwandel*, Wiesbaden: Harrassowitz.
Bortolini, Ugo – Carlo Tagliavini – Adriano Zampolli
1971   *Lessico di frequenza della lingua italiana contemporanea*, Milano: IBM/Garzanti.
Bosque, Ignacio
1980   *Sobre la negación*, Madrid: Cátedra.
Bowen, John T. – T. J. Rhys Jones
1973   *Teach Yourself Welsh*, (first printed 1960), London: The English Universities Press.
Braune, Wilhelm – Ernst A. Ebbinghaus
1981   *Gotische Grammatik. Mit Lesestücken und Wörterverzeichnis*, 19e Auflage (1e Auflage 1880), Tübingen: Niemeyer.
(von) Bremen, Klaus
1986   "Le problème des forclusifs romans", *Lingvisticae Investigationes* 10: 223 – 264.
Brown, D. Richard
1994   "Kresh", in: Peter Kahrel – René van den Berg (eds.), 163 – 189.

Brugmann, Karl– Berthold Delbrück
  1897(ff.)   *Grammatik der indogermanischen Sprachen*, 5 Bde, Straßburg: Trübner.
Brugnatelli, Vermondo
  1987   "La negazione discontinua in berbero e in arabo-magrebino", in: Giuliano
         Bernini–Vermondo Brugnatelli (a cura di), 53–62.
Brunet, Jacqueline
  1981   *Grammaire critique de l'italien*, Vol. 4: *Le démonstratif, les numéraux, les indéfinis*, Paris:
         Université de Paris VIII–Vincennes.
Buchholz, Oda–Wilfried Fiedler
  1987   *Albanische Grammatik*, Leipzig: Enzyklopädie.
Burgers, M. P. O.
  1971   *Afrikaans.* London: Teach Yourself Books.
Burridge, Kate
  1983   "On the development of Dutch negation", in: Hans Bennis–W. U. S. van Lessen
         Kloeke (eds.), *Linguistics in the Netherlands 1983*, Dordrecht: Foris, 31–40.
Bybee, Joan L.
  1985   *Morphology*, Amsterdam: Benjamins.
Callebaut, Bruno
  1992   "Présentation", *Langue française* 94: 3–7.
Campbell, Lyle
  1980   "Towards new perspectives in American Finnish", in: *Congressus Quintus Internationalis
         Fenno-Ugristarum*, Pars III (red. Osmo Ikola), Turku: Suomen Kielen Seura, 341–351.
Cinque, Guglielmo
  1976   "Mica", *Annali della Facoltà di Lettere e Filosofia dell'Università di Padova* 1: 101–112.
Clahsen, Harald
  1988   "Kritische Phasen der Grammatikentwicklung. Eine Untersuchung zum Nega-
         tionserwerb bei Kindern und Erwachsenen", *Zeitschrift für Sprachwissenschaft* 7: 3–31.
Clements, J. Clancy
  1992   "Foreigner talk and the origins of Pidgin Portuguese", *Journal of Pidgin and Creole
         Languages* 7: 75–92.
Collinder, Björn
  1969   "Estonian", in: Björn Collinder (ed.), *Survey of the Uralic Languages*, 2nd edition, Stock-
         holm: Almqvist & Wiksell, 133–179.
Comrie, Bernard
  1981a   "Negation and other verb categories in Uralic languages", in: *Congressus Quintus Intern-
          ationalis Fenno-Ugristarum*, Pars VI (red. Osmo Ikola), Turku: Suomen Kielen Seura,
          350–355.
  1981b   *The languages of the Soviet Union*, Cambridge: Cambridge University Press.
  1989   "Translatability and language universals", in: Michel Kefer–Johan van der Auwera
         (eds.), *Universals of Language*, (Belgian Journal of Linguistics 4), Bruxelles: Editions de
         l'Université de Bruxelles, 53–67.
Comrie, Bernard (ed.)
  1987   *The world's major languages*, London: Croom Helm.
Contini-Morava, Ellen
  1989   *Discourse Pragmatics and Semantic Categorization. The Case of Negation and Tense-Aspect with
         Special Reference to Swahili*, Berlin: Mouton de Gruyter.
Croft, William
  1990   *Typology and Universals*, Cambridge: Cambridge University Press.

1991   "The evolution of negation", *Journal of Linguistics* 27: 1 – 27.
Dahl, Östen
1970   "Some notes on indefinites", *Language* 46: 33 – 41.
1979   "Typology of sentence negation", *Linguistics* 17: 79 – 106.
1985   *Tense and Aspect Systems*, Oxford: Blackwell.
1990   *Standard Average European as an exotic language*, in: Johannes Bechert – Giuliano Bernini – Claude Buridant (eds.), 3 – 8.
Dal Negro
1994   "Strategie di apprendimento della negazione in tedesco L2", *Quaderni del Dipartimento di Linguistica e Letterature Comparate* (Bergamo) 10: 361 – 380.
Danielsen, Niels
1977   "Richieste di chiarimenti epistemologici", in: Raffaele Simone – Ugo Vignuzzi (a cura di), *Problemi della ricostruzione in linguistica*. Atti del Convegno Internazionale di Studi della Società di Linguistica Italiana (Pavia, 1 – 2 ottobre 1975), Roma: Bulzoni, 133 – 142.
De Bhaldraithe, Tomás
1987   *English-Irish Dictionary*, An Deichiú Cló, Baile Átha Cliath: An Gúm an Roinn Oideachais.
Derbyshire, Desmond C. – Geoffrey K. Pullum (eds.)
1986   *Handbook of Amazonian Languages*. Volume 1. Berlin: Mouton de Gruyter.
Diki-Kidiri, Marcel
1977   *Le sango s'écrit aussi... Esquisse linguistique du sango, langue nationale de l'Empire Centrafricain*, (Langues et civilisations à tradition orale 24) Paris: SELAF [Société d'études linguistiques et anthropologiques de France].
Dik, Simon C.
1978   *Functional Grammar*, Dordrecht: North Holland.
1989   *The Theory of Functional Grammar*, Dordrecht: Foris.
Dik, Simon C. – Elseline Vester – Kees Hengeveld – Co Vet
1990   "The Hierarchical Structure of the Clause and the Typology of Adverbial Satellites", in: Jan Nuyts – A. Machtelt Bolkestein – Co Vet (eds.), *Layers and Levels of Representation in Language Theory. A Functional View*, Amsterdam: Benjamins, 25 – 70.
Donadze, Natacha
1981   "Quelques remarques concernant les constructions négatives dans les langues romanes", *Quaderni di Semantica* 2: 297 – 301.
1993   "La négation double dans les langues romanes", *Géolinguistique* 5: 159 – 186.
Dressler, Wolfgang U. – Mayerthaler, Willi – Oswald Panagl – Wolfgang U. Wurzel
1987   *Leitmotifs in Natural Morphology*, Amsterdam: Benjamins.
Doniach, N. S.
1982   *The Concise Oxford English-Arabic Dictionary of Current Usage*, Oxford: Oxford University Press.
Dryer, Matthews S.
1988   "Universals of negative position", in: Michael Hammond – Edith A. Moravcsik – Jessica Wirth (eds.), *Studies in Syntactic Typology*, Amsterdam: Benjamins, 93 – 124.
Ernout, Alfred – Antoine Meillet
1951   *Dictionnaire étymologique de la langue latine*, Paris: Klincksieck.
Faine, Jules
1939   *Le créole dans l'univers*. 1: *Le mauricien*, Port-au-Prince: Imprimerie de l'Etat.

Ferguson, Charles A.
1971   "Absence of copula and the notion of simplicity: A study of normal speech, baby
            talk, foreigner talk, and pidgins", in: Dell Hymes (ed.), *Pidginization and creolization of
            languages*, Cambridge: Cambridge University Press, 141–150.
Ferraz, Luiz – Marius F. Valkhoff
1975   "A comparative study of São-tomense and Cabo-verdiano Creole", in: Marius F. Valk-
            hoff (cur.), 15–39.
Fischer, Wolfdietrich – Otto Jastrow (Hrsg.)
1980   *Handbuch der arabischen Dialekte*, Wiesbaden: Harrassowitz.
Forest, Robert
1983   "'Négation promue', insularité, performatifs et empathie", *Bulletin de la Société de Lin-
            guistique de Paris* 78: 77–97.
1993   *Négations. Essai de syntaxe et de typologie linguistique*, Paris: Klincksieck.
Fraenkel, Ernst
1950   *Die baltischen Sprachen*, Heidelberg: Winter.
Gaatone, David
1971   *Etude descriptive du système de la négation en français contemporain*, Genève: Droz.
Gärtner, Eberhard
1989   "Remarques sur la syntaxe du portuguais en Angola e au Mozambique", *Etudes portu-
            gaises et brésiliennes* (Nouvelle série VI), Université de Haute Bretagne, 21: 29–54 [but
            cover title: *La langue portugaise en Afrique*].
Ghere, S. – N. Skvorzova
1952   *Dizionario russo-italiano*, Roma: Editori Riuniti.
Givón, Talmy
1973   "The time-axis phenomenon", *Language* 49: 890–925.
1975   "Negation in Language: pragmatics, function, ontology", *Working Papers on Language
            Universals* (University of California at Stanford), 18: 59–116 (published in *Syntax and
            Semantics*, Vol. 9, New York, Academic Press, 1978, 69–112).
1984   *Syntax. A Functional-typological Approach*, Amsterdam: Benjamins.
Gonda, Jan
1951   *La place de la particule négative na dans la phrase en vieil indien*, Leiden: Brill.
Goodman, Morris
1987   "Pidgin origins reconsidered", *Journal of Pidgin and Creole Languages* 2: 149–162.
Grégoire, Antoine
1937   *L'apprentissage du langage*, Vol. 1: *Les deux premières années*, Paris: Les Belles Lettres.
Green, John N.
1988   *Romance Creoles*, in: Martin Harris – Nigel Vincent (eds.), 420–473.
Greenberg, Joseph H.
1966   "Some Universals of Grammar with Particular Reference to the Order of Meaningful
            Elements", in: Joseph H. Greenberg (ed.), *Universals of Language*, 2nd edition, Cam-
            bridge (Mass.): M. I. T. Press, 73–113.
Grice H. Paul
1975   "Logic and conversation", in: Peter Cole – J. L. Morgan (eds.), *Syntax and Semantics.
            Speech Acts*, New York: Academic Press, 41–58.
GWN
1984   *Groot Woordenboek der Nederlandse Taal*, Utrecht: Van Dale Lexicographiee.
Hagège, Claude
1982   *La structure des langues*, (Que sais-je? 2006), Paris:Presses Universitaires de France.

Hajičová, Eva
1984   "On Presupposition and Allegation", in: Petr Sgall (ed.), *Contributions to Functional Syntax, Semantics, and Language Comprehension*, Praha: Academia, 99–122.
Halliday, Michael A. K. – Hasan, Ruqaiya
1976   *Cohesion in English*, London: Longman.
Harris, Martin
1978   *The Evolution of French Syntax. A Comparative Approach*, London: Longman.
Harris, Martin – Nigel Vincent (eds.)
1988   *The Romance Languages*, London: Croom Helm.
Haspelmath, Martin
1993   *A typological study of indefinite pronouns*, PhD dissertation, Berlin, Freie Universität.
Heldner, Christina
1981   *La portée de la négation. Examen de quelques facteurs sémantiques et textuels pertinents à sa détermination dans des énoncés authentiques*, Stockholm: Norstedt.
Hemon, Roparz
1975   *A Historical Morphology and Syntax of Breton*, Baile Átha Cliath: Institúid Ard-Léinn.
Hesseling, Dirk Christiaan
1897[1979]   "Dutch in South Africa", in: Dirk Christiaan Hesseling, *On the origin and formation of creoles: a miscellany of articles*, edited and translated by Thomas L. Markey and Paul T. Roberge, Ann Arbor: Karoma, 1–22. [Original title: "Het hollandsch in Zuid Africa"].
Hirt, Hermann
1937   *Indogermanische Grammatik*, Teil VII: *Syntax*, Heidelberg: Winter.
Hirtle, W. H.
1988   "*Some* and *any*: exploring the system", *Linguistics* 26: 443–477.
Holm, John
1988   *Pidgins and Creoles*, Vol. 1: *Theory and Structure*, Cambridge: Cambridge University Press.
1989   *Pidgins and Creoles*, Vol. 2: *Reference Survey*. Cambridge: Cambridge University Press.
Holtus, Günter
1985   "Affirmation und Negation: Beobachtungen zu Syntax und Lexik des gesprochenen und des geschriebenen Italienisch", in: Günter Holtus – Edgar Radtke (Hrsg.), *Gesprochenes Italienisch in Geschichte und Gegenwart*, Tübingen: Narr, 225–235.
Horn, Laurence R.
1978   "Some aspects of negation", in Joseph H. Greenberg – Charles A. Ferguson – Edith A. Moravcsik (eds.), *Universals of Human Language*, Vol. 4: *Syntax*, Stanford: Stanford University Press, 127–210.
1989   *A Natural History of Negation*, Chicago: Chicago University Press.
(van der) Horst, J. M. – M. J. van der Wal
1979   "Negatieverschijnselen en woordvolgorde in de geschiedenis van het Nederlands" [Phenomenology of negation and word order in the history of Dutch], *Tijdschrift voor Nederlandse Taal- en Letterkunde* [Journal of Dutch linguistics and literature] 95: 6–37.
Ineichen, Gustav
1979   *Allgemeine Sprachtypologie*, Darmstadt: Wissenschaftliche Buchgesellschaft.
Jacobs, Joachim
1983   *Fokus und Skalen: zur Syntax und Semantik der Gradpartikeln im Deutschen*, Tübingen: Niemeyer.
Jensen, Hans
1969   *Grammatik der kanaresischen Schriftsprache*, Leipzig: Enzyklopädie.

Jespersen, Otto
1917   "Negation in English and other languages", *Det Kgl. Danske Vidensk. Selskabs Hist.-Filol. Meddeleser* I, 5 [published in: *Selected Writings of Otto Jespersen*, London/Tôkyô: Allen & Unwin/Senjô].
Joly, André
1981   "Structure psychique et structure sémiologique de la négation nexale dans les langues indo-européennes", *Bulletin de la Société de Linguistique de Paris* 76: 99 – 154.
Jones, W. Glyn – Kirsten Gade
1981   *Danish. A Grammar*, København: Gyldendal.
Joseph, Brian D. – Irene Philippaki Warburton
1987   *Modern Greek*, London: Croom Helm.
Kahrel, Peter
in prep.   *A typology of negative sentences.*
Kahrel, Peter – René van den Berg (eds.)
1994   *Typological studies in negation*, Amsterdam/Philadelphia: Benjamins.
Kaczorowska, Elżbieta
1994   "Sur les énoncés existentiels et situatifs en polonais", *Bulletin de la Société Linguistique de Paris* 89/1: 289 – 307.
Kihm, Alain
1994   *Kriyol syntax. The Portuguese-based creole language of Guinea-Bissau*, Amsterdam, Benjamins.
Klein, Horst G. – Petre Ceauşescu
1979   *Einführung in die rumänische Sprache*, 2e überbearbeitete Aufgabe, Tübingen: Niemeyer.
Klein, Wolfgang
1986   *Second language acquisition*, Cambridge: Cambridge University Press.
Klima, Edward S.
1964   "Negation in English", in: J. A. Fodor – J. J. Katz (eds.), *The structure of language: Readings in the philosophy of language*, Englewood Cliffs (N. J.): Prentice Hall, 246 – 323.
Klima, Edward S. – Ursula Bellugi
1966   "Syntactic Regularities in the Speech of Children", in: John Lyons – R. J. Wales (eds.), *Psycholinguistic Papers*, Edinburgh: Edinburgh University Press, 183 – 219.
Kluge, Friedrich – E. Seebold
1989   *Etymologisches Wörterbuch der deutschen Sprache*, Berlin: Mouton de Gruyter.
Koller, Erwin
1988   "Äquivalente Negierung im Deutschen und Portugiesischen. Ein Übersetzungsvergleich", *Sprachwissenschaft* 13: 68 – 117.
Koktová, Eva
1987   "On the scoping properties of negation, focusing particles and sentence adverbials", *Theoretical Linguistics* 14: 173 – 226.
Kouwenberg, Sylvia
1992   "From OV to VO. Linguistic negotiation in the development of Berbice Dutch Creole", *Lingua* 88: 263 – 299.
1994   "Berbice Dutch", in: Peter Kahrel – René van den Berg (eds.), 237 – 266.
Kraft, G. H. – A. H. M. Kirk-Greene
1973   *Teach Yourself Hausa*, Sevenoaks (Kent): Hodder & Stoughton.
Kress, Bruno
1982   *Isländische Grammatik*, Leipzig: Enzyklopädie.
Krivickij, Aleksandr A. – Arnol'd E. Mixnevič – Aleksandr I. Podlužnij
1978   *Belorusskij jazyk dlja nebelorusov* [The Belorussian language for Non-Belorussians], Minsk, Vyšèjšaja škola.

Krivonosov, A. T.
1986   "Otricanie v predloženii i otricanie v umozaključenii: opyt semantičeskogo analiza otricanii v tekste" [Negation in the sentence and negation in the deduction: an experiment of semantic analysis of negation in the text]. *Voprosy Jazykoznanija* [Questions of linguistics], 35/1: 35−49.

Kuruč, Rimma Dmitrievna
1985   *Saamsko-russkij slovar'. Cām'-rūšš soagknèhk'* [Lapp-Russian dictionary], Moskva: Russkij Jazyk.

Lakoff, Robin T.
1969   "Some reason why there can't be any some-any rule", *Language* 45: 608−615.

Lambertz, Max
1959   *Lehrgang des Albanischen*, Teil 3: *Grammatik der albanischen Sprache*, Halle (Saale): Niemeyer.

Lavotha, Ödön
1973   *Kurzgefaßte estnische Grammatik*, (Veröffentlichungen der Societas Uralo-Altaica, Bd. 9) Wiesbaden: Harrassowitz.

Lehmann, Christian
1985   *Der Relativsatz*, Tübingen: Narr.

Lehmann, Winfred P.
1974   *Proto-Indo-European Syntax*, Austin: University of Texas Press.
1986   *A Gothic Etymological Dictionary*, Brill: Leiden.

Lepschy, Anna Laura − Giulio Lepschy
1981   *La lingua italiana. Storia, varietà dell'uso, grammatica*, Milano:Bompiani (English edition: London 1977).

Lerner, Jean-Yves − Wolfgang Sternefeld
1984   "Zum Skopus der Negation im komplexen Satz des Deutschen", *Zeitschrift für Sprachwissenschaft* 3: 159−202.

Leskien, August
1919   *Litauisches Lesebuch mit Grammatik und Wörterbuch*, Heidelberg: Winter.

Lewis, Henry
1988   *Collins-Spurrell Welsh Dictionary*, first published 1960, re-edited by Henry Lewis, London: Collins.

Lipski, John M. − Armin Schwegler
1993   "Creole Spanish and Afro-Hispanic", in: Rebecca Posner − John N. Green (eds.), *Trends in Romance Linguistics and Philology*. Vol.5: *Bilingualism and Linguistic Conflict in Romance*, Berlin: Mouton de Gruyter, 407−432.

Longobardi, Giuseppe
1988   "I quantificatori", in: Lorenzo Renzi (a cura di), *Grande grammatica italiana di consultazione*, Vol. 1: *La frase. I sintagmi nominale e preposizionale*, Bologna: Il Mulino, 647−696.

Lyons, John
1977   *Semantics*, Cambridge: Cambridge University Press.

Macbain, Alexander
1982   *An etymological dictionary of the Gaelic language*, first edition 1896, Glasgow: Gairm Publications.

Macdonell, Arthur A.
1962   *A Vedic Grammar for Students*, 1st edition: 1916, Oxford: Oxford University Press.

Mackinnon, Roderick
1971   *Teach Yourself Gaelic*, London: Hodder & Stoughton.

Manandise, Esméralda
1987   "AUX in Basque", in: Martin Harris – Paolo Ramat (eds.), *Historical Development of Auxiliaries*, Berlin: Mouton de Gruyter, 317 – 344.

Manoliu Manea, Maria
1977   "How can somebody become nobody? Perceptive strategy and Romance negation", *Revue Roumaine de Linguistique* 22: 13 – 19.

Marello, Carla
1984   "Ellissi", in: Lorenzo Coveri (a cura di), *Linguistica testuale*, Atti del XV Congresso Internazionale di Studi della Società di Linguistica Italiana (Genova – S. Margherita Ligure, 8 – 10 maggio 1981), Roma: Bulzoni, 255 – 270.

Marm, Ingvald – Alf Sommerfelt
1981   *Teach Yourself Norwegian*, Twelfth impression, Sevenoaks: Hodder & Stoughton.

Maslov, Jurij S.
1981   *Grammatika bulgarskogo jazyka* [Grammar of the Bulgarian language], Moskva: Vysšaja Škola.

Marvennou, Fanch
1978   *Le breton sans peine*, Tome 1, Chennevières sur Marne: Assimil.

Mathesius, Vilém
1937   "Double negation and grammatical concord", in: *Mélanges van Ginneken*, Paris: Klincksieck, 79 – 83.

Matzel, K.
1966   *Einführung in die singhalesische Sprache*, Wiesbaden: Harrassowitz.

McLaughlin, Barry
1987   *Theories of Second-Language Learning*, London: Arnold.

Meillet, Antoine
1912   *Linguistique historique et linguistique générale*, (2ème éd. 1962) Paris: Champion.
1977[1929] "Sur la négation en grec et en arménien", in: Antoine Meillet, *Etudes de linguistique et de philologie arménienne*, Louvain: Imprimerie Orientaliste, 255 – 257.

Meisel, Jürgen
1983   "Strategies of Second Language Acquisition. More than One Kind of Simplification", in: Roger Andersen (ed.), 120 – 157.

Moeschler, Jacques
1992   "Une, deux ou trois négations?", *Langue française* 94: 8 – 25.

Molinelli, Piera
1984   "Dialetti e italiano: fenomeni di riduzione della negazione", *Rivista Italiana di Dialettologia* 8: 73 – 90.
1988   *Fenomeni della negazione dal latino all'italiano*, Firenze: La Nuova Italia.

Molinelli, Piera – Giuliano Bernini – Paolo Ramat
1987   "Sentence negation in Germanic and Romance languages", in: Paolo Ramat, 165 – 187.

Moreno Cabrera, Juan Carlos
1987   *Fundamentos de Sintaxis General*, Madrid: Síntesis.

Moseley, Christopher – R. E. Asher (eds.)
1994   *Atlas of the world's languages*, London: Routledge.

Muller, Claude
1983   "Les comparatifs du français et la négation", *Lingvisticae Investigationes* 7: 271 – 316.
1984   "L'association négative", *Langue française*, 62: 59 – 94.

1991   *La négation en français: syntaxe, sémantique et éléments de comparaison avec les autres langues romanes*, Genève: Droz.

Naro, Anthony J.
1978   "A study on the origins of pidginization", *Language* 54: 314−347.

Neckel, Gustav
1913   "Zu den germanischen Negationen", *Zeitschrift für vergleichende Sprachwissenschaft* [KZ] 45: 1−23.

Newman, Paul
1987   "Hausa and the Chadic Languages", in: Bernard Comrie (ed.), 705−723.

Nienaber, G. S.
1955   "Iets naders oor die ontkenning in Afrikaans" [Something more precise over negation in Afrikaans], *Hertzog-Annale* 2: 29−45 (published. in G. S. Nienaber, *Taalkundige Opstelle* [Philological essays], Cape Town, Balkema 1965, 22−38).

Nølke, Henning
1992   "Ne...pas. Négation descriptive ou polémique", *Langue française* 94: 48−67.

Nuyts, Jan
1987   "A cognitive-pragmatic reconsideration of negative raising", in: Johan van der Auwera−Louis Goossens (eds.), *Ins and Outs of the Predication*, Dordrecht: Foris, 107−121.

Ó Dónaill, Niall
1977   *Foclóir Gaeilge-Béarla* [Irish-English dictionary] (Eagarthóir comhairleach [consultant editor] De Bhaldraithe, Tomás), Baile Átha Cliath: Oifig an tSoláthair.

Ó Siadhail, Mícheál
1988   *Learning Irish*, New Haven/London: Yale University Press.

Orlandini, Anna
1981   "Semantica e pragmatica dei pronomi indefiniti latini", *Lingua e Stile* 16: 215−234.
1985   "Négation, quantification et modalités", in: *Syntaxe et Latin*, Actes du IIme Congrès International de Linguistique Latine, Aix-en-Provence, 555−568.
1991   "La négation dans la phrase simple en latin", *Bulletin de la Société Linguistique de Paris* 86: 195−210.

Ožegov, Sergej I.
1968   *Slovar' russkogo jazyka* [Dictionary of the Russian language], Moskva: Sovetskaja Enciklopedija.

Palmer, Frank Robert
1986   *Mood and modality*, Cambridge: Cambridge University Press.

Parkinson, Stephen
1987   *Portuguese*, in: Bernard Comrie (ed.), 260−278.

Pauwels, J. L.
1958   *Het dialect van Aarschot en omstreken* [The dialect of Aarschot and environs], Tongeren.

Payne, John R.
1985   "Negation", in Timothy Shopen (ed.), 197−242.
1992   "Negation", in: William Bright (ed.), Vol. 3, New York/Oxford: Oxford University Press, 75−76.

Pokorny, Julius
1959   *Indogermanisches etymologisches Wörterbuch*, Bd. I, Bern: Francke.

Posner, Rebecca
1985   "Post-Verbal Negation in Non-Standard French: A Historical and Comparative View", *Romance Philology* 39: 170−197.

Press, Ian
    1986   *A Grammar of Modern Breton*, Berlin: Mouton de Gruyter.
Price, Glanville
    1986   "Aspects de l'histoire de la négation en français", in: *Actes du XVIIme Congrès Interna-*
                tional de Linguistique et Philologie Romanes, vol. N. 4: *Morphosyntaxe des langues romanes*,
                Aix-en-Provence, 569–75.
Prince, Elene
    1976   "The Syntax and Semantics of NEG-Raising with Evidence from French", *Language*
                52: 404–26.
Queffélec, Ambroise
    1988   "La négation 'explétive' en ancien français. Une approche psycho-mécanique", in:
                André Joly (éd.), *La linguistique génétique. Histoire et théories*, Lille: Presses Universitaires,
                419–443.
Raidt, Edith H.
    1983   *Einführung in Geschichte und Struktur des Afrikaans*, Darmstadt: Wissenschaftliche
                Buchgesellschaft.
Ramat, Paolo
    1987   *Linguistic Typology*, Berlin: Mouton de Gruyter.
    1988a   *Introduzione alla linguistica germanica*, 2a edizione, Bologna: Il Mulino.
    1988b   "Pour une typologie de la négation", in: *Hommage à Bernard Pottier*, Paris: Klincksieck,
                659–669.
    1994   "Negation", in: R. E. Asher (ed.), *The Encyclopedia of language and linguistics*, Vol. 5,
                Oxford: Pergamon Press, 2769–2774.
Ramat, Paolo – Giuliano Bernini
    1990   "Area influence vs. typological drift in Western Europe: the case of negation", in:
                Johannes Bechert – Giuliano Bernini – Claude Buridant (eds.), 25–46.
Ramat, Paolo – Giuliano Bernini – Piera Molinelli
    1986   "La sintassi della negazione romanza e germanica", in: Klaus Lichem – Edith
                Mara – Susanne Knaller (Hrsg.), *Parallela 2. Aspetti della sintassi dell'italiano contemporaneo*,
                Tübingen: Narr, 237–270.
Ranke, Friedrich – Dietrich Hofmann
    1967   *Altnordisches Elementarbuch*, (Sammlung Göschen 1115) Berlin: de Gruyter.
Rivero, María Luísa
    1970   "A surface structure constraint on negation in Spanish", *Language* 46: 640–666.
Rizzi, Luigi
    1982   *Issues in Italian Syntax*, Dordrecht: Foris.
Rohlfs, Gerhard
    1968   *Grammatica storica della lingua italiana e dei suoi dialetti*, Vol.2: *Morfologia*, Torino: Einaudi
                (German edition, Bern 1949).
Rowlands, E. C.
    1969   *Teach Yourself Yoruba*. London: The English Universities Press.
Rudnyćkyj, J. B.
    1964   *Lehrbuch der ukrainischen Sprache*, Wiesbaden: Harrassowitz.
Saagpakk, Paul F.
    1982   *Eesti-inglise sõnaraamat. Estonian-English dictionary*, New Haven: Yale University Press.
Sadock, Jarrold M. – Arnold M. Zwicky
    1985   *Speech act distinctions in syntax*, in: Timothy Shopen (ed.), 155–196.

Saltarelli, Mario
    1988   *Basque*, London: Croom Helm.
Savel'eva, Lidija Vladimirovna
    1989   *Formy otricanija v russkom jazyke donacional'nogo perioda* [Negation forms in the Russian
                language of the pre-national period], Leningrad, Izdatel'stvo Leningradskogo Uni-
                versiteta.
Schmalstieg, William R.
    1974   *An Old Prussian Grammar: The Phonology and Morphology of the Three Catechisms*, University
                Park: The Pennsylvania State University.
Schuchardt, Hugo
    1888   "Beiträge zur Kenntnis des kreolischen Romanisch I. Allgemeineres über das Ne-
                gerportugiesische", *Zeitschrift für romanische Philologie* 12: 242–254.
Schumann, John – Ann-Marie Stauble
    1983   "A Discussion of Second Language Acquisition and Decreolization", in: Roger An-
                dersen (ed.), 260–274.
Schwarze, Christoph
    1988   *Grammatik der italienischen Sprache*, Tübingen: Niemeyer.
Schwegler, Armin
    1983   "Predicate negation and word-order change: A problem of multiple causation", *Lin-
                gua* 61: 297–334.
    1986   "The Chanson de Sainte Foy: Etymology of Cabdorn (with Cursory Comments on
                the Localization of the Poem)", *Romance Philology* 39: 285–304.
    1988   "Word-Order Changes in Predicate Negation Strategies in Romance Languages",
                Diachronica 5: 21–58.
    1991a   "Predicate Negation in Contemporary Brazilian Portuguese – A Change in Pro-
                gress", *Orbis* 34[1985–1987]: 187–214.
    1991b   "Predicate Negation in Palenquero (Colombia) and Other European-Based Creoles",
                Journal of Pidgin and Creole Languages 6: 165–214.
    1992   "La doble negación dominicana y la génesis del español caribeño", *Lingüística* 4.
Seiler, Hansjakob
    1995   "Language universals and typology in the UNITYP framework", in: Masayoshi
                Shibatani – Theodora Bynon (eds.), *Approaches to language typology*, Oxford: Oxford
                University Press, 273–325.
Sheintuch, G. – K. Wise
    1976   "On the pragmatic unity of the rules of neg-raising and neg-attraction", *Chicago
                Linguistic Society* 12: 548–557.
Shopen, Timothy (ed.)
    1985   *Language Typology and Syntactic Description*, Vol. I: *Clause Structure*, Cambridge: Cambridge
                University Press.
Slobin, Daniel
    1971   "Development Psycholinguistics", in: W. O. Dingwall (ed.), *Survey of Linguistics Pro-
                gram*, University of Maryland, 298–400 (Italian translation in: Francesco
                Antinucci – Cristiano Castelfranchi (a cura di), *Psicolinguistica: percezione, memoria e ap-
                prendimento del linguaggio*, Bologna: Il Mulino, 323–363).
    1985   "The child as a linguistic icon-maker", in John Haiman (ed.), *Iconicity in Syntax*, Am-
                sterdam: Benjamins, 221–248.
Smith, A. S. D. – E. G. R. Hooper
    1972   *Cornish Simplified*, Trewolsta: Dyllansow Truran.

Smith, Norval S. H. – Ian E. Robertson – Kay Williamson
1987   "The Ijo element in Berbice Dutch", *Language in Society* 16: 49–90.
Sornicola, Rosanna
1988   "Il relativo in irlandese antico. Una riconsiderazione", *Indogermanische Forschungen* 93: 124–167.
Spitzer, Leo
1976   *Lettere di prigionieri di guerra italiani 1915–1918*, Torino: Boringhieri (German edition: *Italienische Kriegsgefangenenbriefe*, Hanstein: Bonn, 1921).
Stassen, Leon
1985   *Comparison and Universal Grammar*, Oxford: Blackwell.
Stewart, Ann Harleman
1985   "Inference in socio-historical linguistics: the example of Old English word play", *Folia Linguistica Historica* 6: 63–85.
Stickel, Gerhard
1975   "Einige syntaktische und pragmatische Aspekte der Negation", in: Harald Weinrich (Hrsg.), *Positionen der Negativität*, München: Finck, 17–38.
Streitberg, Wilhelm
1971   *Die gotische Bibel*, 6e unveränderte Auflage, Heidelberg: Winter.
Taglicht, Joseph
1984   *Message and emphasis. On focus and scope in English*, London: Longman.
Teyssier, Paul
1986   "La négation dans les créoles portugais", in: *Morphosyntaxe des langues romanes*. Actes du XVIIe Congrès International de Linguistique et Philologie Romanes (Aix-en-Provence, 29 août – 3 septembre 1983). Vol. n°4. Aix-en-Provence: Université de Provence, 591–604.
Tesch, Felicitas
1989   *Die Indefinitpronomina some and any im authentischen englischen Sprachgebrauch und in Lehrwerken*, Tübingen: Narr.
Tesnière, Lucien
1966 [1959]   *Eléments de syntaxe structurale*, 2me éd, Paris: Klincksieck.
Thurneysen, R.
1970   *A Grammar of Old Irish*, 1st edition 1946, Baile Átha Cliath: Institúid Ard-Léinn.
Trepos, P.
1994   *Grammaire bretonne*, Rennes: Simon.
Tóth, László
1964   *Grammatica ungherese*, Bari: Laterza.
Valentin, Paul
1993   "La négation chez Berthold de Ratisbonne", in: D. Buschinger – W. Spiewok (éds.), *Études de littérature et de linguistique en l'honneur d'André Crépin*, Greifswald: Reineke, 419–426.
Valkhoff, Marius F.
1966   *Studies in Portuguese and Creole. With Special Reference to South Africa*, Johannesburg: Witwatersrand University Press.
1972   *New light on Afrikaans and "Malayo-Portuguese"*, Louvain: Peeters.
1975   "L'importance du portugais comme langue mondiale avant le français", in: Valkhoff (cur.), 73–85.
Valkhoff, Marius F. (cur.)
1975   *Miscelânea luso-africana*, Lisboa: Junta de investigações científicas do ultramar.

Vázquez, Cuesta Pilar – Maria Albertina Mendes da Luz
1988   *Gramática da lingua portuguesa*, Lisboa, Edições 70 (Portuguese translation of the 3rd Spanish edition, Madrid 1969).

Veksler, Bunim – Vladimir Jurik
1984   *Latyškij jazyk (Samoucitel')* [The Latvian language (A book for the self-study)], Riga: Zvajgzne.

Vendryes, Joseph
1950   "Sur la négation abusive", *Bulletin de la Société de Linguistique de Paris* 46: 1–18.

Vennemann, Theo
1989   "Language Change as Language Improvement", in: Vincenzo Orioles (a cura di), *Modelli esplicativi della diacronia linguistica*, Atti del Convegno della Società Italiana di Glottologia (Pavia 15–17 settembre 1988), Pisa: Giardini, 11–35.

Vlasto, A. P.
1988   *A Linguistic History of Russia to the End of the Eighteenth Century*, Oxford: Clarendon Press.

Wackernagel, Jacob
1926   *Vorlesungen über Syntax*, 2e Ausgabe 1957, Basel: Birkhäuser.

Wehr, Hans – J. Milton Cowan
1976   *A dictionary of Modern Written Arabic*, Ithaca (N. Y.): Spoken Language Services.

Weijnen, A. A.
1971   *Schets van de geschiedenis van de Nederlandse syntaxis* [An outline of the history of Dutch syntax], Assen: van Gorcum.

Wendt, Heinz F.
1972   *Langenscheidts praktisches Lehrbuch Türkisch*, Berlin: Langenscheidt.

Wheeler, Max W.
1988a   "Catalan", in Martin Harris – Nigel Vincent (eds.), 170–208.
1988b   "Occitan", in Martin Harris – Nigel Vincent (eds.), 246–278.

Whitney, Arthur H.
1984   *Teach Yourself Finnish*, Sixth impression, Sevenoaks (Kent): Hodder and Stoughton Educational.

Whorf, Benjamin Lee
1977   *Linguaggio, pensiero e realtà*, 2a edizione (1a edizione 1970), Torino: Boringhieri (*Language, thought, reality*, Cambridge (Mass.): The M. I. T. Press, 1956).

Wright, W.
1933   *A grammar of the Arabic language*, Third edition, reprinted 1979, Cambridge: Cambridge University Press.

Zanuttini, Raffaella
1987   "Negazione e concordanza negativa in italiano e in piemontese", *Rivista di Grammatica Generativa* 12: 153–172.
1989   "The structure of the negative clauses in Romance", Paper presented at the 12th GLOW Colloquium, Utrecht, April 1989.

Zobl, Helmut
1980   "Developmental and Transfer Errors: Their Common Base and (Possibly) Differential Effects on Subsequent Learning", *TESOL Quarterly* 14: 469–479.

Zwicky, Arnold M. – Geoffrey K. Pullum
1983   "Cliticization vs. inflection: English *n't*", *Language* 59: 502–513.

Appendix

The questionnaire

The questionnaire which was used in the survey of negative structures is recorded below, the English version listed first and followed by the Italian.

a) English version

1. Have you seen John? — *No, I haven't.*
2. John eats fish, but his companions *do not.*
3. John *neither* speaks *nor* moves.
4. *Neither* John *nor* his companions wanted to leave.
5. John *doesn't* eat fish.
6. John *doesn't* eat fish, but he does eat meat.
7. John and Mary met *not* at school, but at a party.
8. "What's your name?" asked Polyphemus.
    "*No-one*" replied Ulysses.
9. "*No-one* has wounded me" cried Polyphemus.
10. "What can you see?" asked John.
    "*Nothing*" replied his companion.
11. *No* people came.
12. Have you seen anything? — No, *nothing.*
13. *Haven't* you seen *anything?* — Yes, I have seen something.
14. Did you see anyone? — No, *nobody.*
15. *Didn't* you see *anyone?* — Yes, I did see someone.
16. *Nobody* saw *anything.*
17. Somebody *didn't* see *anything.*
18. Somebody *didn't* see something.
19. John had *nothing,* he knew *nobody.*
    John *didn't* have *anything,* he *didn't* know *anybody.*
20. *Nobody* could assist them, *nothing* could help them.
21. John had *never* run so fast and he *couldn't* go on *any* longer.
22. John had *no* friend, *no* home *anywhere.*
23. John hoped that *nothing* would happen to him.
24. John *didn't* think that *nothing* would happen to him.
25. John *didn't* think that *anything* would happen to him.
26. John *didn't* think that something would happen to him.
27. John *didn't* forget to take *anything.*
28. There's *nothing* here.
    There *isn't anything* here.

29. There's *nobody* here.
    There *isn't anybody* here.
30. John *isn't* there.
31. There is *no* bread.
    There *isn't any* bread.
32. John *wasn't* there.
33. There was *no* bread.
    There *wasn't any* bread.
34. In the contest of wits, Ulysses − more often than *not* − came out the winner.
35. *No* idea!
36a. John thinks that it *is not* possible.
    b. John *does not* think that it is possible.
37a. *Do not* cross, John!
    b. Cross the road, John!
38a. *Do not* cross, my children!
    b. Cross the road, my children!

b) Italian version

1. Hai visto Giovanni? − *No*.
2. Giovanni mangia pesce, i suoi compagni *no*.
3. Giovanni *non* parla *né* si muove.
4. *Né* Giovanni *né* i suoi compagni volevano andarsene.
5. Giovanni *non* mangia pesce.
6. Giovanni *non* mangia pesce, ma carne.
7. Giovanni e Maria si incontrarono *non* a scuola, ma a una festa.
8. "Come ti chiami?" chiese Polifemo.
    "*Nessuno*" rispose Ulisse.
9. "*Nessuno* mi ha ferito" gridò Polifemo.
10. "Che cosa riesci a vedere?" chiese Giovanni.
    "*Niente*" rispose il suo compagno.
11. *Nessuno* venne.
12. Hai visto qualcosa? − No, *niente*.
13. (*Non*) hai visto *niente*? − Sì, qualcosa.
14. Hai visto qualcuno? − No, *nessuno*.
15. (*Non*) hai visto *nessuno*? − Sì, qualcuno.
16. *Nessuno* vide niente.
17. Qualcuno *non* vide *niente*.
18. Qualcuno *non* vide qualcosa.

19. Giovanni *non* aveva *niente*, *non* conosceva *nessuno*.
20. *Nessuno* poteva aiutarli, *niente* poteva essere utile.
21. Giovanni *non* era *mai* corso così velocemente e *non* ce la faceva più.
22. Giovanni *non* aveva amici, *non* aveva casa *in nessun luogo*.
23. Giovanni sperava che *non* gli succedesse *niente*.
24. Giovanni *non* pensava che *non* gli sarebbe successo *niente*.
25. Giovanni *non* pensava che gli sarebbe successo *niente*.
26. Giovanni *non* pensava che gli sarebbe successo qualcosa.
27. Giovanni *non* dimenticò di prendere *niente*.
28. Qui *non* c'è *niente*.
29. Qui *non* c'è *nessuno*.
30. Giovanni *non* è qui.
31. *Non* c'è pane.
32. Giovanni *non* era qui.
33. *Non* c'era pane.
34. Nelle gare di astuzia, Ulisse era più spesso vincitore che *no*.
35. *Non* ne ho idea!
36a. Giovanni pensa che *non* sia possibile.
   b. Giovanni *non* pensa che sia possibile.
37a. Giovanni, *non* attraversare!
   b. Attraversa la strada, Giovanni!
38a. Bambini, *non* attraversate!
   b. Attraversate la strada, bambini!

Index of languages

Index of authors